Java™ Enterprise Best Practices

The O'Reilly Java Authors

O'REILLY®

Beijing · Cambridge · Farnham · Köln · Paris · Sebastopol · Taipei · Tokyo

Java™ Enterprise Best Practices
by The O'Reilly Java Authors

Copyright © 2003 O'Reilly & Associates, Inc. All rights reserved.
Printed in the United States of America.

Published by O'Reilly & Associates, Inc., 1005 Gravenstein Highway North, Sebastopol, CA 95472.

O'Reilly & Associates books may be purchased for educational, business, or sales promotional use. Online editions are also available for most titles (*safari.oreilly.com*). For more information contact our corporate/institutional sales department: (800) 998-9938 or *corporate@oreilly.com*.

Editor:	Robert Eckstein
Production Editor:	Matt Hutchinson
Cover Designer:	Hanna Dyer
Interior Designer:	David Futato

Printing History:

December 2002:   First Edition.

ISBN: 0-596-00384-6

[M]

Table of Contents

Preface

For several years now, we've been programming with the Java™ 2 Enterprise Edition (J2EE), watching it grow from an infant since its introduction in the late 1990s to the woolly mammoth of multitier development environments that it is today. And now, with the introduction of J2EE Version 1.4, thousands of us have opened the chest to access a treasure trove of APIs that can help us organize, modernize, and get our enterprise systems in order. However, while most Java Enterprise texts scramble to document the latest in J2EE APIs, we've noticed that few texts talk openly about the dos and don'ts of developing with the Enterprise APIs. This book attempts to bridge that gap by providing solid advice, backed up with experience. This advice is what we at O'Reilly like to call "best practices."

Audience

Put succinctly, this book is for anyone who is interested in picking up solid experience in the Java Enterprise APIs. Note that I use the word "solid." It's one thing to learn an API; it's another thing to learn an API so well that you know which areas to use and which areas to stay away from. That doesn't mean the material in this book will turn you into a J2EE expert overnight—obviously, learning any development environment takes many months of development experience. However, after reading some of these chapters, you should be able to get a feel for the right and wrong approaches to tackling common problems in a particular API space. After all, you're likely learning from other people's mistakes.

One important point that should be made is that these chapters are not tutorials for learning the java Enterprise APIs. For that, you should consult a wide array of books from O'Reilly that cover each Java Enterprise API (see Chapter 1 for an exhaustive list). However, the authors expect that you will have at least some degree of familiarity with the Enterprise APIs in each chapter, even if you don't consider yourself ready to give presentations on J2EE programming at the next JavaOne conference. Obviously, it helps if you've done some programming with that particular API before. If you're reasonably familiar with the structure of the Java Enterprise APIs, you shouldn't feel lost when reading any of these chapters.

Organization

This book consists of 11 chapters:

Chapter 1, *Java Enterprise Best Practices (Robert Eckstein, O'Reilly editor)*
Contains a brief introduction as to why best practices are important, and what to expect from each chapter in this book.

Chapter 2, *EJB Best Practices (Sasha Nikolic, EJB author)*
Contains important information on how to effectively develop and deploy Enterprise JavaBeans™ (EJBs).

Chapter 3, *Servlet Best Practices (Jason Hunter, author of Java Servlet Programming)*
Tips and tricks from one of O'Reilly's bestselling authors on how to efficiently work with servlets and frameworks.

Chapter 4, *JDBC Best Practices (George Reese, author of Database Programming with JDBC and Java)*
Includes wisdom on configuring, storing, and retrieving information from various databases using the latest version of JDBC.

Chapter 5, *XML Best Practices (Brett McLaughlin, author of Java and XML and O'Reilly editor)*
Contains practical advice on structuring XML, as well as using both the SAX and DOM APIs. Brett also covers using the new JAXP APIs in some detail.

Chapter 6, RMI Best Practices (William Grosso, author of Java RMI)
Includes a plethora of tips for making sure you don't pull your hair out working with Java's Remote Method Invocation (RMI).

Chapter 7, *Java Management Extensions (J. Steven Perry, author of Java Management Extensions)*
Our newest Java author, J. Steven Perry, shows you some common and arcane pitfalls to watch out for when working with the Java Management Extensions.

Chapter 8, *Enterprise Internationalization (David Czarnecki and Andy Deitsch, authors of Java Internationalization)*
Contains a thorough explanation as to why J2EE developers need to plan for internationalization from the start, as well as common design principles to ensure that your first internationalized project won't be your last.

Chapter 9, *JSP Best Practices (Hans Bergsten, author of Java ServerPages)*
Offers practical wisdom for using JavaServer Pages (JSPs) on your web server, as well as the new JavaServer Pages Standard Tag Library (JSTL) elements.

Chapter 10, *JavaMail Best Practices (William Crawford, co-author of Java Enterprise in a Nutshell)*

Talks about how to get the most out of the JavaMail APIs and provides tips and tricks for using attachments effectively.

Chapter 11, *Enterprise Performance Tuning Best Practices (Jack Shirazi, author of Java Performance Tuning)*

Contains good advice on how to make sure that your J2EE applications are not painfully slow.

Conventions Used in This Book

Italic is used for:

- Pathnames, filenames, and program names
- New terms where they are defined
- Internet addresses, such as domain names and URLs

`Constant width` is used for:

- Anything that appears literally in a JSP or Java program, including keywords, data types, constants, method names, variables, class names, and interface names
- Command lines and options that should be typed verbatim on the screen
- All JSP and Java code listings
- HTML documents, tags, and attributes

`Constant width italic` is used for:

- General placeholders that indicate that an item is replaced by some actual value in your own program

`Constant width bold` is used for:

- Text that is typed in code examples by the user

 This icon designates a note, which is an important aside to the nearby text.

 This icon designates a warning relating to the nearby text.

How to Contact Us

We have tested and verified all the information in this book to the best of our abilities, but you may find that features have changed or that we have let errors slip through during the production of this book. Please let us know of any errors that you find, as well as suggestions for future editions, by writing to:

O'Reilly & Associates, Inc.
1005 Gravenstein Highway North
Sebastopol, CA 95472
(800) 998-9938 (in the U.S. or Canada)
(707) 829-0515 (international/local)
(707) 829-0104 (fax)

You can also send messages electronically. To be put on our mailing list or to request a catalog, send email to:

info@oreilly.com

To ask technical questions or to comment on the book, send email to:

bookquestions@oreilly.com

We have a web site for the book, where we'll list examples, errata, and any plans for future editions. You can access this page at:

http://www.oreilly.com/catalog/javaebp

For more information about this book and others, see the O'Reilly web site:

http://www.oreilly.com

Acknowledgments

From the editor's desk in Round Rock, Texas, the first thing I would like to do is thank all the Java Enterprise authors at O'Reilly who were generous enough with their time to return and divulge their experiences. This book represents a logical next step for our Java publishing program, as many of our authors are now considered field experts in the areas they wrote about. And all of the authors have brought a wealth of knowledge that they have picked up—not only by writing their own books, but also by talking to readers like you after their particular books were published. Thank you all.

On the personal side, I'd like to thank Mike Loukides, mentor and friend, who encouraged me to take on such an ambitious project with so many authors so quickly. I found myself brooding about how I would go about tackling this project at our booth at JavaOne 2002 (just before I got sick), and, as usual, Mike helped me see both the forest and the trees. He was also instrumental in getting me some medicine.

As the author byline hints, this is not a typical O'Reilly book, but I think after reading it you'll agree that it meets O'Reilly's high standards.

Finally, I'd also like to pass my thanks to my wife, Michelle, who is always ready with a healthy dinner and a hug, even when I have to work late into the night. There's nothing quite like shutting down the computer at 8 P.M., coming out to watch some comedy on TV, and finding a nice, warm quesadilla waiting for me along with a family that wants to do nothing but relax and laugh.

"Surely, the best of times."

—Robert Eckstein

First, I'd like to thank my co-author David Czarnecki for convincing me to write yet another book. It's a lot of work and I wouldn't have had the motivation if it wasn't for David. I'd also like to thank Bob Eckstein for pulling this project together. It's not easy to get a bunch of scattered people to collaborate on a book like this and have it done in record time. My acknoweldgments would not be complete without thanking my wife Marie, who continues to support me through all my crazy antics. Finally, I'd like to dedicate this book to my mother Rochelle Solomons.

—Andy Deitsch

There are a number of people I would like to acknowledge for their direct and indirect support and understanding in writing our chapter: Anthony, Lorraine, and Pam Czarnecki; Chad Morrison; Jim and Donna Morrison; Joel, Nancy, Amanda, Korey, Jordan, and Brandon Morrison; and Jeff, Stacey, Joseph, and Emily Baker. I would also be remiss if I did not acknowledge my colleagues at GE Global Research, in particular, Rick Arthur, Marc Garbiras, and Dan Morrill.

Finally, I would like to dedicate our chapter to Joseph James Baker and Emily Anna Baker. I have learned a great deal from the both of you in such a short time. These include, but are not limited to: the tractor is a definitive piece of farm equipment even if you refuse to acknowledge it by name, and you can never have too many shoes. But most importantly, I have learned how much fun it can be to have a picnic in front of a refrigerator eating cheese and olives.

—David Czarnecki

CHAPTER 1

Introduction to Java Enterprise Best Practices

Robert Eckstein

Ever since Java programmers have downloaded their first virtual machine, their ears have been glued to the ground, constantly on the lookout for tips and tricks for using the latest Java APIs. After all, there's nothing quite as satisfying as grasping a new technique for solving a common programming problem. Remember the first time you learned the power of Model-View-Controller (MVC), or developed your first singleton class? It was clear that someone out there had thought through the same problems you were having and, best of all, developed a solution that worked.

However, as any Java programmer can tell you now, learning tips and tricks for the Java APIs isn't as easy anymore. Java has grown in the past seven years to include a ghastly number of APIs, classes, and methods. In fact, Java is so big that it is now separated into three distinct areas: the Java 2 Standard Edition (J2SE), the Java 2 Enterprise Edition (J2EE), and the Java 2 Micro Edition (J2ME). And each area now has an enormous range of classes and methods available from which to choose. Quite frankly, it's nearly impossible to become an expert in all areas of 21st-century Java.

That being said, programmers discover a number of lessons after using the Java APIs for a while. At O'Reilly, we like to call these lessons "best practices." Best practices come in many flavors. Some recommend that you always use a specific design, while others advise you to avoid a particular class or method. Still others illustrate that design and implementation choices are often not black and white, but instead shades of gray. Best practices help you decide which strategies and approaches are right for you by illustrating the pros and cons of each side.

This book focuses on the J2EE APIs. The J2EE APIs include such alphabet-soup acronyms as EJB, JDBC, RMI, XML, and JMX. Because the J2EE is the most popular area of Java right now, it seems logical that we put together a volume of experience that programmers like you can learn from. However, we have not limited this book exclusively to J2EE. This book is a companion to *Java Best Practices*, also published by O'Reilly, which covers J2SE APIs such as Swing, the collections classes, performance tuning, and NIO.

How Does a Best Practice Come About?

Slowly, and with experience. But let's take a step back first and look at how anyone becomes an expert in a specific environment. A programmer goes through four steps when learning to program with any modern language, including Java:[*]

1. You learn the syntax of the language, usually through a tutorial of some sort. In the case of Java, you quickly learned, for example, that, unlike with C++, there was no "delete" keyword for memory deallocation. The garbage collector took care of that automatically. You also learned that the Java language designers included a "synchronized" keyword to help you avoid common threading issues.

2. You learn the environment that you're programming toward. Is it on a 2 GHz PC, or an embedded controller with limited memory on a cell phone? Are you targeting a PDA with access to a business network? Are you compiling toward a supercomputer Internet server that must handle millions of connections per day? Perhaps it's only one of the above. Perhaps all.

3. You learn how to use one or more specialized libraries and APIs with the language. Often, this involves a more direct tutorial or reference book. For example, a good many of you learned how to use the servlet API by reading one of our books, *Java Servlet Programming*. Or perhaps you learned from some other book,[†] or even from an article on the Internet.

4. You slowly begin to gain experience, gleaning tips and tricks for using both the language and the APIs in the defined environment. More precisely, you learn—from your own or others' mistakes—that there are things you should *always* do, things you should *consider* doing only under specific circumstances, and things you should *never* do, even if the documentation says it's OK.

As we hinted earlier, the exclusive province of this book is the fourth area, and it pinpoints the J2EE APIs. This book compresses advice from nearly all of O'Reilly's Java Enterprise authors, each of whom has gained a wealth of experience, not only while writing his book, but also while interacting with programmers like you since their publication. Some of these tips will surprise you; some you might have already learned yourself. But we think you'll agree that *all* are valuable.

Now, having said that, we can tell you what this book is not. This book is *not* a tutorial or a reference on using the specific APIs, as you might find in the third point. We expect that as you peruse these chapters, you are at least modestly familiar with the

---

[*] Guy Steele uses a humorous analogy of real-world languages at the beginning of *Effective Java* (Addison-Wesley) to demonstrate this, although he boils it down to three points. I tend to stress environment to my authors much more heavily, as that often decides whether a practice is good or bad (e.g., massive lookup tables don't work well on cell phones). These four points also fall more in line with the types of books were generate at O'Reilly.

[†] Shame on you. :-)

APIs in question, and have some programming experience with them. However, if you need a quick refresher on any of the APIs in question, we recommend any of the following books from O'Reilly's Java catalog:

Ant: The Definitive Guide
Building Java Enterprise Applications Volume I: Architecture
Database Programming with JDBC and Java, Second Edition
Enterprise JavaBeans, Third Edition
Java and SOAP
Java and XML, Second Edition
Java and XML Data Binding
Java and XSLT
Java Distributed Computing
Java Enterprise in a Nutshell, Second Edition
Java Internationalization
Java Management Extensions
Java Message Service
Java Performance Tuning
Java Programming with Oracle JDBC
Java Programming with Oracle SQLJ
Java RMI
Java ServerPages, Second Edition
Java Servlet Programming, Second Edition
Java Web Services
JXTA in a Nutshell

If you're really in a hurry, we highly recommend *Java Enterprise in a Nutshell*, Second Edition. This book provides an excellent balance of tutorial and reference that can help any aspiring Java Enterprise programmer come up to speed in no time.

Can Best Practices Be Arguable?

Absolutely. As I've frequently scribbled on early drafts of these chapters, the term "best practice" implies that there is a "not-so-best practice" that should be avoided. However, you might disagree. It could be that you've found something that works well for you that was in fact discouraged by one of our authors. Or maybe you have something to add. Perhaps you've even found a better solution and you'd like to share it.

With that in mind, we certainly don't want this compendium of advice to degenerate into a stale set of obsolete guidelines. We actively seek and encourage your comments! Hence, we've set up a discussion forum for these books on the O'Reilly Network web site, which is located at:

http://www.oreillynet.com

Here, you can discuss with others (and occasionally with me and even the authors) what works best or worst for you and in which environments.

What's in This Book?

We've tried to cover as many useful J2EE APIs as possible. That being said, we haven't included all of them, sometimes because we felt that the API isn't in widespread use, and sometimes because there just wasn't much to say about it. However, the majority of the central J2EE APIs are represented in this book.

This book consists of 10 additional chapters:

EJB Best Practices by Sasha Nikolic, EJB author
> Chapter 2 contains important information on how to effectively develop and deploy Enterprise JavaBeans (EJBs).

Servlet Best Practices by Jason Hunter, author of Java Servlet Programming
> Chapter 3 has tips and tricks from one of O'Reilly's bestselling authors on how to efficiently work with servlets and frameworks.

JDBC Best Practices by George Reese, author of Database Programming with JDBC
> Chapter 4 includes wisdom on configuring, storing, and retrieving information from various databases using the latest version of JDBC.

XML Best Practices by Brett McLaughlin, author of Java and XML and O'Reilly editor
> Chapter 5 contains practical advice on structuring XML, as well as using both the SAX and DOM APIs. Brett also covers using the new JAXP APIs in some detail.

RMI Best Practices by William Grosso, author of Java RMI
> Chapter 6 includes a plethora of tips for making sure you don't pull your hair out working with Java's Remote Method Invocation (RMI).

Java Management Extensions by J. Steven Perry, author of Java Management Extensions
> In Chapter 7, our newest Java author, Steve Perry, shows you some common and arcane pitfalls to watch out for when working with the Java Management Extensions.

Enterprise Internationalization by David Czarnecki and Andy Deitsch, authors of Java Internationalization
> Chapter 8 contains a thorough explanation as to why J2EE developers need to plan for internationalization from the start, as well as common design principles to ensure that your first internationalized project won't be your last.

JSP Best Practices by Hans Bergsten, author of JavaServer Pages
> Chapter 9 offers practical wisdom for using JavaServer Pages (JSPs) on your web server, as well as the new Java Standard Tag Library (JSTL) elements.

JavaMail Best Practices by William Crawford, co-author of Java Enterprise in a Nutshell
> Chapter 10 talks about how to get the most out of the JavaMail APIs and provides tips and tricks for using attachments effectively.

Enterprise Performance Tuning Best Practices by Jack Shirazi, author of Java Performance Tuning
> Chapter 11 contains good advice on how to make sure that your J2EE applications are not painfully slow.

About the Practices Themselves

Once you start reading the chapters, you'll find that almost all the best practices start with a header that briefly summarizes the author's advice. For example, in Chapter 4, one of the headers is:

Do Not Rely on Built-in Key Generation

Following this summary in Chapter 4 is an introduction to the type of problem the author encountered that prompted this dilemma in the first place, and after that the author explains why he came to that conclusion. But more importantly, you'll find that each best practice documented in this book does more than state problems and solutions. They tend to shift your mode of thinking on using the APIs from the start. For instance, with the previous example, you might be tempted to use built-in key generation with your databases initially, then switch to a manual system later on. However, as this text demonstrates, this is often more trouble than it's worth and should be avoided at all costs. Of course, each practice originated with the author's personal experience, or experience learned from others since publication. In some cases, a recommendation might be obvious (e.g., "Always Close Your Database Connections"), but we've chosen to include it because it's so commonly executed incorrectly that it bears repeating.

> Many of the best practices include examples that illustrate either correct or incorrect usage of the API. In these cases, we have occasionally omitted package names at the beginning of the code listing, as well as other elements that are not required to demonstrate the point of the best practice. We assume that you are already familiar with the APIs to the point at which this is not an issue. If, however, you want to download the complete examples, you can do so at the web site for this book (*http://www.oreilly.com/catalog/javaebp*).

Enterprise Java Programming Resources Online

As I mentioned earlier, this book is not a tutorial for the individual J2EE APIs. However, you can find several excellent choices online if you need a place to start. In addition to the books listed earlier, many free sources of information about Java and J2EE programming are available.

Sun's official Java web site is *http://java.sun.com*, which can also be reached by the now deprecated *http://www.javasoft.com*. Another web site specifically for Java and J2EE developers is the Java Developer Connection: *http://developer.java.sun.com*. Most of the technical articles and beta software on this developer site is password-protected, and access to it requires registration. However, registration is free, and you can allow the site to automatically log in through the use of cookies.

Don't forget O'Reilly's Java web sites: *http://java.oreilly.com* and *http://www.onjava.com*. These sites contain links to our catalog of latest books, as well as insightful tips and tricks for every level of Java programmer. Some other useful sites that you can access are those for *Javaworld* magazine, at *http://www.javaworld.com*; *JavaPro* magazine, at *http://www.javapro.com*; and IBM *developerWorks*, at *http://www.ibm.com/developerworks*.

Finally, if you've just started with the J2EE and want to come up to speed quickly, you should probably be aware that several of the Enterprise APIs covered in this book are now part of the core Java 2 platform. Hence, if you have downloaded the Java Development Kit (JDK), you already have the classes for APIs such as JDBC, RMI, and parts of XML. Other APIs are standard extensions, however, so if you want to use, say, JSP or servlets, you have to download the classes separately. The best way to get the latest API information is to start on Sun's Products and APIs page at *http://java.sun.com/products* and find the appropriate API.

CHAPTER 2

EJB Best Practices

Sasha Nikolic

The Enterprise JavaBean (EJB) component model provides a very powerful platform for distributed enterprise computing. In fact, it is one of the most widely used enterprise platforms around. Because of this, an enormous amount of developer experience and practical knowledge has accumulated with EJBs. In this chapter, I'll present best practices for a range of EJB topics. Most of these topics cannot be covered completely in one chapter, so I'll focus on conventions and techniques that will enable you to write solid Java 2 Enterprise Edition (J2EE) applications.

Design

Application design is the first step in J2EE application development, as any text on the topic will attest. The reason for this is simple: changing the design is usually much more expensive than adding a new feature, or fixing a bug in the application. Design of the EJBs will also significantly impact the performance of a J2EE application.

Know When to Use EJBs

Even though EJBs are great, they are not always the right solution to the problem at hand. Developers often refer to this as "using a sledgehammer to crack a nut." Whenever you are considering how to implement your application, bear in mind the following basic guidelines:

Design
> The EJB component model, and the J2EE architecture in general, are meant to solve a particular class of problems. If your application naturally separates into standard layers (persistence, domain objects, business logic, presentation), you should consider using EJBs.

Implementation
> A proper J2EE application takes time to develop. A typical EJB consists of at least four files (home, remote, implementation, and deployment descriptor), so

even a small application requires some work before it can run. If you are proto-typing an application, consider using only JavaServer Pages (JSPs) and servlets, and then refactoring and expanding that code to include EJBs.

Performance

Application servers are meant to run applications that need scalability. The services that the server provides (i.e., transaction management and instance and connection pooling) are very useful for writing scalable applications, but they also take up a good number of computer resources. If your application does not use these services to its advantage, EJBs might actually slow down your application by, for instance, unnecessarily caching objects, or checking security descriptors.

In general, deciding whether EJBs are the right choice for your application comes from experience. Knowing exactly what you will gain and what you will lose by using EJBs will also help you make the right decision.

Use Standard Design Architecture

As I mentioned earlier, it is usually a good idea to design most of the application before implementing it. This is especially true of J2EE applications, which regularly contain many different components.

Even though every developer or system architect has a unique approach to application design, most people follow some general principles. The first of these principles is the layered structure of a J2EE application:

Presentation layer

This is the UI of the application. It usually contains servlets, JSP files, applets, and various presentation and display logic. This layer is considered to be a client of the business logic layer because it exclusively uses that layer to complete its operations.

Business logic layer

This is the most important layer of the application, at least from the perspective of an EJB programmer. This layer contains the business workflow and various services used by the client. It relies on the persistence layer for storing and retrieving data.

Persistence layer

This layer is obviously used to persist application data. Most of the code here will comprise entity beans, and possibly some other layers of persistence abstraction, such as data access objects (which abstract the source of the data).

These layers are by no means set in stone. You might encounter a situation in which adding an additional logical layer will make the application design cleaner and easier to implement. Or you might find that you don't need a presentation layer if your application is used by another application. In any case, the layout of an application is flexible, but there are some definite advantages to using this three-layer structure, given that the J2EE specification encourages it by classloader schemes and packaging rules. Also, different types of components that can be built in J2EE (servlets, entity beans, session beans, etc.) lend themselves to this type of structure.

The second principle of design has to do with the order in which the application layers are developed. Even though every programmer has his own philosophy and way of developing an application, you should follow these rules if you follow the layout described earlier:

1. Define requirements and use cases. This will help you understand what the application has to do and how flexible it must be, and it might help you decide which technologies to use.

2. Clearly define the domain object model (i.e., your data objects) and business interfaces that will be exposed to the clients.

3. Possibly write stubs for various components so that development can start.

4. Implement the persistence layer.

5. Define and write *services*, which are independent components of the system that are used in the implementation.

6. Implement the business logic layer.

7. Implement the presentation layer.

 Writing functional prototype applications is almost as involved as writing a full application. You have to define and partially implement most of the components if your strategy will extend the prototype into a proper application. For this reason, design patterns similar to business delegates are commonly used (see "Use Business Delegates for Clients"), and simple implementations of these can be used in place of EJB components and layers.

Use CMP Entity Beans

Whenever possible, try to use container-managed persistence (CMP) for entity beans. Most application servers have highly optimized handling mechanisms for CMP beans, and even though CMP beans might be a little harder to configure and deploy properly, they are well worth the effort. Some of the benefits of CMP are:

- Better transaction management
- Configurable database layout
- No SQL or persistence logic in source code
- Container-managed relationships between entity beans

Use Design Patterns

Learn and use as many EJB design patterns as possible. Most patterns will save you development time, improve the performance of your application, and make it more maintainable. It's fair to say that without patterns, writing solid J2EE applications would be very hard.

Because this is not a design patterns book, we will not examine in detail the multitude of EJB patterns that exist out there. Instead, we'll focus on several patterns that most EJB developers will find useful in their work.

Session façade

A *session façade* is the most frequently used EJB design pattern. It's a way to encapsulate business workflow logic to get better performance and to have more maintainable code. The basic idea is very simple: put all business workflow logic into stateless session beans, and have clients call those beans instead of calling the different components of the application. This concept is shown in Figure 2-1.

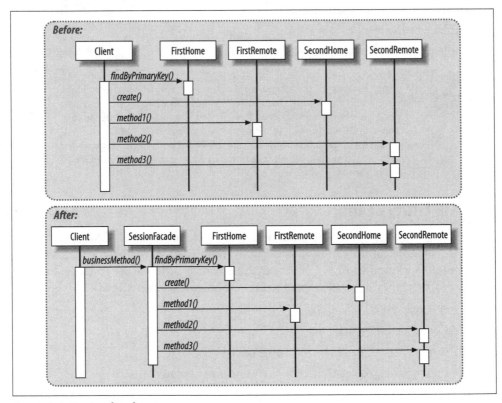

Figure 2-1. Session façade pattern

There are many advantages to this pattern. The most significant is that moving all business logic into its own layer makes the code a lot cleaner and more manageable. Because each workflow operation corresponds to one business method in the session bean, all implementation logic for that operation is executed under one transaction. This means you need to set the transaction attributes for the session bean methods to "Required" for this aspect of the façade to work correctly.

Having session façades will also enable you to use local interfaces in the persistence layer, and expose only the remote session bean interface to the client.

Value objects

Value objects, or data transfer objects, are a way to transfer "bulk" data between remote components, with minimal network traffic. For example, suppose you have a User entity bean. To get the user's first name, last name, address, and other data, you would usually have to call a get method for each piece of data that you need. If you have to do this through a remote interface, the network overhead will be very large. The natural solution to this problem is to create an object that can hold all the data you need, and use that object to transfer the data. This is exactly what a value object is. Figure 2-2 illustrates this pattern.

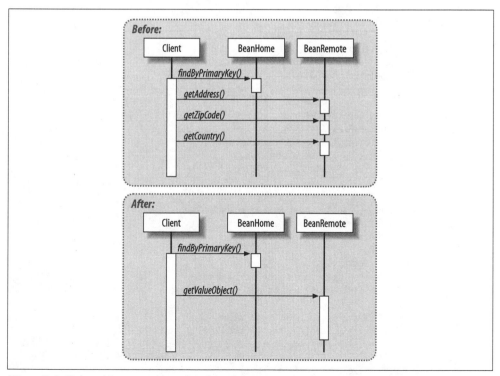

Figure 2-2. Value object pattern

A common practice is to use the value object in the entity bean, instead of constructing it every time a client requests it. Another common practice is to expose several different value objects from a single entity bean so that clients can get only the data they are interested in. This is ordinarily used when the entity bean contains large amounts of data, and sending everything over the network becomes impractical.

When the number of value objects is very large and their management becomes tedious, it might be a good idea to implement a generic HashMap value object that can be used to transfer arbitrary data. Now, a generic value object would have only a couple of getField/setField methods, and it would be hard to implement some kind of validation code to ensure that the right value object fields are being set. In contrast, a simple value object has getXXX/setXXX methods for each field, which makes it impossible to make that mistake. A compromise is to implement all value objects as interfaces, and then use a DynamicProxy with a HashMap to store the value object fields. Example 2-1 shows a dynamic proxy implementation, and how it's used in an entity bean.

Example 2-1. Use of a dynamic proxy implementation in an entity bean

```
public class ValueObjectProxy implements InvocationHandler, Serializable
{
    protected HashMap fieldMap;
    protected Class valueObjectClass;

    protected ValueObjectProxy (Class valueObjectClass) {
        this.valueObjectClass = valueObjectClass;
        fieldMap = new HashMap( );
    }

    public static Object createValueObject (Class valueObjectClass) {
        return Proxy.newProxyInstance (
            valueObjectClass.getClassLoader( ),
            new Class[ ] {valueObjectClass},
            new ValueObjectProxy(valueObjectClass));
    }

    public Object invoke (Object proxy, Method method, Object[ ] args)
    throws Exception {
        String methodName = method.getName( );

        if (methodName.startsWith ("get")) {
            // Remove "get" to get the field name.
            String fieldName = methodName.substring(3);

            // It's a get, so return the value.
            if (!fieldMap.containsKey ("fieldName"))
                throw new ValueObjectException ("Field " + fieldName
                                                + " does not exist");
            return fieldMap.get(fieldName);

        } else if (methodName.startsWith ("set")) {
```

```
                // Remove "set" to get the field name.
                String fieldName = methodName.substring(3);

                // Put it into the hashmap.
                // Assume we received one argument in the set method.
                fieldMap.put (fieldName, args[0]);

        // It's neither a get nor a set.
        } else {
                throw ValueObjectException ("Invalid method");
        }
    }
}

public SomeBean implements EntityBean
{
    // Skipping irrelevant methods...

    public SomeValueObject getValueObject()
    {
        // Create the value object.
        SomeValueObject vo = (SomeValueObject)
                ValueObjectProxy.createValueObject (SomeValueObject.class);

        // Set its values.
        vo.setName ("John Smith");
        vo.setAddress ("140 Maple Drive");

        return vo;
    }
}
```

Because local interfaces are implemented in EJB 2.0, there is really no need to expose entity beans with remote interfaces. However, you still need to handle domain objects, such as the User object in the example, whether the entity bean is directly available to the client or not. So, in this case, you still have to use value objects in to transfer this data between application layers.

Implementation

Now, let's discuss some implementation best practices.

Use Local Interfaces for Entity Beans

As I said before, letting clients access entity beans directly is a bad idea, and this is why session façades should be used as the intermediate layer between entity beans and the client. Because all (or most) of your entity beans will be called by session beans, it makes perfect sense to make these calls use local interfaces. So, if you made your entity beans expose local interfaces, you would eliminate all network calls occurring between business logic and persistence layers. On the other hand, the session beans making up the façade would still have remote interfaces, and clients would access them remotely, which is what you want.

Use Business Interfaces

Because the bean implementation class does not inherit from the bean interface, it's a fairly common error to get a mismatch in business method signatures between the implementation and the interface. Typically, you would have to package and deploy the EJBs to see the error. Needless to say, this can be very frustrating at times, especially because most of these errors are simple typos or missed method parameters.

One common practice is to use business interfaces to enforce compile-time checks. To do this, create a new interface that contains only business methods of your bean, and let both the remote/local bean interface and the implementation class inherit from it. However, even though this method will work for all types of beans (CMP, BMP, local, or remote), there are some inconveniences when dealing with remote beans. Namely, because remote bean interfaces must throw RemoteException, you are also forced to do this in your business interface. Also, a minor inconvenience is that all method parameters must be Serializable.

Example 2-2 shows the key interfaces for a remote bean.

Example 2-2. The order interfaces and implementation

```
// Business interface

public interface Order
{
    public int getQuantity( ) throws RemoteException;
    public void setQuantity (int quantity) throws RemoteException;
    public double getPricePerItem( ) throws RemoteException;
    public void setPricePerItem (double price) throws RemoteException;

    public double getTotalPrice( ) throws RemoteException;
}

// Remote interface

public interface OrderRemote extends Order, EJBObject
{
    // All methods are inherited from Order and EJBObject.
}

// Implementation

public class OrderBean extends Order, EntityBean
{
```

Example 2-2. The order interfaces and implementation (continued)

```
    private int quantity;
    private double pricePerItem;

    // Business interface implementation

    public int getQuantity( ) {
          return quantity;
    }
    public void setQuantity (int quantity) {
          this.quantity = quantity;
    }
    public double getPricePerItem( ) {
          return pricePerItem;
    }
    public void setPricePerItem (double price) {
          this.pricePerItem = pricePerItem;
    }
    public double getTotalPrice( ) {
          return quantity*pricePerItem;
    }

    // Other EntityBean methods go here...
}
```

Notice that you did not declare RemoteException in the throws clause of the implementation class. This is not necessary because although you are allowed to override methods with definitions that have fewer exceptions, the opposite doesn't work (i.e., you can't add new exceptions to a superclass method). Beans with local interfaces would use a business interface in the same way, except that there are no RemoteException and Serializable rules to follow.

Now, you might be tempted to use a business interface instead of the real local/remote interface so that whenever you get an interface to a bean, you cast it to its business interface and use it as if it's not an EJB but a standard Java class. In general, this is usually a bad idea because an EJB exposes other methods and functionality to the client (create, remove, find, getHandle, getPrimaryKey, etc.). If you expose these methods, there is no point in having a separate business interface because it would be identical to the remote/local interface. If you don't expose these methods, you would still have to perform a lot of extra EJB management (i.e., handle remote exceptions, terminate sessions, etc.). If you need the client to work with simple Java classes, you can write a separate class that internally handles all EJB details, and possibly exposes the business interface to the client. This is called a "business delegate," and we'll talk about it later in the chapter. So, to recap this discussion: it's a bad idea to use business interfaces for anything other than compile-time syntax checking.

Handle Exceptions in EJB Code Correctly

Handling exceptions in a distributed J2EE environment can be confusing and very messy at times. Because most exceptions are never thrown in a properly debugged application, you might tend to ignore them, or just print them out to see where the error is. Nevertheless, writing a robust application requires you to properly deal with all possible error conditions that might appear.

To see how and where to handle various EJB exceptions, it's useful to separate them into three basic types:

RemoteException

> This exception is declared in all remote interfaces exposed by an EJB. It is meant to be caught by the client of an EJB, and it usually indicates a network problem. A class implementing an EJB really cannot throw this type of exception. If you need to propagate a network problem (i.e., call another remote object and receive a RemoteException), you should always wrap it in an EJBException, as you'll see next.

EJBException *and its subclasses*

> This exception is thrown by the developer in the EJB implementation class and it's caught by the container. Throwing an EJBException usually signifies a major error, in which case the container will always do a rollback of the current transaction. This exception should be treated as a NullPointerException: it's a runtime exception, and in most cases, it should never be caught by the developer. To help diagnose errors, EJBException can be constructed with a causedBy exception— effectively wrapping another exception. A common use of this is to rethrow an SQLException by wrapping it into an EJBException.

Application-level exceptions

> Unlike the previous two types of exceptions, application-level exceptions are considered "normal," as far as the container is concerned. They are meant to be used in the spirit of standard Java exceptions to report various application errors such as: "user Bob is too old." An EJB can declare and throw these exceptions, and the client will receive them just like it would any normal Java exception, but because these exceptions might potentially travel over the network (from the EJB to the client), they must implement the Serializable interface. Good examples of application-level exceptions are the ones already predefined in the EJB framework, such as CreateException or FinderException.

Know When to Use Compound Primary Keys

If you decide to write a compound primary key class for an entity bean, you must override the hashCode( ) and equals( ) methods. It is also common practice to override the toString( ) method for debugging purposes. Overriding hashCode( ) and equals( ) is important because the container uses these methods to compare primary keys and to look up cached entity bean instances.

Implementing the equals( ) method is pretty simple—all you have to do is compare various components of the primary key. On the other hand, implementing hashCode( ) is harder because a poorly implemented hashCode( ) method can slow down entity bean lookups, especially if there are a lot of instantiated beans. This happens because application servers use HashMap-type structures to store primary keys, and the performance of these structures relies on the fact that hashCode( ) returns different values for different objects.

In most cases, the implementation of hashCode( ) should depend on the data that the primary key contains. However, there are a few generic algorithms that work well. The one shown in Example 2-3 is taken from the java.util.List.hashCode( ) method. This algorithm simply adds all hashcodes of the primary key fields, multiplying each intermediate result by 31 (so that it's not a simple sum of hashcodes).

Example 2-3. Compound primary key

```
public class CompoundPK implements Serializable
{
    private String str1;
    private String str2;
    private int int1;
    private Date date1;

    // Omitting irrelevant code here

    public int hashCode( )
    {
        int hash = 0;
        hash = hash * 31 + str1.hashCode( );
        hash = hash * 31 + str2.hashCode( );
        hash = hash * 31 + int1;
        hash = hash * 31 + date1.hashCode( );
        return hash;
    }

    public boolean equals (Object obj)
    {
        if (!(obj instanceof CompoundPK)) returns false;
        CompoundPK other = (CompoundPK)obj;

        return str1.equals (other.str1)
            && str2.equals (other.str2)
            && int1 == other.int1
            && date1.equals (other.date1);
    }
}
```

Using compound primary keys is usually not a preferred way of identifying records in a database. If possible, it's always better to have a primary key column. With a primary key column, you can index the database, which will accelerate the querying process. A primary key column is also easier on developers because the primary key will be only one number, and not a whole object.

Know How to Handle Large Queries

One of the biggest performance problems with entity beans is doing queries on data that return large collections of objects. This usually happens, for example, when you need to display a list of items to a user, each corresponding to a domain object handled by an entity bean. Simply using a finder method and then getting value objects from the returned entity beans will not work very well, especially if you need this data in the read-only form just for display purposes.

A good solution is to bypass entity beans entirely and query the database directly. You can have a stateless session bean that is responsible for query operations, and it can internally do a database query and return a list of plain value objects. A problem with this scheme is that the database records might change while the client is still using the query results. This is an accepted drawback of read-only query methods, and there is nothing you can do about it.

To see how this querying scheme might be implemented, suppose you have a User value object that contains name and country fields. Example 2-4 shows how to implement your stateless session bean.

Example 2-4. A stateless session bean

```
public class UserQueryBean implements SessionBean
{
    // Skipping EJB methods

    public LinkedList findCanadianUsers() {
        // Do a SELECT * FROM USERS WHERE COUNTRY='Canada' ORDER BY ID
        // and get a result set back.
        return createListFromRS (rs);
    }

    protected LinkedList createListFromRS (ResultSet rs) throws SQLException {
        // This is what you'll return.
        LinkedList list = new LinkedList();

        while (rs.next()) {
            // Create value object with primary key value.
            UserValueObject user = new UserValueObject (rs.getInt(1));

            // Add other fields to it.
            user.setName (rs.getString(2));
            user.setCountry (rs.getString(3));
```

Example 2-4. A stateless session bean (continued)
```
                // Add it to the list.
                list.add (user);
        }

        return list;
    }
}
```

Note that you would frequently need to display results in pages, so it doesn't make sense to read all records into memory. In this case, you would need to have a ranged query (i.e., with "from" and "to" parameters). Implementing a ranged query is somewhat complicated. One way to do it is to use a JDBC 2.0 scrollable result set and move to the required row, as shown in Example 2-5.

Example 2-5. Implementation of a ranged query
```
// Assume you have "from" and "to" parameters.

// Create a scrollable statement.
Statement stmt = conn.createStatement (ResultSet.TYPE_SCROLL_INSENSITIVE,
    ResultSet.CONCUR_UPDATABLE);

// Give hints to the driver.
stmt.setFetchSize (to-from+1); // how many rows to fetch
stmt.setFetchDirection (ResultSet.FETCH_FORWARD);

// Create result set.
ResultSet rs = stmt.executeQuery ("SELECT * FROM MYTABLE");
rs.absolute(from);

for (int i=0; i<(to-from+1); i++) {
    // Read a row from the result set.

    rs.next();
}
```

This method assumes the driver will not read rows you skipped with the rs.absolute() call, and that it will read only the number of rows specified in the hint. This is not always the case, so you might have to rely on database-specific ways of accomplishing the ranged query.

Use Dirty Flags in ejbStore

The ejbStore() method is usually called at the end of each transaction in which an entity bean participates. Given that the container cannot know if a bean-managed persistence (BMP) entity bean actually changed (and thus needs to be saved), it will always call the entity's ejbStore(). Because a typical transaction involves many entity beans, at the end of the transaction the container will call ejbStore() on all these beans, even though only a few might have actually changed. This is usually a big performance bottleneck because most entity beans will communicate with the database.

To solve this problem, a common solution is to use "dirty flags" in your EJB implementation. Using them is very simple: have a boolean flag indicate whether the data in the entity bean has changed. Whenever one of the business methods modifies the data, set the flag to true. Then, in ejbStore( ), check the flag and update the database if needed. Example 2-6 illustrates this.

Example 2-6. Using dirty flags in ejbStore

```
public class MyBean implements EntityBean
{
   // Your dirty flag
   private boolean isModified;

   // Some data stored in this entity bean
   private String someString;

   // You've skipped most of the unrelated methods...

   public void ejbLoad( )
   {
        // Load the data from the database.

        // So far, your data reflects the database data.
        isModified = false;
   }

   public void ejbStore( )
   {
        // No need to save?
        if (!isModified) return;

        // Data has been changed; update the database.
        // ...
   }

   // Some business methods

   public String getSomeString( )
   {
        return someString;
   }

   public void setSomeString (String str)
   {
        someString = str;
        isModified = true;
   }
}
```

For further optimization, you might also want to consider having several dirty flags, one for each update statement in your ejbStore( ).

Use Lazy Loading

Most BMP entity beans are implemented so that ejbLoad( ) populates all data fields in the bean. In nearly every case this is fine because all this data will be used at some point. However, there are instances when you should delay loading parts of the data until it's actually needed. This process, called *lazy-loading*, will save memory and decrease database access times.

The most common example of this is an entity bean that contains large binary or text data in Blob or Clob form. If this data is accessed less often than other data fields in the entity bean, it makes sense to delay reading this data until the client requests it. To implement this lazy-loading technique, you simply have to use a flag to indicate whether the data has been loaded. Example 2-7 shows a basic instance of this.

Example 2-7. Using a lazy-loading technique

```
public class ForumMessageBean implements EntityBean
{
    // Persisted fields
    private Integer id;
    private String title;
    private String author;

    private String messageText; // This is your large data field.
    private boolean isMessageTextLoaded;

    // Skipping irrelevant EJB methods...

    public Integer ejbCreate (String title, String author,
                        StringBuffer message) throws CreateException {
        // Create new record in the database:
        //    INSERT INTO message VALUES (.....)
        // and get ID back.

        this.id = id;
        this.title = title;
        this.author = author;
        this.messageText = messageText;

        // Indicate that the text is in the bean.
        isMessageTextLoaded = true;
    }

    public void ejbLoad() {
        // Load data with an SQL statement such as:
        //    SELECT id, title, author FROM message where id=?
```

Example 2-7. Using a lazy-loading technique (continued)

```
        // Delay loading of the message text.
        isMessageTextLoaded = false;
    }

    // Accessor methods
    public String getMessageText( ) {
        // Call helper method to load the text if needed.
        loadMessageText( );

        return messageText;
    }

    public void setMessageText (String text) {
        messageText = text;

        // Set the lazy-load flag to true so that getMessageText
        // doesn't overwrite this value.
        isMessageTextLoaded = true;
    }

    private void loadMessage( ) throws SQLExcpetion {
        // If it's already loaded, you have nothing to do...
        if (isMessageTextLoaded) return;

        // Load the text from the database.
        // ...

        isMessageTextLoaded = true;
    }
}
```

Even though lazy-loading is a useful technique, people often use it improperly. From a design perspective, check if your lazy-loaded data can be better represented as a dependant object. If it can, splitting your object into two separate entities might be better: you will have a more natural design, and there will be no need for lazy-loading. An even better alternative is to use CMP entities with container-managed relationships between them. However, a lot of CMP engines do not support Clob and Blob data types, so if you take this approach, you will have to use BMP.

Cache JNDI Lookup Objects

To get a DataSource, or an EJB home interface, you typically create an InitialContext, and then do a lookup for the needed resource. These operations are usually very expensive, considering the fact that you perform them all the time throughout your code.

Fortunately, you can optimize these lookups fairly easily by doing the lookup only once, and then reusing the lookup result whenever you need it again—effectively caching it. This is usually done with a singleton class. The singleton can be very simple and cache only specified objects, or it can be a sophisticated service locator that caches many arbitrary objects. An extra benefit of the singleton scheme is that you centralize the Java Naming and Security Interface (JNDI) names of your objects, so if the names change, you have to change your code in only one place: the singleton class.

Example 2-8 shows a singleton that stores several EJB home objects.

Example 2-8. Using a singleton class to cache lookup objects

```
public class EJBHomeCache
{
    private static EHBHomeCache instance;

    protected Context ctx = null;
    protected FirstEJBHome firstHome = null;
    protected SecondEJBHome secondHome = null;

    private EJBHomeCache( )
    {
        try {
            ctx = new InitialContext( );
            firstHome = (FirstEJBHome)PortableRemoteObject.narrow (
                ctx.lookup ("java:comp/env/FirstEJBHome"),
                FirstEJBHome.class);
            secondHome = (SecondEJBHome)PortableRemoteObject.narrow (
                ctx.lookup ("java:comp/env/SecondEJBHome"),
                FirstEJBHome.class);

        } catch (Exception e) {
            // Handle JNDI exceptions here, and maybe throw
            // application-level exception.
        }
    }
    public static synchronized EJBHomeCache getInstance( )
    {
        if (instance == null) instance = new EJBHomeCache( );
        return instance;
    }
    public FirstEJBHome getFirstEJBHome( )
    {
        return firstHome;
    }

    public SecondEJBHome getSecondEJBHome( )
    {
        return secondHome;
    }
}
```

The main shortcoming of this caching scheme is that it was assumed the JNDI names would always be the same, across all components using the singleton. In fact, every J2EE component separately declares the names of the resources it uses (through its deployment descriptor). In most cases, however, all references to a particular resource have the same name because it would be very confusing if you referred to the same EJB by different names, for example.

It's also possible to cache other factories provided by the J2EE environment, such as JMS, or custom connector factories. As a general rule, most resource factories stored in the JNDI are cacheable, but whether you should cache them will probably depend on how often they are used in the application.

Use Business Delegates for Clients

A business delegate is a plain Java class that delegates all calls to an EJB. It might seem too simple to be useful, but it's actually commonly used. The main reason to use a business delegate is to separate the EJB handling logic (e.g., getting remote interfaces, handling remote exceptions, etc.) from the client so that developers working on the client code don't have to know and worry about various EJB details.

Another benefit of business delegates is that you can initially leave all their business methods empty and, by doing so, give client developers something to work with so that they don't have to wait for EJBs to be developed. It's also not uncommon to implement straight JDBC code in the business delegate, instead of leaving it blank, in case you'd like to have a functional prototype. Even in a fully implemented J2EE application, delegates are useful for caching common client requests and computation results from the business layer.

Example 2-9 contains a business delegate that demonstrates some of the basic benefits discussed here. It delegates its calls to a remote stateless session bean that is actually a session façade, retrying several times in case of a network problem.

Example 2-9. A business delegate

```
public class BeanDelegate
{
    private static final int NETWORK_RETRIES = 3;
    private BeanRemote bean;

    public void create() throws ApplicationError
    {
        // Here you get a bean instance.
        try {
            InitialContext ctx = new InitialContext();
            BeanHome home = (BeanHome) PortableRemoteObject.narrow (
                    ctx.lookup ("ejb/BeanExample"),
                    BeanHome.class);

            // Retry in case of network problems.
            for (int i=0; i<NETWORK_RETRIES; i++)
                try {
                    bean = home.create();
                    break;
                } catch (RemoteException e) {
```

Example 2-9. A business delegate (continued)

```
                              if (i+1 < NETWORK_RETRIES) continue;
                              throw new ApplicationError ("Network problem "
                                      + e.toString( ));
                      }
              }
      } catch (NamingException e) {
              throw new ApplicationError ("Error with bean");
      }
}

public void remove( ) throws ApplicationError
{
      // Release the session bean here.

      // Retry in case of network problems
      for (int i=0; i<NETWORK_RETRIES; i++)
              try {
                      bean.remove( );
                      break;
              } catch (RemoteException e) {
                      if (i+1 < NETWORK_RETRIES) continue;
                      throw new ApplicationError ("Network problem "
                              + e.toString( ));
              }
      }
}

public int doBusinessMethod (String param) throws ApplicationError
{
      // Call a bean method here.
      for (int i=0; i<NETWORK_RETRIES; i++)
              try {
                      return bean.doBusinessMethod (param);
              } catch (RemoteException e) {
                      if (i+1 < NETWORK_RETRIES) continue;
                      throw new ApplicationError ("Network problem "
                              + e.toString( ));
              }
      }
  }
}
```

You probably noticed the repeated network retry code in all the methods. If you want to make a cleaner implementation, the best solution is an intermediate wrapper class implemented as a dynamic proxy.

Write Dual CMP/BMP Entity Beans

If you are deploying on different platforms, some of which do not support CMP, the usual practice is to write a bean that can support both CMP and BMP, and then set the appropriate implementation in the deployment descriptors. The advantage of this method is that you gain the performance benefits of CMP where it is available, but the application will still work in BMP mode if necessary. Obviously, there is no need to implement BMP if you know CMP will always be available, but on the other hand, it's not uncommon to write specialized BMP versions to take advantage of particular database features, or even different persistence media.

The dual beans are actually fairly simple to implement. All you have to do is write a CMP implementation class, and then write a BMP implementation that overrides accessor methods and persistence-related methods (ejbCreate( ), ejbRemove( ), etc.). You don't have to override ejbActivate( ), ejbPassivate( ), ejbSetEntityContext( ), ejbUnsetEntityContext( ), or any business methods in the CMP class because these do not deal with the persistence directly.

Example 2-10 shows a pair of CMP and BMP classes.

Example 2-10. CMP and BMP classes

```
public class TheCMPBean implements EntityBean
{
    protected EntityContext ctx;

    public abstract String getName( );
    public abstract void setName (String name);
    public abstract String getAddress( );
    public abstract void setAddress (String address);

    public String ejbCreate (String name, String address)
    throws CreateException
    {
        setName (name);
        setAddress(address);
        return name;
    }

    // Skipping other EJB methods...

    // The business methods...
    public String getMailingAddress( )
    {
        return name + "\n" + address;
    }
}

public class TheBMPBean extends TheCMPBean
{
    protected String name;
    protected String address;

    // Overriding accessor methods
```

Example 2-10. CMP and BMP classes (continued)

```
public String getName( ) {
    return name;
}
public abstract void setName (String name) {
    this.name = name;
}
public abstract String getAddress( ) {
    return address;
}
public abstract void setAddress (String address) {
    this.name = name;
}

// Overriding persistence methods
public String ejbCreate (String name, String address)
throws CreateException
{
    // Insert it into the database with SQL statements.
    // ...

    setName (name);
    setAddress(address);
    return name;
}

// Override other persistence methods:
// ejbRemove, ejbLoad, ejbStore.
}
```

Create Domain Object Factories

If you need to support different persistence media such as the filesystem or database, there are alternatives to writing different BMP implementations for each persistence type. The problem with writing different BMP implementations is that you have to replicate code that deals with EJB semantics in each different implementation. Also, switching implementations involves either changing deployment descriptors for many components, or switching JAR files.

A good solution is to separate the details of persisting data from entity bean implementations. This is especially useful when you have to deal with persisting domain objects because a natural solution is to create abstract factories for domain objects. With or without domain objects, it's easy to see that this additional implementation layer would have to allow entity beans to load, save, and find data. To illustrate this implementation model, consider a User domain object that is handled by an entity bean. In Example 2-11, the entity bean will expose fine-grained get/set methods, but will use a UserFactory to persist the User domain object.

Example 2-11. Using domain object factories

```
public class UserBean implements EntityBean
{
    private EntityContext ctx;
    private transient UserFactory userFactory;
    private UserDomainObject user;

    public void setEntityContext (EntityContext ctx) {
        this.ctx = ctx;

        // Get the factory object for:
        userFactory = UserFactory.getInstance( );
    }

    public void unsetEntityContext( ) {
        ctx = null;
        userFactory = null;
    }

    public void ejbActivate( ) {
        userFactory = UserFactory.getInstance( );
    }

    public void ejbPassivate( ) {
    }

    public Integer ejbCreate (String name, String password)
    throws CreateException {
        // Get the factory to create the user.
        try {
            user = userFactory.createUser (name, password);
            return user.getId( );

        } catch (PersistenceException e) {
            throw new EJBException (e);
        }
    }

    public Integer ejbFindByPrimaryKey (Integer id)
    throws FinderException {
        // Use the factory to find the user.
        if (userFactory.existsUser(id)) return id;

        throw FinderException ("User " + id + " not found");
    }

    public void ejbLoad( ) {
        try {
            user = userFactory.loadUser (user.getId( ));

        } catch (PersistenceException e) {
            throw new EJBException (e);
        }
    }
```

Example 2-11. Using domain object factories (continued)

```
    public void ejbStore( ) {
        try {
            userFactory.saveUser (user);
        } catch (PersistenceException e) {
            throw new EJBException (e);
        }
    }

    // Exposed business methods
    public String getName( ) {
        return user.getName( );
    }

    public void setName (String name) {
        user.setName (name);
    }
}

public interface UserFactory {
    public static synchronized UserFactory getInstance( ) {
        // In this example, you'll hardcode a particular factory.
        return new DBUserFactory( );
    }

    public User create (String name, String password) throws PersistenceException;
    public boolean existsUser (int id);
    public User loadUser (int id) throws PersistenceException;
    public void saveUser (User user) throws PersistenceException;
}
```

I'll leave the implementation of the DBUserFactory to you because the factory contains standard JDBC code familiar to all EJB developers. The important detail to notice is the getInstance( ) method, which returns the appropriate factory. Instead of hardcoding the concrete factory, you can implement a flexible lookup. Some simple lookup methods include reading the factory class from JNDI, or using the ClassLoader to find the concrete class.

Deployment and Packaging

Finally, let's briefly look at some best practices for deployment and packaging of EJBs.

Create a Build Environment

Having a build environment for your application is very important. Even if you use a sophisticated integrated development environment (IDE) for your development that can create EJB JARs and WAR files, a proper build environment will pay off in the long run.

The biggest benefit is that you will have total control over the structure of the produced files. It will also be very easy to produce WAR files, or a separate component, without having to run the IDE every time a change in the code is made. The most obvious benefit is that you won't have to depend on a particular IDE and its features for your builds.

A commonly used open source tool for making build environments is Ant. It's written in Java and is easily customizable for any task. Ant can effortlessly compile and package Java code, and make different J2EE archives. Writing Ant build files, which are XML files, if fairly simple, even for J2EE applications.

I won't go into the details of writing Ant build files because that is a very large topic, but you can find a lot of information about this process on the official Ant site at *http://jakarta.apache.org/ant/index.html*.

Separate Components and Create Shared Libraries

J2EE programmers usually tend to write one big application, with one JAR file containing all EJBs, because it is easy to develop this way. This is bad when it comes to maintenance of a deployed application because a bug fix in one EJB would mean a redeployment of the whole application.

It's not hard to see the benefits of packaging EJBs into related groups. Aside from easing redeployment, this also facilities maintenance of the source code and deployment descriptors. Reusing different parts of the system is also easier if you can split up and package the application into separate components.

Frequently, classes and interfaces are shared among components and layers of the system—usually domain objects, utility classes, and various service interfaces. These can easily be packaged into shared libraries and used by other components. We use a shared library by putting it into the main EAR file, and then referencing the library in the manifest file of each JAR file that needs to use it. Here is an example:

```
Manifest-Version: 1.0
Created-By: Apache Ant 1.5
Class-Path: SharedLibrary1.jar log4j.jar
```

You can use the same method to specify interdependencies among EJB JARs as well.

Write Testing and Diagnostics Code

This might seem like one of those textbook best practices that people tend to ignore, but you might be surprised to know that this best practice is probably the biggest timesaver covered in this chapter. The reason is very simple: J2EE applications are big and generally harder to debug than normal applications.

The standard approach to testing is to use a testing framework such as JUnit (*http://www.juinit.org*) to test different application layers separately. This is a good approach because layer interdependency makes a bug in one layer appear very different in other layers. So, by testing layers separately you usually isolate the bugs early on.

It's also a good practice to include runtime diagnostic code in the final production version of the application. Many components and systems need to be deployed and configured properly for an application to run correctly. For example, missing initial data in the database, a CMP bean that failed to deploy, or firewall problems would not prevent an application from running, but would cause strange errors that are hard to diagnose unless you could look at server logs.

This is why a certain degree of diagnostic code should be put into the application. It might be as simple as a JSP page that checks if the database connection is still working, or it might involve all components of the applications having a method for self-diagnostics. Obviously, the more elaborate the diagnostics, the simpler it will be to find the source of a problem. Generally, if the application runs on diverse platforms and in flexible environments, it has more sophisticated diagnostics.

CHAPTER 3
Servlet Best Practices

Jason Hunter

Since their introduction in 1996, servlets have dominated the server-side Java landscape and have become the standard way to interface Java to the Web. They are the foundation technology on which Java developers build web applications and, increasingly, web services. This chapter discusses best practices for servlet-based development and deployment.

Working Effectively with Servlets

We start with a look at servlet frameworks. Frameworks (e.g., Apache Struts) are becoming increasingly popular because they increase programmer efficiency by providing a skeleton on which applications can be built. In the first section, we examine what servlet frameworks offer, and I give a quick overview of the most popular frameworks. After that, we jump from the high level to the low level with a discussion on how using pre-encoded characters can optimize your servlet's performance. Next, we tackle the thorny issue of loading configuration files and provide some code to make the task easier, and after that I give some tips on when you should (or should not) use the `HttpSession` and `SingleThreadModel` features. As we near the end of the chapter, I explain how to reliably control caching to improve the user's experience. Then I address the frequently asked question: "How do I download a file to the client so that the client sees a 'Save As' pop up?" As you'll see, the answer lies in setting the right HTTP headers.

Choose the Right Servlet Framework

When writing web applications, it's good to remember that servlets are an enabling technology. This is easy to forget because in the early days, the Servlet API was all we had for server-side Java web programming. If the Servlet API didn't include something, we had to build it ourselves. It was a little like the Old West, where times were tough and real programmers wrote servlets by hand. Specs weren't written yet. Heck, we felt lucky just to have out.println( ).

These days, times have changed. The crowds have come, and with them we see a multitude of servlet-based technologies designed to make web application development easier and more effective. The first area of innovation has been happening at the presentation layer. Technologies such as JavaServer Pages (JSP), WebMacro, and Velocity give us more productive alternatives to the vast fields of out.println( ) that came before. These technologies make it easier than ever before to quickly develop, deploy, and maintain dynamic web content. You can find a full discussion of these and other templating technologies in my book *Java Servlet Programming*, Second Edition (O'Reilly).

Today, we're seeing a new area of innovation happening below the presentation layer, at the framework level (see Figure 3-1). These new frameworks provide a solid scaffolding against which new web applications can be built, moving from building pages quickly to building full applications quickly. Frameworks take the best designs of the experts and make them available to you for reuse. Good frameworks help improve your application's modularization and maintainability. Frameworks also bring together disparate technologies into a single bundled package and provide components that build on these technologies to solve common tasks. If you choose the right servlet framework, you can greatly enhance your productivity and leverage the work of the crowds. Consequently, I advise you to consider using a framework and provide some helpful tips in this section on selecting the right framework.

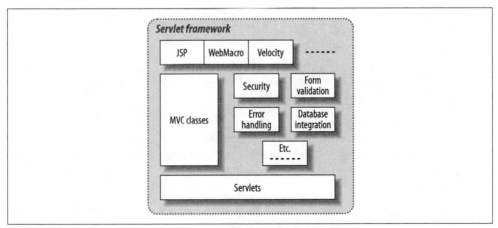

Figure 3-1. Servlets, template technologies, and frameworks

Tips for selecting a framework

When choosing a servlet framework, it's important that you consider its feature list. Here are some of the features that frameworks provide. Not all frameworks support all these features, nor should this short list be considered exhaustive.*

Integration with a template language
> Some frameworks integrate with a specific template language. Others have a pluggable model to support many templates, although they're often optimized for one template language. If you prefer a particular template language, make sure the framework supports it well.

Support (ideally, enforcement) of designer/developer separation
> One of the common goals in web application development is to effectively separate the developer's duties from the designer's. Choosing the right template language helps here, but the framework choice can have even more impact. Some enable the separation of concerns; some enforce it.

Security integration
> The default servlet access control and security model works for simple tasks but isn't extensible for more advanced needs. Some frameworks provide alternative security models, and many support pluggable security models. If you've ever wanted more advanced security control, the right framework can help.

Form validation
> Frameworks commonly provide tools to validate form data, allowing the framework to sanity-check parameters before the servlet even sees the data, for example. Some allow for easy development of "form wizards" with Next/Previous buttons and maintained state.

Error handling
> Some frameworks include advanced or custom error handling, such as sending alert emails, logging errors to a special data store, or autoformatting errors to the user and/or administrator.

Persistence/database integration
> One of the most powerful features of frameworks can be their close and elegant integration with back-end data stores such as databases. These frameworks let the user think in objects rather than in SQL.

Internationalization
> Internationalization (i18n) is always a challenge, but some frameworks have features and idioms that simplify the process.

---

* There's actually a research project underway with the goal of tracking servlet framework features and implementing the same demonstration web application across every framework. See *http://www.waferproject.org* for more information.

IDE integration

Some frameworks provide integrated development environments (IDEs) for development and/or have features that plug in to third-party IDEs.

Mechanisms to support web services

With the growing interest in web services, it's common to see new frameworks centered around web services, or existing frameworks touting new web services features.

Beyond features, a second important criterion when examining a framework is its license. My advice is to stick with open source projects or standards implemented by multiple vendors. This protects your investment. Both open source and common standards avoid the single-vendor problem and ensure that no one entity can terminate support for the framework on which your application depends.

A third consideration is for whom the framework is targeted (e.g., news sites, portal sites, commerce sites, etc.). Different sites have different needs, and frameworks tend to be optimized toward a certain market segment. You might find it useful to investigate which frameworks are used by others implementing similar applications.

High-profile frameworks

While it would be wonderful to do a full comparison between frameworks here, that's not what this book is about. What we can do instead is briefly discuss the four most popular servlet frameworks available today: Java 2 Enterprise Edition (J2EE) BluePrints, Apache Struts, JavaServer Faces, and Apache Turbine.

You might be thinking to yourself, "Just skip the summary and tell me which is best!" Unfortunately, there's no all-encompassing answer; it depends entirely on your application and personal taste. This is one place where working with server-side Java follows Perl's slogan: "There's more than one way to do it."

J2EE BluePrints

J2EE BluePrints (*http://java.sun.com/blueprints/enterprise*) is more accurately described as a guidebook than a framework. Authored by Sun engineers, the book provides guidelines, patterns, and code samples showing how best to use J2EE and the constituent technologies. For example, the book shows how to implement a Model-View-Controller (MVC) framework that encapsulates back-end web operations into three parts: a model representing the central data, the view handling the display of the data, and the controller handling the alteration of the data. To support this MVC model BluePrints suggests using an `Action` class in the style of the "Command" pattern:

> The sample application defines an abstract class Action, which represents a single application model operation. A controller can look up concrete Action subclasses by name and delegate requests to them.

The book gives code samples for how to implement an `Action` but doesn't provide any production-quality support code. For production code, the J2EE Blue-Prints book points readers to Apache Struts.

Apache Struts

Apache Struts (*http://jakarta.apache.org/struts*) might very well be the most popular servlet framework. It follows very closely the MVC pattern discussed in BluePrints (from what I can tell, the ideas have flowed in both directions):

> Struts is highly configurable, and has a large (and growing) feature list, including a Front Controller, action classes and mappings, utility classes for XML, automatic population of server-side JavaBeans, Web forms with validation, and some internationalization support. It also includes a set of custom tags for accessing server-side state, creating HTML, performing presentation logic, and templating. Some vendors have begun to adopt and evangelize Struts. Struts has a great deal of mindshare, and can be considered an industrial-strength framework suitable for large applications.

In Struts, requests are routed through a controller servlet. `Action` objects control request handling, and these actions use components such as JavaBeans to perform business logic. Struts elegantly creates a full dispatch mechanism on top of servlets with an external configuration, eliminating the artificial tie between URLs and online activities. Nearly all requests come in through the same servlet, client requests indicate as part of the request the action they'd like to take (i.e., login, add to cart, checkout), and the Struts controller dispatches the request to an `Action` for processing. JSP is used as the presentation layer, although it also works with Apache Velocity and other technologies. Struts is an open source project and was developed under the Apache model of open, collaborative development.

JavaServer Faces

JavaServer Faces (JSF) is a Sun-led Java Community Process effort (JSR-127) still in the early development stage. It's just reaching the first stage of Community Review as of this writing, but already it's gaining terrific mindshare. The JSF proposal document contains plans to define a standard web application framework, but the delivery appears to focus on the more limited goal of defining a request-processing lifecycle for requests that include a number of phases (i.e., a form wizard). It's a JSF goal to integrate well with Struts.

Apache Turbine

Apache Turbine might be one of the oldest servlet frameworks, having been around since 1999. It has services to handle parameter parsing and validation, connection pooling, job scheduling, caching, database abstractions, and even XML-RPC. Many of its components can be used on their own, such as the Torque tool for database abstraction. Turbine bundles them together, providing a solid platform for building web applications the same way J2EE works for enterprise applications.

Turbine, like the other frameworks, is based on the MVC model and action event abstraction. However, unlike the rest, Turbine provides extra support at the View layer and has dubbed itself "Model 2+1" as a play on being better than the standard "Model 2" MVC. Turbine Views support many template engines, although Apache Velocity is preferred.

We could discuss many more frameworks if only we had the space. If you're interested in learning more, Google away on these keywords: TeaServlet, Apache Cocoon, Enhydra Barracuda, JCorporate Expresso, and Japple.

Use Pre-Encoded Characters

One of the first things you learn when programming servlets is to use a `PrintWriter` for writing characters and an `OutputStream` for writing bytes. And while that's stylistically good advice, it's also a bit simplistic. Here's the full truth: just because you're outputting characters doesn't mean you should always use a `PrintWriter`!

A `PrintWriter` has a downside: specifically, it has to encode every character from a char to a byte sequence internally. When you have content that's already encoded—such as content in a file, URL, or database, or even in a `String` held in memory—it's often better to stick with streams. That way you can enable a straight byte-to-byte transfer. Except for those rare times when there's a charset mismatch between the stored encoding and the required encoding, there's no need to first decode the content into a `String` and then encode it again to bytes on the way to the client. Use the pre-encoded characters and you can save a lot of overhead.

To demonstrate, the servlet in Example 3-1 uses a reader to read from a text file and a writer to output text to the client. Although this follows the mantra of using Reader/Writer classes for text, it involves a wasteful, needless conversion.

Example 3-1. Chars in, chars out

```
import java.io.*;
import java.util.prefs.*;
import javax.servlet.*;
import javax.servlet.http.*;

public class WastedConversions extends HttpServlet {

  // Random file, for demo purposes only
  String name = "content.txt";

  public void doGet(HttpServletRequest req, HttpServletResponse res)
                         throws ServletException, IOException {

    String file = getServletContext().getRealPath(name);

    res.setContentType("text/plain");
    PrintWriter out = res.getWriter();

    returnFile(file, out);
  }
```

Example 3-1. Chars in, chars out (continued)

```
  public static void returnFile(String filename, Writer out)
                          throws FileNotFoundException, IOException {
    Reader in = null;
    try {
      in = new BufferedReader(new FileReader(filename));
      char[] buf = new char[4 * 1024];  // 4K char buffer
      int charsRead;
      while ((charsRead = in.read(buf)) != -1) {
        out.write(buf, 0, charsRead);
      }
    }
    finally {
      if (in != null) in.close();
    }
  }
}
```

The servlet in Example 3-2 is more appropriate for returning a text file. This servlet recognizes that file content starts as bytes and can be sent directly as bytes, as long as the encoding matches what's expected by the client.

Example 3-2. Bytes in, bytes out

```
import java.io.*;
import java.util.prefs.*;
import javax.servlet.*;
import javax.servlet.http.*;

public class NoConversions extends HttpServlet {

  String name = "content.txt";  // Demo file to send

  public void doGet(HttpServletRequest req, HttpServletResponse res)
                          throws ServletException, IOException {
    String file = getServletContext().getRealPath(name);

    res.setContentType("text/plain");
    OutputStream out = res.getOutputStream();

    returnFile(file, out);
  }

  public static void returnFile(String filename, OutputStream out)
                          throws FileNotFoundException, IOException {
    InputStream in = null;
    try {
      in = new BufferedInputStream(new FileInputStream(filename));
      byte[] buf = new byte[4 * 1024];  // 4K buffer
      int bytesRead;
      while ((bytesRead = in.read(buf)) != -1) {
        out.write(buf, 0, bytesRead);
      }
```

Example 3-2. Bytes in, bytes out (continued)

```
    }
    finally {
      if (in != null) in.close( );
    }
  }
}
```

How much performance improvement you get by using pre-encoded characters depends on the server. Testing these two servlets against a 2 MB file accessed locally shows a 20% improvement under Tomcat 3.*x*. Tomcat 4.*x* shows a whopping 50% improvement. Although those numbers sound impressive, they of course assume that the application does nothing except transfer text files. Real-world numbers depend on the servlet's business logic. This technique (illustrated in Figure 3-2) are most helpful for applications that are bandwidth- or server CPU–bound.

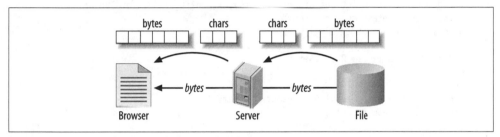

Figure 3-2. Taking advantage of pre-encoded characters

The principle "Use Pre-encoded Characters" applies whenever a large majority of your source content is pre-encoded, such as with content from files, URLs, and even databases. For example, using the ResultSet getAsciiStream( ) method instead of getCharacterStream( ) can avoid conversion overhead for ASCII strings—both when reading from the database and writing to the client. There's also the potential for cutting the bandwidth in half between the server and database because ASCII streams can be half the size of UCS-2 streams. How much benefit you actually see depends, of course, on the database and how it internally stores and transfers data.

In fact, some servlet developers preencode their static String contents with String.getBytes( ) so that they're encoded only once. Whether the performance gain justifies going to that extreme is a matter of taste. I advise it only when performance is a demonstrated problem without a simpler solution.

To mix bytes and characters on output is actually easier than it probably should be. Example 3-3 demonstrates how to mix output types using the ServletOutputStream and its combination write(byte[ ]) and println(String) methods.

Example 3-3. ValueObjectProxy.java

```java
import java.io.*;
import java.sql.*;
import java.util.Date;
import javax.servlet.*;
import javax.servlet.http.*;

public class AsciiResult extends HttpServlet {

  public void doGet(HttpServletRequest req, HttpServletResponse res)
                            throws ServletException, IOException {
    res.setContentType("text/html");
    ServletOutputStream out = res.getOutputStream( );

    // ServletOutputStream has println( ) methods for writing strings.
    // The println( ) call works only for single-byte character encodings.
    // If you need multibyte, make sure to set the charset in the Content-Type
    // and use, for example, out.write(str.getBytes("Shift_JIS")) for Japanese.
    out.println("Content current as of");
    out.println(new Date( ).toString( ));

    // Retrieve a database ResultSet here.

    try {
      InputStream ascii = resultSet.getAsciiStream(1);
      returnStream(ascii, out);
    }
    catch (SQLException e) {
      throw new ServletException(e);
    }
  }

  public static void returnStream(InputStream in, OutputStream out)
                            throws FileNotFoundException, IOException {
    byte[ ] buf = new byte[4 * 1024]; // 4K buffer
    int bytesRead;
    while ((bytesRead = in.read(buf)) != -1) {
      out.write(buf, 0, bytesRead);
    }
  }
}
```

Although mixing bytes with characters can provide a performance boost because the bytes are transferred directly, I recommend you use this technique sparingly because it can be confusing to readers and can be error-prone if you're not entirely familiar with how charsets work. If your character needs to extend beyond ASCII, be sure you know what you're doing. Writing non-ASCII characters to an output stream should not be attempted by a novice.

Load Configuration Files from the Classpath

From Servlet API 1.0 through Servlet API 2.3, servlets have distinctly lacked a standard mechanism to retrieve external configuration files. Although many server-side libraries require configuration files, servlets have no commonly accepted way to locate them. When a servlet runs under J2EE, it receives support for JNDI, which can provide a certain amount of configuration information. But the common web server configuration file problem remains.

The best solution (or perhaps I should call it the "lesser evil" solution) is to locate files with a search of the classpath and/or the resource path. This lets server admins place server-wide configuration files in the web server's classpath, or place per-application configuration files in *WEB-INF/classes* found in the resource path. It also works equally well for locating configuration files placed within WAR files and/or deployed across multiple back-end servlet containers. In fact, using files for configuration has several advantages, even when JNDI is available. The component provider can include a set of "sample" or "default" configuration files. One configuration file can be made to work across the entire server. And finally, configuration files are trivially easy to understand for both the developer and deployer.

Example 3-4 demonstrates the search technique with a class called Resource. Given a resource name, the Resource constructor searches the class path and resource path attempting to locate the resource. When the resource is found, it makes available the resource contents as well as its directory location and last modified time (if those are available). The last modified time helps an application know, for example, when to reload the configuration data. The class uses special code to convert file: URL resources to File objects. This proves handy because URLs, even file: URLs, often don't expose special features such as a modified time. By searching both the class path and the resource path this class can find server-wide resources and per-application resources. The source code for this class can also be downloaded from *http://www.servlets.com*.

Example 3-4. A standard Resource locator

```java
import java.io.*;
import java.net.*;
import java.util.*;

/**
 * A class to locate resources, retrieve their contents, and determine their
 * last modified time. To find the resource the class searches the CLASSPATH
 * first, then Resource.class.getResource("/" + name). If the Resource finds
 * a "file:" URL, the file path will be treated as a file. Otherwise, the
 * path is treated as a URL and has limited last modified info.
 */
public class Resource implements Serializable {
```

Example 3-4. A standard Resource locator (continued)

```java
private String name;
private File file;
private URL url;

public Resource(String name) throws IOException {
  this.name = name;
  SecurityException exception = null;

  try {
    // Search using the CLASSPATH. If found, "file" is set and the call
    // returns true.  A SecurityException might bubble up.
    if (tryClasspath(name)) {
      return;
    }
  }
  catch (SecurityException e) {
    exception = e;  // Save for later.
  }

  try {
    // Search using the classloader getResource(). If found as a file,
    // "file" is set; if found as a URL, "url" is set.
    if (tryLoader(name)) {
      return;
    }
  }
  catch (SecurityException e) {
    exception = e;  // Save for later.
  }

  // If you get here, something went wrong. Report the exception.
  String msg = "";
  if (exception != null) {
    msg = ": " + exception;
  }

  throw new IOException("Resource '" + name + "' could not be found in " +
    "the CLASSPATH (" + System.getProperty("java.class.path") +
    "), nor could it be located by the classloader responsible for the " +
    "web application (WEB-INF/classes)" + msg);
}

/**
 * Returns the resource name, as passed to the constructor
 */
public String getName() {
  return name;
}

/**
 * Returns an input stream to read the resource contents
 */
```

Example 3-4. A standard Resource locator (continued)

```
public InputStream getInputStream( ) throws IOException {
  if (file != null) {
    return new BufferedInputStream(new FileInputStream(file));
  }
  else if (url != null) {
    return new BufferedInputStream(url.openStream( ));
  }
  return null;
}

/**
 * Returns when the resource was last modified. If the resource was found
 * using a URL, this method will work only if the URL connection supports
 * last modified information. If there's no support, Long.MAX_VALUE is
 * returned. Perhaps this should return -1, but you should return MAX_VALUE on
 * the assumption that if you can't determine the time, it's
 * maximally new.
 */
public long lastModified( ) {
  if (file != null) {
    return file.lastModified( );
  }
  else if (url != null) {
    try {
      return url.openConnection( ).getLastModified( );  // Hail Mary
    }
    catch (IOException e) { return Long.MAX_VALUE; }
  }
  return 0;  // can't happen
}

/**
 * Returns the directory containing the resource, or null if the resource
 * isn't directly available on the filesystem. This value can be used to
 * locate the configuration file on disk, or to write files in the same directory.
 */
public String getDirectory( ) {
  if (file != null) {
    return file.getParent( );
  }
  else if (url != null) {
    return null;
  }
  return null;
}

// Returns true if found
private boolean tryClasspath(String filename) {
  String classpath = System.getProperty("java.class.path");
  String[ ] paths = split(classpath, File.pathSeparator);
  file = searchDirectories(paths, filename);
  return (file != null);
}
```

Example 3-4. A standard Resource locator (continued)

```java
  private static File searchDirectories(String[ ] paths, String filename) {
    SecurityException exception = null;
    for (int i = 0; i < paths.length; i++) {
      try {
        File file = new File(paths[i], filename);
        if (file.exists( ) && !file.isDirectory( )) {
          return file;
        }
      }
      catch (SecurityException e) {
        // Security exceptions can usually be ignored, but if all attempts
        // to find the file fail, report the (last) security exception.
        exception = e;
      }
    }
    // Couldn't find any match
    if (exception != null) {
      throw exception;
    }
    else {
      return null;
    }
  }

  // Splits a String into pieces according to a delimiter.
  // Uses JDK 1.1 classes for backward compatibility.
  // JDK 1.4 actually has a split( ) method now.
  private static String[ ] split(String str, String delim) {
    // Use a Vector to hold the split strings.
    Vector v = new Vector( );

    // Use a StringTokenizer to do the splitting.
    StringTokenizer tokenizer = new StringTokenizer(str, delim);
    while (tokenizer.hasMoreTokens( )) {
      v.addElement(tokenizer.nextToken( ));
    }

    String[ ] ret = new String[v.size( )];
    v.copyInto(ret);
    return ret;
  }

  // Returns true if found
  private boolean tryLoader(String name) {
    name = "/" + name;
    URL res = Resource.class.getResource(name);
    if (res == null) {
      return false;
    }

    // Try converting from a URL to a File.
    File resFile = urlToFile(res);
```

Example 3-4. A standard Resource locator (continued)

```
    if (resFile != null) {
      file = resFile;
    }
    else {
      url = res;
    }
    return true;
  }

  private static File urlToFile(URL res) {
    String externalForm = res.toExternalForm( );
    if (externalForm.startsWith("file:")) {
      return new File(externalForm.substring(5));
    }
    return null;
  }

  public String toString( ) {
    return "[Resource: File: " + file + " URL: " + url + "]";
  }
}
```

Example 3-4 shows a fairly realistic example of how the class can be used. Assume your servlet library component needs to load some chunk of raw data from the filesystem. This file can be named anything, but the name must be entered in a *library.properties* main configuration file. Because the data, in some situations, takes a while to process in its raw form, the library keeps a serialized version of the data around in a second file named *library.ser* to speed up load times. The cache file, if any, resides in the same directory as the main configuration file. Example 3-5 gives the code implementing this logic, building on the Resource class.

Example 3-5. Loading configuration information from a Resource

```
import java.io.*;
import java.util.*;
import javax.servlet.*;
import javax.servlet.http.*;

public class LibraryLoader {

  static final String CONFIG_FILE = "library.properties";
  static final String CACHE_FILE =  "library.ser";

  public ConfigData load( ) throws IOException {
    // Find the configuration file and fetch its contents as Properties.
    Resource config = new Resource(CONFIG_FILE);
    Properties props = new Properties( );
    InputStream in = null;
    try {
      in = config.getInputStream( );
      props.load(in);
```

```
    }
    finally {
      if (in != null) in.close( );    // IOException propagates up.
    }

    // Determine the source directoru of the configuration file and look for a cache file
    // next to it containing a full representation of your program state.
    // If you find a cache file and it is current, load and return that data.
    if (config.getDirectory( ) != null) {
      File cache = new File(config.getDirectory( ), CACHE_FILE);
      if (cache.exists( ) &&
          cache.lastModified( ) >= config.lastModified( )) {
        try {
          return loadCache(new FileInputStream(cache));
        }
        catch (IOException ignored) { }
      }
    }

    // You get here if there's no cache file or it's stale and you need to do a
    // full reload. Locate the name of the raw datafile from the configuration file
    // and return its contents using Resource.
    Resource data = new Resource(props.getProperty("data.file"));
    return loadData(data.getInputStream( ));
  }

  private ConfigData loadCache(InputStream in) {
    // Read the file, perhaps as a serialized object.
    return null;
  }

  private ConfigData loadData(InputStream in) {
    // Read the file, perhaps as XML.
    return null;
  }

  class ConfigData {
    // An example class that would hold configuration data
  }
}
```

The loading code doesn't need to concern itself with where the resource might be located. The Resource class searches the class path and resource path and pulls from the WAR if necessary.

Think of Sessions as a Local Cache

Servlet sessions as implemented by HttpSession provide a simple and convenient mechanism to store information about a user. While sessions are a useful tool, it's important to know their limitations. They are not a good choice for acting as the back-end storage in real-world applications, no matter how tempting it might be to try it. Rather, sessions are best thought of as a handy local cache—a place to store information which, if lost, can be recovered or safely ignored.

To understand why this is, we should quickly review how sessions work. Sessions generally use cookies to identify users. During a client's first request to a server, the server sets a special cookie on the client that holds a server-generated unique ID. On a later request the server can use the cookie to recognize the request as coming from the same client. The server holds a server-side hashtable that associates the cookie ID keys with HttpSession object values. When a servlet calls request.getSession(), the server gets the cookie ID, looks up the appropriate HttpSession, and returns it. To keep memory in check, after some period of inactivity (typically 30 minutes) or on programmer request, the session expires and the stored data is garbage-collected.

Session data is inherently transient and fragile. Session data will be lost when a session expires, when a client shuts down the browser,* when a client changes browsers, when a client changes machines, or when a servlet invalidates the session to log out the user. Consequently, sessions are best used for storing temporary information that can be forgotten—because either it's nonpermanent or is backed by a real store.

When information needs to be persistent, I recommend using a database, an EJB backed by a database, or another formal back-end data store. These are much safer, portable, and reliable, and they work better for backups. If the data must have a long-term association with a user, even when he moves between machines, use a true login mechanism that allows the user to relogin and reassociate. Servlet sessions can help in each case, but their role should be limited to a local cache, as we'll see in the next section.

Architecture of a shopping cart

Let's look at how you can architect session tracking for a shopping-cart application (think Amazon.com). Here are some requirements for your shopping cart:

- Logged-in users get a customized experience.
- Logins last between browser shutdowns.
- Users can log out and not lose cart contents.
- Items added to a cart persist for one month.
- Guests are allowed to place items in the cart (although contents are not necessarily available to the guest for the long term or from a different browser).
- Purchasing items in the cart requires a password for safety.

---

* The session data isn't lost immediately when a browser is shut down, of course, because no notification is sent to the server. However, the session data will be lost because the browser will lose its session cookies, and after a timeout the server will garbage-collect the abandoned session data.

Servlet sessions alone don't adequately satisfy these requirements. With the right server you might be able to get sessions to persist for a month, but you lose the information when a user changes machines. Trying to use sessions as storage, you also need to take pains to expire individual items (but not the whole session) after a month, while at the same time making sure to put nothing into the session that shouldn't be kept indefinitely, and you need a way to log out a user without invalidating his cart contents. There's no way to do this in API 2.3!

Here's one possible architecture for this application that takes advantage of sessions as a local cache: if the user has not logged in, he is a guest, and the session stores his cart contents. The items persist there as long as the session lasts, which you have deemed sufficient for a guest. However, if the user has logged in, the cart contents are more safely recorded and pushed through to a back-end database for semi-permanent storage. The database will be regularly swept to remove any items added more than a month earlier. For performance, the user's session should be used to store cart contents even if the user is logged in, but the session should act as a local cache of the database—allowing later requests to display cart information without going across the wire to the database on each request.

The user logins can be tracked with a manually set cookie with a long expiration time. After a form-based login, the cookie stores a hash of the user's ID; the hash corresponds to the database records. On later visits, the user can be automatically recognized and his cart contents loaded into the session. For safety, on checkout the server logic asks for password verification before proceeding. Even though the server knows the client's identity, because the login is automatic the billing activity should be protected. The marker stating that the password was verified would, of course, be stored in the session, with a 30-minute timeout being fairly appropriate! A user-request logout would require only the removal of the cookie. The full architecture is shown in Figure 3-3.

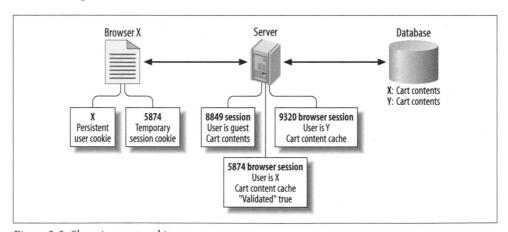

Figure 3-3. Shopping-cart architecture

In this example you proposed custom login management. The default servlet form-based login could be used—however, it's designed for single-session login to restrict access to secure content. It is not designed for multisession login to identify users for shopping-cart applications.

When to use sessions

As shown in the shopping-cart example, sessions are useful but aren't a panacea. Sessions make the best sense in the following situations:

Storing login status
> The timeout is useful, and changes between browsers or machines should naturally require a new login.

Storing user data pulled from a database
> The local cache avoids an across-the-wire database request.

Storing user data that's temporary
> Temporary data includes search results, form state, or a guest's shopping-cart contents that don't need to be preserved over the long term.

Don't Use SingleThreadModel

Now, onto a servlet feature for which there's never a good use. SingleThreadModel. Here's my advice: don't use it. Ever.

This interface was intended to make life easier for programmers concerned about thread safety, but the simple fact is that SingleThreadModel does not help. It's an admitted mistake in the Servlet API, and it's about as useful as a dud firecracker on the Fourth of July.

Here's how the interface works: any servlet implementing SingleThreadModel receives a special lifecycle within the server. Instead of allocating one servlet instance to handle multiple requests (with multiple threads operating on the servlet simultaneously), the server allocates a pool of instances (with at most one thread operating on any servlet at a time). From the outside this looks good, but there's actually no benefit.

Imagine a servlet needing access to a unique resource, such as a transactional database connection. That servlet needs to synchronize against the resource regardless of the servlet's own thread model. There's no difference if two threads are on the same servlet instance or on different servlet instances; the problem is that two threads are trying to use the connection, and that's solved only with careful synchronization.

Imagine instead that multiple copies of the resources are available, but access to any particular one needs to be synchronized. It's the same situation. The best approach is not to use SingleThreadModel, but to manage the resources with a pool that all servlets share. For example, with database connections it's common to have connection pools. You could instead use `SingleThreadModel` and arrange for each servlet instance to hold its own copy of the resource, but that's a poor use of resources. A server with hundreds of servlets might require thousands of resource instances.

As a book author, I've kept my eye out for a compelling use for `SingleThreadModel`. (After all, I need to write book examples showing how best to use this feature.) The most justifiable use I found was given to me by a development manager who said the programmers he hired were used to C global variables. By implementing `SingleThreadModel` they could pass data between servlet method calls using instance variables rather than parameters. While `SingleThreadModel` accomplishes that, it's poor form and inadvisable unless you're hiring Java newbies. When that's the best use case, you know there's no good use case. The bottom line: don't use `SingleThreadModel`.

Caching with Servlets

Here are some tips to consider that will help things move quickly with your servlets.

Pregenerate Content Offline and Cache Like Mad

Pregeneration and caching of content can be key to providing your site visitors with a quality experience. With the right pregeneration and caching, web pages pop up rather than drag, and loads are reduced—sometimes dramatically—on the client, server, and network. In this section I'll provide advice for how best to pregenerate content and cache at the client, at the proxy, and at the server. By the end of this section you'll feel compelled to generate new content during request handling only in worst-case scenarios.

There's no need to dynamically regenerate content that doesn't change between requests. Yet such regeneration happens all the time because servlets and JSPs provide an easy way to template a site by pulling in headers, footers, and other content at runtime. Now this might sound like strange guidance in a chapter on servlets, but in many of these situations servlets aren't the best choice. It's better to "build" the content offline and serve it as static content. When the content changes, you can build the content again. Pull the content together once it is offline rather than during every request.

Take, for example, an online magazine, newspaper, or weblog ('blog). How do the pros handle templatization without burdening the server? By pregenerating the content. Articles added to a site are written and submitted in a standard format (often XML-based) which, when run through a build process, produces a comprehensive update to the web site. The build reformats the article into HTML, creates links to the article from other pages, adds the content into the search engine (before the HTML reformatting), and ultimately prepares the site to handle heavy loads without extreme resources. You can see this in action with 'blog tools such as MovableType.

It's a Perl application, but it generates content statically, so Perl doesn't even need to run on the production server.

As another example, think of an e-tailer with millions of catalog items and thousands of visitors. Clearly, the content should be database-backed and regularly updated, yet because much of the content will be identical for all visitors between updates, the site can effectively use pregeneration. The millions of catalog item description pages can be built offline, so the server load will be greatly reduced. Regular site builds keep the content fresh.

The challenge comes where the static and dynamic content meet. For example, the e-tailer might need servlets to handle the dynamic aspects of its site, such as an item review system or checkout counter. In this example, the item review can invoke a servlet to update the database, but the servlet doesn't necessarily need to immediately update the page. In fact, you see just such a delay with Amazon.com updates— a human review and subsequent site build must take place before you see new comments. The checkout pages in our example, however, can be implemented as a fully servlet-based environment. Just make sure special coordination is implemented to ensure that the template look and feel used by the servlets matches the template look and feel implemented during the offline build.

Pregeneration tools

Unfortunately, few professional-quality, reasonably priced standard tools are available to handle the offline build process. Most companies and webmasters either purchase high-end content management systems or develop custom tools that satisfy their own needs. Perhaps that's why more people don't practice offline site building until their site load requires it.

For those looking for a tool, the Apache Jakarta project manages its own content using something called Anakia. Built on Apache Velocity, Anakia runs XML content through an XSL stylesheet to produce static HTML offline. Apache Ant, the famous Java build system, manages the site build. Others have had success with Macromedia Dreamweaver templates. Dreamweaver has the advantage of viewing JSP, WebMacro, Velocity, and Tea files as simple template files whose HTML contents are autoupdated when a template changes, providing a helpful bridge between the static and the dynamic.

There's a need here for a good common tool. If you think you have the right tool, please share it or evangelize it. Maybe it's out there and we just haven't heard of it yet.

Cache on the client

Pregeneration and caching go hand in hand because caching is nothing more than holding what you previously generated. Browsers (a.k.a. clients) all have caches, and it behooves a servlet developer to make use of them. The `Last-Modified` HTTP header provides the key to effective caching. Attached to a response, this header tells the browser when the content last changed. This is useful because if the browser requests the same content again, it can attach an `If-Modified-Since` header with the previous `Last-Modified` time, telling the server it needs to issue a full response only if the content has changed since that time. If the content hasn't changed, the server can issue a short status code 304 response, and the client can pull the content from its cache, avoiding the `doGet()` or `doPost()` methods entirely and saving server resources and bandwidth.

A servlet takes advantage of `Last-Modified` by implementing the `getLastModified()` method on itself. This method returns the time as a `long` at which the content was last changed, as shown in Example 3-6. That's all a servlet has to do. The server handles issuing the HTTP header and intercepting `If-Modified-Since` requests.

Example 3-6. The getLastModified() method

```
public long getLastModified(HttpServletRequest req) {
  return dataModified.getTime() / 1000 * 1000;
}
```

The `getLastModified()` method is easy to implement and should be implemented for any content that has a lifespan of more than a minute. For details on `getLastModified()`, see my book, *Java Servlet Programming*, Second Edition (O'Reilly).

Cache at the proxy

While implementing `getLastModified()` to make use of client caches is a good idea, there are bigger caches to consider. Oftentimes, especially at companies or large ISPs, browsers use a proxy to connect to the Web. These proxies commonly implement a shared cache of the content they're fetching so that if another user (or the same user) requests it again, the proxy can return the response without needing to access the original web server. Proxies help reduce latency and improve bandwidth utilization. The content might come from across the world, but it's served as if it's on the local LAN—because it is.

The `Last-Modified` header helps web caches as it does client caches, but web caches can be helped more if a servlet hints to the cache when the content is going to change, giving the cache a timeframe during which it can serve the content without even connecting to the server. The easiest way to do this is to set the `Expires` header, indicating the time when the content should be considered stale. For example:

```
// This content will expire in 24 hours.
response.setDateHeader("Expires",
                       System.currentTimeMillis() + 24*60*60*1000);
```

If you take my earlier advice and build some parts of your site on a daily basis, you can set the Expires header on those pages accordingly and watch as the distributed proxy caches take the load off your server. Some clients can also use the Expires header to avoid refetching content they already have.

A servlet can set other headers as well. The Cache-Control header provides many advanced dials and knobs for interacting with a cache. For example, setting the header value to only-if-cached requests the content only if it's cached. For more information on Cache-Control, see *http://www.servlets.com/rfcs/rfc2616-sec14.html#sec14.9*. A great overview of caching strategies is also available at *http://www.mnot.net/cache_docs*. This site also includes tips for how to count page accesses even while caching.

Cache on the server

Caching at the client and proxy levels helps if requests came from the same person or organization, but what about the multitude of requests from all the different browsers? This is why the last level of caching needs to happen on the server side. Any content that takes significant time or resources to generate but doesn't generally change between requests is a good candidate for server-side caching. In addition, server-side caching works for both full pages and (unlike other caching technologies) parts of pages.

Take, for example, an RSS text feed. In case you're not familiar, RSS stands for Rich Site Summary and is an XML-based file format with which publishers advertise new content. Affiliates can pull the RSS files and display links between sites. Servlets.com (*http://www.servlets.com*), for example, pulls and links to servlet-related articles, using RSS with O'Reilly's Meerkat (*http://meerkat.oreillynet.com*) as the RSS news-feed hub.

Suppose you want to display an RSS feed for an affiliate site, updated every 30 minutes. This data should absolutely be cached on the server side. Not only would it be slow to pull an RSS feed for every request, but it's also terribly poor form. The cache can be implemented using an internal timer or, more easily, a simple date comparator. The code to pull the stories can check on each access if it's time to refetch and reformat the display. Because the data is small, the formatted content can be held in memory. Example 3-7 demonstrates sample code that would manage the story cache. On top of this cache might be another cache holding the actual String (or bytes) to be displayed.

Example 3-7. Caching RSS feeds

```
public Story[] getStories(String url) {
  Story[] stories = (Story[]) storyCache.get(url);
  Long lastUpdate = (Long) timeCache.get(url);
  long halfHourAgo = System.currentTimeMillis() - 30*60*1000;
```

Example 3-7. Caching RSS feeds (continued)

```
  if (stories == null || stories.length == 0 ||
      lastUpdate == null || (lastUpdate.longValue() < halfHourAgo)) {
    refetch();
  }
  return stories;
}
```

As a second example, take a stock chart diagram as found on any financial site. This presents a more significant challenge because such a site can support thousands of stock symbols, each offering charts of different sizes with different time spans and sometimes even allowing graphical comparisons between stocks. In this application caching will be absolutely necessary because generating a chart takes significant time and resources, and dynamically generating every chart would balloon the server requirements.

A good solution would be multifaceted. Some charts can be statically built offline (as discussed earlier in this section). These charts would be served as files. This technique works for most commonly accessed charts that don't change more than once a day. Other charts, perhaps ones that are accessed heavily but change frequently, such as a day's activity charts for popular stocks, would benefit from being cached in memory and served directly. They might be stored using a SoftReference. Soft references free the memory if the Java Virtual Machine (JVM) gets low. Still other charts, perhaps ones that are less popular or actively changing, would benefit from being cached by servlets to the filesystem, stored in a semirandom temporary file whose contents can be pulled by a servlet instead of generated by the servlet. The File.createTempFile() method can help manage such files.

Many potential solutions exist, and this shouldn't be taken as gospel. The main point is that memory caches, temporary file caches, and prebuilt static files are good components of any design for caching on the server.

Beyond the server cache, it's important to remember the client and proxy caches. The chart pages should implement getLastModified() and set the Expires and/or Cache-Control headers. This will reduce the load on the server and increase responsiveness even more.

...Or don't cache at all

Even though caching makes sense most of the time and should be enabled whenever possible, some types of content are unsuitable for caching and must always be refreshed. Take, for example, a current status indicator or a "Please wait..." page that uses a Refresh tag to periodically access the server during the wait. But because of the sheer number of locations where content might be cached—at the client, proxy, and server levels—and because of several notorious browser bugs (see *http://www.web-caching.com/browserbugs.html*), it can be difficult to effectively turn off caching across the board.

After spending hours attempting to disable caching, programmers can feel like magicians searching in vain for the right magic spell. Well, Harry Potter, Example 3-8 provides that magic spell, gathered from personal experience and the recommendations of the Net Wizards.

Example 3-8. The magic spell to disable caching

```
// Set to expire far in the past.
res.setHeader("Expires", "Sat, 6 May 1995 12:00:00 GMT");

// Set standard HTTP/1.1 no-cache headers.
res.setHeader("Cache-Control", "no-store, no-cache, must-revalidate");

// Set IE extended HTTP/1.1 no-cache headers (use addHeader).
res.addHeader("Cache-Control", "post-check=0, pre-check=0");

// Set standard HTTP/1.0 no-cache header.
res.setHeader("Pragma", "no-cache");
```

The Expires header indicates that the page expired long ago, thus making the page a poor cache candidate. The first Cache-Control header sets three directives that each disable caching. One tells caches not to store this content, another not to use the content to satisfy another request, and the last to always revalidate the content on a later request if it's expired (which, conveniently, it always is). One directive might be fine, but in magic spells and on the Web, it's always good to play things safe.

The second Cache-Control header sets two caching "extensions" supported by Microsoft Internet Explorer. Without getting into the details on nonstandard directives, suffice to say that setting pre-check and post-check to 0 indicates that the content should always be refetched. Because it's adding another value to the Cache-Control header, we use addHeader( ), introduced in Servlet API 2.2. For servlet containers supporting earlier versions, you can combine the two calls onto one line.

The last header, Pragma, is defined in HTTP/1.0 and supported by some caches that don't understand Cache-Control. Put these headers together, and you have a potent mix of directives to disable caching. Some programmers also add a getLastModified( ) method that returns a time in the past.

Other Servlet Tips

Here are some other things to keep in mind when working with servlets.

Use Content-Disposition to Send a File

While we're on the subject of magic header incantations, servlet developers often struggle with finding the right header combination to send a browser a file that's intended for saving rather than viewing and thus triggers a "Save As" dialog. For the solution to this problem, I have some good news and some bad news.

The bad news is that although the HTTP specification provides a mechanism for file downloads (see HTTP/1.1, Section 19.5.1), many browsers second-guess the server's directives and do what they think is best rather than what they're told. These browsers—including Microsoft Internet Explorer and Opera—look at the file extension and "sniff" the incoming content. If they see HTML or image content, they inline-display the file contents instead of offering a Save As dialog.* Turns out there's no 100% reliable way to download a file across all browsers. Perhaps, with this effort, programmers are more like alchemists than magicians, trying in vain to turn lead into gold.

The good news is that the right combination of headers will download files well enough to be practical. With these special headers set, a compliant browser will open a Save As dialog, while a noncompliant browser will open the dialog for all content except HTML or image files. For these types it will display the content inline, where a user can use the menu to save the content. Example 3-9 shows the best technique for sending files.

Example 3-9. Sending a file for download

```
// Set the headers.
res.setContentType("application/x-download");
res.setHeader("Content-Disposition", "attachment; filename=" + filename);

// Send the file.
OutputStream out = res.getOutputStream( );
returnFile(filename, out);  // Shown earlier in the chapter
```

First, set the Content-Type header to a nonstandard value such as application/x-download. It's very important that this header is something unrecognized by browsers because browsers often try to do something special when they recognize the content type.† Then set the Content-Disposition header to the value attachment; filename=foo, in which foo is substituted with the filename to be used by default in the Save As dialog. Finally, send the file content as bytes. The bytes can come from the filesystem or be dynamically generated.

---

* Microsoft documents Internet Explorer's deviant behavior at *http://msdn.microsoft.com/workshop/ networking/moniker/overview/appendix_a.asp*, although I've found that reality doesn't exactly match the documentation.

† The HTTP specification recommends setting the Content-Type to application/octet-stream. Unfortunately, this causes problems with Opera 6 on Windows (which will display the raw bytes for any file whose extension it doesn't recognize) and on Internet Explorer 5.1 on the Mac (which will display inline content that would be downloaded if sent with an unrecognized type).

Using these headers, the file content in the response will be saved by most browsers or, in worst cases, displayed inline where the user can save the file. There's no standard way to download multiple files in one response.

Finally, it can be useful to include the download file's name as extra path information to the servlet. The servlet can use the filename to learn which file to download, or it can ignore the extra path info. Either way, it's useful because the name appears to the browser as the name of the resource being retrieved, and browsers often use that name in the Save As dialog prompt. For example, instead of serving content from */servlet/ FileDownload?fileid=5*, serve it from */servlet/FileDownload/inventory.pdf?fileid=5*.

Hire a UI Designer

My last piece of personal advice comes not from fellow servlet programmers, but from the users we all serve: "Please, please, please hire a user interface designer."

Here are the facts: only a handful of people can be good designers, and only a handful of people can be good Java programmers. The rare odds of one person being in both handfuls can barely be measured with an IEEE double. Therefore, the odds are you're not a good UI designer. Please hire someone who is, and spend your time hacking back-end code with the rest of us who can't tell kerning from a kernel. We back-end folks are more fun anyway, in a laugh-through-the-nose kind of way.

CHAPTER 4
JDBC Best Practices

George Reese

The JDBC API is the ideal interface for database access, independent of the constraints of any particular database engine. In theory, you can take your JDBC application and deploy it on any operating system within any application server talking to any relational database. In reality, however, it's easy for a programmer to write seemingly database-independent JDBC code that results in wildly different behavior on different database engines. In this chapter, I have compiled a list of best practices that can help ensure both database independence and optimal performance of your JDBC code.

Configuration

JDBC configuration has very little to do with programming, per se. Instead, JDBC configuration assists you in configuring your applications in their runtime environments. Through proper JDBC configuration, you can take advantage of many of the performance features of your database of choice without burdening your applications with proprietary code. Proper configuration provides your database engine of choice with all the information it needs to tailor itself to your application's needs.

Avoid Type 1 and Type 3 Drivers

Sun classifies JDBC drivers into four categories, as shown in Table 4-1.

Table 4-1. JDBC drivers

Driver	Description
Type 1	A bridge between JDBC and another database-independent API, such as ODBC. The JDBC-ODBC driver that comes with the Java SDK is the primary example of a Type 1 driver.
Type 2	Translates JDBC calls into native API calls provided by the database vendor.
Type 3	Network bridges that enable an application to take advantage of the WORA (write once, run anywhere) capabilities of Type 4 drivers, even when your database of choice supports only Type 2 drivers.
Type 4	Talks directly to a database using a network protocol. Because it makes no native calls, it can run on any Java Virtual Machine (JVM).

Most programmers learn JDBC using the JDBC-ODBC Bridge, which is a Type 1 JDBC driver. Nevertheless, the JDBC-ODBC Bridge is a *bridging driver*. In other words, it's a driver that falls into the Type 1 or Type 3 categories. These types of drivers provide much weaker database performance than direct access drivers, and the reason for the weakness is fairly simple: bridging technologies require more hops to communicate with the database.

Though avoiding Type 1 and Type 3 drivers is a good rule of thumb, sometimes they cannot be avoided. Not all databases are supported by a Type 2 or Type 4 driver. For example, if you want an application to talk to Microsoft Access, you must use a Type 1 or Type 3 driver.

When to use a Type 1 or Type 3 driver

You should use a Type 1 driver under the following circumstances:

- No Type 2 or Type 4 driver exists for your database engine.
- Your application has a specific target platform or must run standalone.
- Your database engine supports an open API such as ODBC that has a bridging driver.

You should use a Type 3 driver when:

- No Type 4 driver exists for your database engine.
- Your application is a WORA client/server application or no Type 1 driver exists for your database engine.
- Your database engine has either a Type 1 or Type 2 driver supported by your Type 3 driver.

Choosing between Type 2 and Type 4 drivers

As I just mentioned, you should always try to use a Type 2 or Type 4 driver whenever possible. The only time you should choose a Type 3 driver rather than a Type 2 driver is when your application requires portability. It never makes sense to use a Type 1 bridging driver instead of a Type 2 or Type 4 driver.

That said, which is better, a Type 2 or a Type 4? This largely depends on how you intend to use it. The choice between Type 2 and Type 4 comes down to portability and an understanding of the underlying mechanics of the two drivers. Here are some guidelines:

- Always choose a Type 4 driver when portability is critical.
- For standalone applications or server applications, favor Type 2 drivers unless you understand the mechanics of how the two drivers are implemented.
- If the Type 4 driver is proven to be more efficient, use the Type 4 driver.

Use DataSource Whenever Possible

If you have a choice, you always should use `javax.sql.DataSource` to get a JDBC connection. Data sources, which were introduced with JDBC 2.0, make the job of configuring a database connection and connecting to a database nearly foolproof. Consider the following data source code fragment:

```
InitialContext ctx = new InitialContext();
DataSource ds = (DataSource)ctx.lookup("dsname");
Connection conn = ds.getConnection();
```

This code contains nothing proprietary, involves no parsing of configuration files, and uses no information dependent on the deployment environment other than a data source name. Now, compare that code to the following:

```
Connection conn;

Class.forName("org.gjt.mm.mysql.Driver").newInstance();
conn = DriverManager.getConnection("jdbc:mysql://carthage:/db", "user", "password");
```

This code is the simplest alternative to using a data source. However, the latter example is harder to read, contains proprietary code (i.e., specific reference to the `Driver` implementation class, which is the JDBC URL for a specific driver), and requires hard-coded information about the runtime environment (e.g., the host and database in the URL, the username, and the password). In short, you have to compile the `DriverManager` version for a specific target runtime environment.

To be fair, it is possible to achieve the same level of portability with the driver manager approach as with the data source approach. However, doing so makes your application code much more complex. In this case, you would have to specifically introduce code to parse a resource file containing the formerly hardcoded information. In addition, you would need to handle exceptional cases in which information is missing from your resource file. Finally, you would need to write in logic to handle any proprietary connection properties that help optimize the performance of your JDBC driver. All these items are better handled with the `DataSource` class.

Leverage Proprietary Connection Properties

Java has conditioned us to embrace open, generic standards and shy away from technology-specific tools. The JDBC API, however, allows databases to specify options that enable you to optimize the functionality of your database applications without impacting their openness. These options are called *connection properties*.

Every JDBC driver comes with a set of connection properties that allow you to specially configure it. Put another way, they allow you to tell the driver a bit about your application so that it can efficiently communicate with the database on the other side. These properties answer common JDBC questions, such as how big the result sets tend to be, which sorting rules should be used, and how long the driver should wait for information from the database before timing out. The properties that are available to you, and how they are best set, depend extensively on the database you are using and how your application is using that database. However, you should always take advantage of these properties in a production environment.

The two most common methods of specifying connection properties are to hardcode them when you configure your data source, or to place them inside a driver manager resource file. However, the following code snippets show a simpler way to keep your code free of platform-dependent property strings: use the system properties hashtable to embed the connection properties.

First, pass the system properties into the constructor of an InitialContext object:

```
InitialContext ctx = new InitialContext(System.getProperties());
DataSource ds = (DataSource)ctx.lookup("dsname");
Connection conn = ds.getConnection();
```

Or, if you use the DriverManager class (see my earlier warning against this), pass the system properties hashtable into the getConnection( ) method:

```
Connection conn = DriverManager.getConnection(url, System.getProperties());
```

You can then pass in JDBC connection properties by specifying them directly on the command line, configuring them accordingly based on the database that is used:

```
java -Duser=uid -Dpassword=pw -Dencoding=8859-1 -Dautocommit=true DBApp
```

Pool Database Connections

A sure way to bog down any JDBC application is to repeatedly open and close database connections. This problem is especially troublesome for high-volume applications such as web sites and enterprise applications. The clear and obvious answer to this problem is *connection pooling*. Connection pooling allows your application to use preexisting database connections by "loaning out" from a pool of connection objects.

Before JDBC 2.0, you had to write your own connection pooling support or look for a third-party tool. Put succinctly, connection pooling was a coding problem. Thanks to JDBC 2.0, however, connection pooling is now just a configuration issue. This means you simply have to convert your data source to a pooled data source; the code to access data from the connection remains the same, regardless of whether you use connection pooling. However, even though connection pooling is becoming more commonplace in JDBC code, it should still be included as a JDBC best practice.

How you configure your application to use a pooled connection depends on the environment in which you are running it. First, you must use a DataSource that supports connection pooling, which typically means obtaining an object that implements the javax.sql.ConnectionPoolDataSource interface. Your application then grabs its pooled connections from this data source. The only part that varies from one environment to the next is how to configure the environment to use a particular data source. For example, in a Java 2 Enterprise Edition (J2EE) application server, you will typically configure an XML file to store that data source for JNDI lookups. In other environments, you might manually configure and serialize a data source to be read later by the application.

Example 4-1 shows code used to obtain and release a pooled connection.

Example 4-1. Obtaining and releasing a pooled database connection

```
import javax.sql.*;
import javax.naming.*;

public void connectToDatabase() {

  try {

      InitialContext ctx = new InitialContext(parms);

      ConnectionPoolDataSource poolDataSource =
          (ConnectionPoolDataSource)ctx.lookup(
              cpsource);
      poolDataSource.setLoginTimeout(30); // seconds

      PooledConnection poolConnection =
          poolDataSource.getPooledConnection();

      Connection connection = poolConnection.getConnection();

      //  Do whatever you would typically do with the connection
      //  here.

  } catch (Exception e) {
      //  Handle exceptions.
  } finally {
      connection.close();
  }
}
```

Design

Design best practices tend to favor the creation of manageable database applications and rarely enhance performance. In fact, you might find that some of these best practices come with performance costs. Design, however, is never the place to second-guess performance issues. In any kind of programming, you should always put forth the best design first and optimize later.

Separate Application, Persistence, and JDBC Logic

The single most critical best practice in design is the proper separation of application and database logic through a generic persistence interface. Figure 4-1 shows an example of this separation.

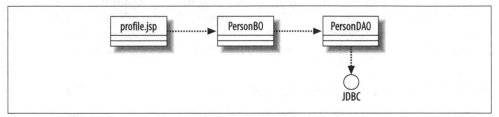

Figure 4-1. The division of labor in database programming

Note that in this approach, database logic is never mixed with application logic. (Here, the person bean object is separate from the person data access object.) This division not only makes code easier to read and manage, but it makes it possible for your data model and application logic to vary without impacting one another.

The ideal approach involves encapsulating application logic in components often referred to as business objects and developing a pattern through which these components persist, without knowing anything about the underlying persistence mechanism. Figure 4-2 is a class diagram showing how this approach works for bean-managed Enterprise JavaBean (EJB) entity beans.

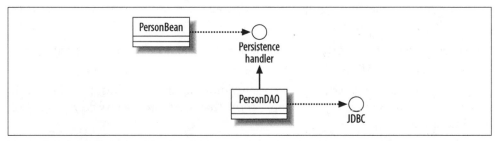

Figure 4-2. Entity bean persistence

The PersonBean entity bean contains no JDBC code or other database logic. Instead, it delegates all persistence operations to a generic persistence API. Underneath the covers, an implementation of that API performs the actual mapping of bean values to the database through the data access object. In fact, the implementation could persist to any entirely different data storage technology, such as an object database or directory service, without the entity bean being any wiser.

Avoid Long-Lived Transactions

Transactions are intrinsically part of another Java API, but their abuse of databases deserves mention here. Nothing will slow down a system quite like long-lived transactions. Whenever you start a transaction, you put others on hold waiting to access some of the resources of your transaction. Consequently, you should always design your applications to begin transactions only when they are ready to talk to the database and end them once that communication is done. Nothing other than database communication should occur between the beginning and end of a transaction.

Do Not Rely on Built-in Key Generation

Every database engine provides a feature that enables applications to automatically generate values for identity columns. MySQL, for example, has the concept of AUTO_INCREMENT columns:

```
CREATE TABLE Person (
    personID   BIGINT UNSIGNED NOT NULL PRIMARY KEY AUTO_INCREMENT,
    lastName   VARCHAR(30)     NOT NULL,
    firstName  VARCHAR(25)     NOT NULL
);
```

When you insert a new person into this table, you omit the primary key columns:

```
INSERT INTO Person ( lastName, firstName)
VALUES ( 'Wittgenstein', 'Ludwig' );
```

MySQL will automatically generate the value for the personID column based on the highest current value. For example, if one row exists in the database with a personID of 1, Ludwig Wittgenstein's personID will be 2.

However, using the supported key generation tools of your database of choice presents several problems:

- Every database engine handles key generation differently. Thus, it is difficult to build a truly portable JDBC application that uses proprietary key generation schemes.
- Until JDBC 3.0, a Java application had no clear way of finding out which keys were generated on an insert.
- Automated key generation wreaks havoc with EJBs.

You can avoid the difficulties of proprietary key generation schemes by writing your own. Your first inclination might be to create a table in the database to hold the generated keys, and this inclination is correct. It comes with some caveats, however.

Relying solely on a database table to hold the keys requires two trips to the database for each insert. To avoid too many trips to the database, it is best to generate the keys in memory based on a seed from the database. The heart of this database-independent scheme is the following table code:

```
CREATE TABLE Sequencer (
    name        VARCHAR(20)      NOT NULL,
    seed        BIGINT UNSIGNED  NOT NULL,
    lastUpdate  BIGINT UNSIGNED  NOT NULL,
    PRIMARY KEY ( name, lastUpdate )
);
```

Here's the strategy: the first time your application generates a key, it grabs the next seed from this database table based on the name you give it, increments the seed, and then uses that seed to generate keys until the seed is exhausted (at which point, it increments to get another one) or until the application terminates. Examples 4-2 through 4-4 show how to create a database-independent utility class called Sequencer that uses this strategy to uniquely generate key numbers. This enables your application to use the following two lines of code to create primary keys, an approach which guarantees that you will receive a value that is unique across all values in the specified sequence (i.e., personID):

```
Sequencer seq = Sequencer.getInstance("personID");
personID = seq.next( );
```

You probably noticed that you are not using the lastUpdate field yet. Don't worry, this field is being kept in reserve until the next section.

Example 4-2 shows part of the Sequencer class, which uses static elements that employ a singleton design pattern to hand out shared sequencers.

Example 4-2. Sequencer.java

```
public class Sequencer {

    static private final long    MAX_KEYS   = 1000000L;
    static private final HashMap sequencers = new HashMap( );

    static public final Sequencer getInstance(String name) {
        synchronized( sequencers ) {
            if( !sequencers.containsKey(name) ) {
                Sequencer seq = new Sequencer(name);

                sequencers.put(name, seq);
                return seq;
            }
            else {
                return (Sequencer)sequencers.get(name);
            }
        }
    }

    ...
}
```

The code in Example 4-2 provides two critical guarantees for sequence generation:

- All code that needs to create new numbers for the same sequence (e.g., personID) will share the same sequencer object.
- Because of the synchronized block, two attempts to get a previously unreferenced sequence at the same instant will not cause two different sequencers to be instantiated.

Example 4-3 continues the Sequencer class with three fields and a constructor. The nonstatic fields have two private variables that mirror values in the Sequencer database table (name and seed) as well as a third attribute (sequence) to track the values handed out for the current seed.

Example 4-3. Sequencer.java (constructors)

```java
public class Sequencer {
    ...
    private String name    = null;
    private long   seed    = -1L;
    private long   sequence = 0L;

    private Sequencer(String nom) {
        super();
        name = nom;
    }
    ...
}
```

Finally, the core element of the sequencer is its public next( ) method. This method contains the algorithm for generating unique numbers, and uses the following process:

1. First, it checks to see if the seed is valid. The seed is invalid if this is a newly created sequencer or if the seed is exhausted. A seed is exhausted if the next sequence has a value greater than MAX_KEYS.
2. If the seed is not valid based on the preceding criteria, it gets a new seed from the database.
3. It increments the sequence.
4. It generates the unique key by multiplying the seed by MAX_KEYS and adding the current sequence value.

Example 4-4 contains the algorithm.

Example 4-4. Sequencer.java (next() method)

```java
public class Sequencer {

    static public final String DSN_PROP = "myapp.dsn";
    static public final String DEFAULT_DSN = "jdbc/default";
```

Example 4-4. Sequencer.java (next() method) (continued)

```
    ...

    public synchronized long next( ) throws PersistenceException {

        Connection conn = null;

        // When seed is -1 or the keys for this seed are exhausted,
        // get a new seed from the database.

        if( (seed == -1L) || ((sequence + 1) >= MAX_KEYS) ) {
            try {
                String dsn = System.getProperty(DSN_PROP, DEFAULT_DSN);
                InitialContext ctx = new InitialContext( );
                DataSource ds = (DataSource)ctx.lookup(dsn);

                conn = ds.getConnection( );

                // Reseed the database.

                reseed(conn);
            }
            catch( SQLException e ) {
                throw new PersistenceException(e);
            }
            catch( NamingException e ) {
                throw new PersistenceException(e);
            }
            finally {
                if( conn != null ) {
                    try { conn.close( ); }
                    catch( SQLException e ) { }
                }
            }
        }

        // Up the sequence value for the next key.

        sequence++;

        // Return the next key for this sequencer.

        return ((seed * MAX_KEYS) + sequence);
    }

    ...
}
```

The rest of the code is the database access that creates, retrieves, and updates seeds in the database. The next( ) method triggers a database call via the reseed( ) method when the current seed is no longer valid. The logic for reseeding the sequencer is not shown, but it is fairly straightforward:

1. Fetch the current values (e.g., the seed) for the sequence name in question from the database.

2. If the sequence does not yet exist in the database, create it.

3. Increment the seed from the database.

4. Update the database.

5. Set the new seed and reset the sequence attribute to -1 (this makes the first number generated 0).

Example 4-5 contains the implementation of everything but the creation of a new sequence. You can find the full code for the Sequencer class on O'Reilly's FTP site under the catalog index for this book. (See *http://www.oreilly.com/catalog/javaebp*.)

Don't Be Afraid to Use Optimistic Concurrency

Depending on your database engine, you might have the ability to choose between optimistic or pessimistic concurrency models. If your database supports pessimistic concurrency, you can enforce it through either database configuration or JDBC configuration.

The concurrency model you select determines whether you or the database engine is responsible for preventing *dirty writes*—that is, preventing one person from overwriting changes made by another based on old data from the database. Under optimistic concurrency, changes can be made to a row between the time it is read and the time updates are sent to the database. Without special logic in your application, systems that rely on optimistic concurrency run the risk of the following chain of events:

1. User A fetches a data record for a specific person from the database.

2. User B fetches the same data record.

3. User A changes a field in that data (e.g., the marital status of the person) and sends the update to the database.

4. User B changes another field in that data (e.g., the home phone number of the person) and sends the update to the database.

The consequence of this chain of events is an invalid marital status in the database. The status is no longer valid because User B overwrote the change in marital status of User A with the dirty data from its original read.

Pessimistic concurrency prevents dirty writes. How it prevents dirty writes depends on your database engine. Put succinctly, pessimistic concurrency causes User A to get a lock on the row or table with the user data and hold up User B until the marital status change is committed. User B reads the new marital status and will not overwrite the change of User A unless it is intended.

Because maintaining data integrity is the single most important principle of database programming, it might appear that pessimistic concurrency is a must. Unfortunately, pessimistic concurrency comes with a huge performance penalty that few applications should ever accept. Furthermore, because many database engines do not even support pessimistic concurrency, reliance on it will make it difficult to port your application to different databases.

The answer to the problem of using pessimistic concurrency without sacrificing data integrity is to use a smart optimistic concurrency scheme. Under optimistic concurrency, the burden of data integrity lies squarely on the shoulders of the application developer. The problem you face managing optimistic concurrency is how you allow people to make changes to the database between reading a row from a table and writing updates back to the database. To prevent dirty writes, you need some mechanism of row versioning, and then you must specify updates only to a particular version of that row.

Programmers use many different schemes for versioning rows; some database engines even have built-in row versioning. Two of the more common approaches are to use either a timestamp or a combination of a timestamp and another identifying information such as a user ID. Earlier in this chapter, we discussed a scheme for generating unique primary keys. The Sequencer table responsible for storing the state of the primary key generation tool had a compound primary key of both the sequence name and the time it was last updated. Example 4-5 contains the JDBC calls that make updates to that table using optimistic concurrency, which is shown in the fully implemented reseed( ) method.

Example 4-5. Sequencer.java (reseed() method using optimistic concurrency)

```java
public class Sequencer {
    ...
    static private final String FIND_SEQ =
        "SELECT seed, lastUpdate " +
        "FROM Sequencer " +
        "WHERE name = ?";

    static private final int SEL_NAME   = 1;

    static private final int SEL_SEED   = 1;
    static private final int SEL_UPDATE = 2;

    static private String UPDATE_SEQ =
        "UPDATE Sequencer " +
        "SET seed = ?, " +
        "lastUpdate = ? " +
        "WHERE name = ? AND lastUpdate = ?";

    static private final int UPD_SEED         = 1;
    static private final int UPD_SET_UPDATE   = 2;
    static private final int UPD_NAME         = 3;
    static private final int UPD_WHERE_UPDATE = 4;
```

Example 4-5. Sequencer.java (reseed( ) method using optimistic concurrency) (continued)

```java
private void reseed(Connection conn) throws SQLException {
    PreparedStatement stmt = null;
    ResultSet rs = null;

    try {

        // Keep in this loop as long as you encounter concurrency errors.

        do {
            stmt = conn.prepareStatement(FIND_SEQ);
            stmt.setString(SEL_NAME, name);
            rs = stmt.executeQuery();
            if( !rs.next() ) {

                // If there is no such sequence, create it.

                {
                    // Close resources.
                    try { rs.close(); }
                    catch( SQLException e ) { // Handle }
                    rs = null;
                    try { stmt.close(); }
                    catch( SQLException e ) { // Handle }
                    stmt = null;
                }

                // Create the sequence in the database.

                create(conn);
            }
            else {

                long ts;

                seed = rs.getLong(SEL_SEED) + 1L;
                ts = rs.getLong(SEL_UPDATE);

                {
                    // Close resources.
                    try { rs.close(); }
                    catch( SQLException e ) { // Handle }
                    rs = null;
                    try { stmt.close(); }
                    catch( SQLException e ) { // Handle }
                    stmt = null;
                }

                // Increment the seed in the database.

                stmt = conn.prepareStatement(UPDATE_SEQ);
                stmt.setLong(UPD_SEED, seed);
                stmt.setLong(UPD_SET_UPDATE,
                                System.currentTimeMillis());
```

Example 4-5. Sequencer.java (reseed() method using optimistic concurrency) (continued)

```
                    stmt.setString(UPD_NAME, name);
                    stmt.setLong(UPD_WHERE_UPDATE, ts);

                    if( stmt.executeUpdate( ) != 1 ) {
                        // Someone changed the database! Try again!
                        seed = -1L;
                    }
                }

            } while( seed == -1L );

            sequence = -1L;
        }

        finally {
            if( rs != null ) {
                try { rs.close( ); }
                catch( SQLException e ) { // Handle }
            }
            if( stmt != null ) {
                try { stmt.close( ); }
                catch( SQLException e ) { // Handle }
            }
        }
    }
    ...
}
```

Without optimistic concurrency in place, you would either have to rely on pessimistic concurrency or risk the generation of a series of duplicate identifiers. This code prevents duplicate keys without resorting to pessimistic concurrency by using the last update time—accurate to the millisecond—as a versioning mechanism. The last update time is part of the primary key, and it is updated with every change. Now, an attempted dirty write will take the following course:

1. User A will request a unique ID for the Person table.

2. User A's sequencer will read the values of the row from the Sequencer table for the "personID" sequence.

3. User B will request a unique ID for the Person table.

4. User B's sequencer will read the same values just read for User A.

5. User A's sequencer will increment the current seed and update the Sequencer table with the incremented seed and the value of System.currentTimeMillis( ) using the old lastUpdate value in its WHERE clause.

6. User B's sequencer will increment its current seed to the same value User A's sequencer incremented it to and then attempt to update the Sequencer table with the incremented seed and the value of System.currentTimeMillis( ) using the old

lastUpdate value in its WHERE clause. This attempt will fail because the old lastUpdate value no longer matches what is in the database.

7. User B's sequencer will make a second attempt to reseed itself.

This approach works because the SQL statement specified by the static string UPDATE_SEQ will update a table only in the event that both the name and the lastUpdate timestamp are identical to the values it read earlier from the database. Otherwise, the call to executeUpdate( ) will return -1.

Figure 4-3 illustrates how optimistic concurrency works.

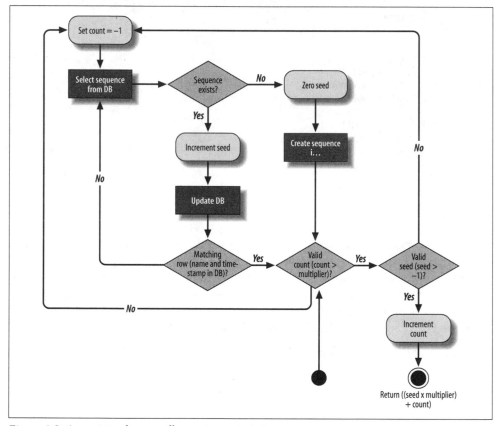

Figure 4-3. An activity diagram illustrating optimistic concurrency

This approach works only if versioning using milliseconds sufficiently guarantees distinct row versions. In other words, it will fail if three requests to read and update the row can occur in the same millisecond, or if the updates are occurring from a set of hosts with serious time synchronization issues. However, in the scenario of ID generation, these issues do not materialize into a serious concern.

Alternative forms of optimistic concurrency management can address clock synchronization. In older systems, it was impossible even to get the current time down to the millisecond. Though the read-three-and-update scenario was unlikely in a single millisecond for unique identifier generation, doing it in a second is not so inconceivable. Similarly, in client/server applications where the client clocks can be severely out of whack, System.currentTimeMillis( ) is not reliable. The solution is to add more information to the update clause. In client/server applications, for example, it is common to use a timestamp combined with the user ID of the last person to update the table. Because different clients tend to represent different users in a client/server environment—and they rarely do work that would risk multiple updates in the same second—the combination of user ID and timestamp addresses both the rapid operation and clock synchronization issues.

That said, the use of user IDs in multitier applications is unreliable because an application server in such an environment tends to use the same user ID for all database access, no matter who the client is. The moral here is that there is no definitive answer; you always need to tailor your optimistic concurrency management to the needs of the environment in which you are working.

Finally, it is important to note that while operating a database using optimistic concurrency has major performance advantages over operating with pessimistic concurrency, the data integrity management schemes I have introduced come with performance hits on updates. Specifically, you are updating unique keys in your database on every insert and update. Updating keys can be an expensive operation. Normally, this performance hit is well worth the cost, as read operations significantly outnumber write operations most of the time. If you are in a heavy write situation, however, you might want to consider other options. If you are performing some limited timeframe write operation, such as a batch update, you might even want to turn off indexing completely.

Code

In the previous section, I mentioned the principle of "design first and optimize later." Code is where optimization is realized. Most of the following coding best practices are aimed at improving database performance or getting around deficiencies in different JDBC drivers or database engines.

Use PreparedStatement

JDBC provides three kinds of statement classes: Statement, PreparedStatement, and CallableStatement. All too often, however, discussions of which kind of statement to use focus purely on performance. That's not to say that the choice of statement class doesn't impact performance. As a general rule, CallableStatement instances based on database-stored procedures provide the best performance, with PreparedStatement instances close behind. Finally, Statement instances generally perform significantly worse than the other kinds of statements. Focusing purely on performance, however, disguises two important facts:

- The difference between CallableStatement and PreparedStatement is generally negligible.
- There are nontrivial situations in which a Statement gives you optimal performance.

The primary difference in performance among the different statement types concerns how the SQL parsing occurs. With Statement-based calls, the driver sends the SQL to the database, which parses it every time you execute the statement. Calls through a PreparedStatement (as the name implies) are "prepared" before they are executed. In other words, the driver sends the SQL to the database for parsing when the statement is created but before it is executed. By the time you call execute( ), the statement has been preparsed by the database. And if you're truly lucky, the same SQL has already been executed, and no parsing even needs to occur. Finally, a CallableStatement is "precompiled" in the database. The actual statement is stored in the database and referenced by your JDBC application by name. Consequently, there is no overhead for the initial call, and your application has the power to tweak the database configuration to support that call.

Sounds good, right? Wrong. Unfortunately, everything described here is the ideal. The truth is that every database engine handles these different statements in very different ways. Under mSQL, for example, a prepared statement will always perform a bit worse than a regular statement because the mSQL driver is only simulating prepared statement behavior—mSQL does not inherently support prepared statements. Furthermore, many databases do not actually precompile stored procedures and thus provide absolutely no performance benefits at all.

In spite of the few odd situations in which a Statement does perform best, you should unconditionally avoid the use of Statement in production systems. Not only does it generally perform more slowly than other kinds of statements, but it also makes for ugly, error-prone JDBC. Consider the following SQL code fragment:

```
conn = ds.getConnection( );
stmt = conn.createStatement( );
stmt.executeUpdate("UPDATE Person " +
                "SET lastName = '" + lastName + "', " +
                "firstName = '" + firstName + "', " +
                "biography = '" + clean(biography) + "' " +
                "WHERE personID = " + personID);
```

First and foremost, this code is a mess to read with all the string additions. Readability is just a start to the maintenance problems of this very simple example, however. In this example, the biography is assumed to be free-form text pulled from user-supplied data. You cannot trust it to validly fit within the single quotes that signify a SQL string literal. What if there is a possessive in the biography, such as "his wife's car?" In that case, your application breaks. You therefore have to include code—captured in a nonportable clean( ) method in this object—to clean out any special SQL symbols and escape codes. And to make matters worse, what if strings such as the last name and first name need cleaning that you did not consider ahead of time?

Fortunately, you can do the same thing much more elegantly with a prepared statement:

```
conn = ds.getConnection( );
stmt = conn.prepareStatement("UPDATE Person " +
                    "SET lastName = ?, firstName = ?, biography = ? " +
                    "WHERE personID = ?");
stmt.setString(1, lastName);
stmt.setString(2, firstName);
stmt.setString(3, biography);
stmt.setLong(4, personID);
stmt.executeUpdate( );
```

The only string concatenation in this code is done for readability. Because concatenation of string literals occurs at compile time, you also get a nice performance boost that has nothing to do with statement versus prepared statement processing. The real benefit here, however, is that your code elements are more compact, and there is a significant reduction in the risk of bugs. You no longer have to write your own database-specific routine to remove symbols from the raw strings—the driver or database handles that for you. In short, the prepared statement code has significantly increased:

- Readability
- Reliability
- Portability

Not performance? Maybe the PreparedStatement performs better; maybe the Statement performs better. It depends on the driver and database you are using. To be honest, this exact JDBC code can yield wildly different results depending on the driver/database combination and how many times you call this prepared statement. The only thing you really know for sure is that the Statement will never significantly outperform the PreparedStatement. If you are making repeated calls, you can bet that the prepared statement will significantly outperform the statement.

Of course, if the elegant PreparedStatement code is such a good thing, shouldn't the more elegant stored procedure code be even better? For example:

```
conn = ds.getConnection( );
stmt = conn.prepareCall("{call update_person(?, ?, ?, ?)}");
stmt.setString(1, lastName);
stmt.setString(2, firstName);
stmt.setString(3, biography);
stmt.setLong(4, personID);
stmt.executeUpdate( );
```

This code doesn't contain long strings requiring concatenation for readability's sake! In fact, this code almost turns database access into a function call, as if the database were some black box. In general, this level of abstraction is the desirable form of an interface between two separate technologies. Unfortunately, there are absolutely no clues in this code as to what you are doing to the database. In a persistence engine, this separation makes maintenance difficult. The reason for this problem is that JDBC is the proper demarcation between the database and the application. The SQL is part of the persistence code and therefore belongs with the rest of the persistence code, not with the data storage logic of the database engine.

 In spite of my recommendations to avoid stored procedures, there are valid reasons for using them. Specifically, stored procedures can significantly speed up some very complex database operations and encapsulate complex transaction logic. The rule of thumb in these situations is to write the application using prepared statements first and identify the bottlenecks and complexities. Once you have identified them, manage them by moving special cases to the database in the form of stored procedures. If the changes are designed to improve performance and are successful, keep the changes just in those bottlenecks. Also, stored procedures allow the DBA to handle the database logic and allow the programmer to use just the exposed hooks. But, no matter what, never resort to placing business logic into stored procedures!

Beyond abstract platitudes about the proper separation of systems behind clean interfaces, however, stored procedures also have one serious drawback: poor portability. Though JDBC provides a database-independent form for stored procedure calls, different database engines do not support stored procedures in even remotely similar fashions. Access times for retrieving data from a database in Oracle through PL/SQL can be wildly different from retrieving data from SQL Server through TransactSQL. In Oracle, for example, you need to use out parameters. TransactionSQL, however, supports retrieving data as result sets. Finally, the underlying stored procedure languages are very different. You will consequently have to rewrite all stored procedures to port an application to a new database engine.

Leverage PreparedStatement Pooling

You are guaranteed to see a performance boost from prepared statements only when the underlying database supports prepared statements and you repeatedly use the same PreparedStatement instance. Your application will probably receive a performance boost if you repeatedly use the same prepared SQL statement. However, a performance boost is very unlikely when you use a prepared statement only once.

To maximize the likelihood that you will see a performance boost in a cross-platform environment, you need to find ways to reuse your PreparedStatement instances. Unfortunately, pooling prepared statements is not quite as straightforward as pooling database connections. Because closing a connection closes any associated statements, you cannot pool statements across connection closures. The new JDBC 3.0 specification has stepped in to address the problem by supporting prepared statement pooling inside the specification.

The ability to use pooled prepared statements in JDBC 3.0 is hidden behind connection pooling. To take advantage of it, you must:

- Use a JDBC 3.0 driver that supports pooled prepared statements.
- Configure a data source for pooled connections that provide statement pooling.

Let's review how connection pooling works. When an application requests a database connection, it receives a logical connection that at some point becomes associated with a physical database connection. Note that the application never has direct access to the physical database connection. A call to close the connection closes only the logical connection—the physical database connection remains open and returns to the connection pool. The same principle works for prepared statements. The code that you have always used to execute prepared statements works with prepared statement pooling. Use of statement pooling simply depends on proper data source configuration.

This best practice is not an absolute, as the costs of prepared statement pooling can outweigh the benefits. Specifically, if your application uses a significant number of distinct statements with little repeated calling of those statements, you will burden the system with an inordinate number of open statements. To get around this, you need to balance the repetition of the same statement against the number of statements your system will use. If the number of repeated calls to the same statement is significant, you should favor statement pooling. If your application consists of many calls to distinct statements, however, you should disfavor statement pooling.

The use of JDBC 3.0 is, as of yet, not widespread. What do you do if you cannot use a JDBC 3.0 driver? One alternative is to write your own statement pooling behind a JDBC 2.0 façade! To accomplish this task, you need to write implementations of `javax.sql.ConnectionPoolDataSource`, `java.sql.Connection`, and `java.sql.PreparedStatement`. In fact, you will need two separate `Connection` implementations. On O'Reilly's FTP and web sites, an implementation based on a combination of the JDBC 3.0 specification and ideas from Morgan Catlin that aid in statement pooling for JDBC 2.0 applications are provided.

Question Using Nonstandard SQL

You should try to use only ANSI SQL in your JDBC calls. This best practice might seem obvious, but it is amazing how often people fall back on database-specific SQL simply because it is a nice crutch. On occasion, some behavior will demand proprietary SQL. For example, you may find that your project simply cannot live without the proprietary features of a specific database, and that is more important than portability.

If this is the case, then so be it. Your first reaction, however, should always be to question your use of proprietary SQL and justify it to yourself and your team.

Delay Access to Metadata

Most people do not realize just how expensive *metadata operations*—that is, calls to `DatabaseMetaData`, `ResultSetMetaData`, and `ParameterMetaData` methods—can be. When calling for a result set's metadata, for example, many database engines need to finish pulling all rows in the current fetch batch before they can get the metadata for that result set. Consider the following code fragment:

```
conn = ds.getConnection();
stmt = conn.prepareStatement("SELECT * FROM Person");
rs = stmt.excecuteQuery();
md = rs.getMetaData();
while( rs.next() ) {
```

For some database engines and drivers, you will not be able to read anything from the first row until the driver retrieves all the rows from the server. Of course, you cannot avoid calling metadata. The solution is therefore to delay accessing metadata until you need it.

Reference Columns by Number

This best practice is related to the previous one. Column names are part of the metadata for a result set. A JDBC driver might not have access to a column's name when you process the first row. If you are retrieving the data by column name, the retrieval will wait until the name is available to the driver. Because retrieving columns by name could penalize some database engines over others in terms of performance, the ability to retrieve columns by name was not even part of the original JDBC specification.

Most programmers prefer to retrieve results by name instead of by number because names are easier to remember, and the order of the parameters in the SQL can change without impacting code. This objection, however, is based on the faulty practice of including naked literals in code. In other words:

```
id = rs.getLong(1);
```

and:

```
id = rs.getLong("personID");
```

are equally improper. You should instead use:

```
static private final int PERSON_ID = 1;

...

id = rs.getLong(PERSON_ID);
```

With this format, it does not matter from a maintenance perspective whether you are using retrieval by name or number.

You can maximize the maintainability and performance of your code by placing the constants for the parameter values with a constant containing the SQL itself, as shown in Example 4-5.

Navigate a ResultSet Forward Only

This best practice is also related to the inconsistency in the way databases transfer results from the server to the client. Specifically, the only sure way to achieve the best database performance without optimizing your JDBC code for a specific database engine is to use only forward navigation with your results. In other words, you should ignore the support for scrollable result sets added in JDBC 2.0.

In fact, the need to do fancy navigation in a result set is generally reflective of an application design flaw. Except for batch programs, normal Java applications should simply grab data from the database and construct Java objects. Application processing should operate on those Java objects. Consequently, the application should not need to do anything except move forward through a result set instantiating Java objects from the data.

Close Statements and Result Sets

According to the JDBC specification, closing a database connection closes all open statement and result set resources associated with that connection. Theoretically, you should never have to close anything but connection instances unless you are intentionally keeping the connection open for a long time. Unfortunately, there are several drivers that do not appropriately clean up the underlying result set and statement resources unless you explicitly close them.

The following code can be used as a template for all JDBC access to ensure that all resources are properly cleaned up:

```
PreparedStatement stmt = null;
Connection conn = null;
ResultSet rs = null;

try {
    InitialContext ctx = new InitialContext();
    DataSource ds = (DataSource)ctx.lookup("dsn");

    conn = ds.getConnection();
    // Do your database access here!
}
catch( SQLException e ) {
    // Handle the error appropriately here.
}
catch( NamingException e ) {
```

```
        // Handle the error appropriately here.
    }
    finally {
        if( rs != null ) {
            try { rs.close( ); }
            catch( SQLException e ) { // Handle}
        }
        if( stmt != null ) {
            try { stmt.close( ); }
            catch( SQLException e ) { // Handle}
        }
        if( conn != null ) {
            try { conn.close( ); }
            catch( SQLException e ) { // Handle}
        }
    }
```

This code ensures that no matter what awful things occur in your application, you will never leave any database resources open! The only truly controversial element in this code lies in the eating of the SQL exceptions when the resources are closed. If you like, you can do something with those exceptions; however, it is unlikely you will encounter such exceptions in a situation in which you will care and be able to do something about it.

Thread JDBC Code in Swing Applications

Swing events are not made to support complex application processing. In fact, if you perform any extensive processing in the same thread that triggered a Swing event—the click of a button, for example—you will create odd behavior in your user interface. Windows will stop redrawing, and menu items will cease to behave as expected.

Any network calls, especially JDBC calls that trigger database activity, require too much processing to place into a Swing event thread. Your Swing applications should therefore disable the appropriate user interface elements and start a new thread when the user triggers some event that needs to go to the database. All database access should take place in the spawned thread. When that thread is done, it should notify the Swing event queue that it is time to reenable the appropriate user interface elements.

The book *Database Programming with JDBC and Java* (O'Reilly) goes into more detail on the topic of database access from Swing access than is appropriate for this chapter. You can see some example code, however, by downloading its examples from *ftp://ftp.oreilly.com/pub/examples/java/jdbc2*.

Minimize Database Calls and Perform Lazy-Loading

One of the nastiest things about the object/relational mismatch is the fact that proper object-oriented coding implies that you should make an inordinate number of database calls. The canonical object-oriented search looks like this:

- Get all the primary keys from the database that match search criteria.
- For each match, go to the database to load its primary attributes.
- Also for each match, go to the database once for each object attribute.

This degree of database access is not only unnecessary, but it will also render your application totally unusable. Therefore, this area is where compromising on object-oriented principles is not only acceptable, but also a requirement.

As you've probably guessed, your Java application should do whatever it can to minimize the number of trips it makes to the database to support a single logical operation. Selecting the columns necessary to instantiate objects as part of the search will reduce the number of calls immensely. In the true object-oriented way, a search returning 100 rows results in at least 101 calls to the database. By selecting the necessary columns in your search, you can potentially drop this number to just the single search query.

Of course, selecting all the columns when you are probably going to use only one or two can itself be a performance problem. Your application needs to balance the need to minimize calls to the database with the reality of how many rows you will actually use.

Another trick to create the illusion of good performance is to perform *lazy-loading* on any extra database calls that must happen. In other words, return from a JDBC search immediately with objects incompletely populated from whatever the database could offer from a single query. Then in a background thread (or perhaps on demand), the individual objects can populate the missing data without impacting the speed with which search results are returned, no matter how many database calls are necessary to populate the objects with data. A Person object that needs to make a second call to get all addresses associated with that person might have a getAddresses( ) method that looks like this:

```
public synchronized Iterator getAddresses( ) {
    if( addresses == null ) {

        // This method will go to the database to load the addresses.
        addresses = Address.getAddressesFor(this);
    }
    return addresses.iterator( );
}
```

Cache Lookup Tables

This practice is a kind of corollary of the last best practice. Lookup tables are tables that contain fairly static lists such as states, countries, type codes, etc. Applications generally need to reference this data frequently. Because the data does not change, you can avoid repeated lookups against these tables by caching the data in memory.

Use wasNull( ) Checks

SQL NULL is a very useful tool that, unfortunately, is frequently abused. A good database application uses NULL in situations in which a row lacks a value. For example, if you have an application in which one of the attributes of the Person table is numPets, you should use NULL to indicate that you do not know how many pets they have. Without NULL, you would have to use a bogus value such as -1.

Your JDBC code should always be checking for possible NULL values from nullable columns using the wasNull( ) method in ResultSet. The actual value that JDBC returns for NULL values in getter methods is undefined. Your code to check the number of pets, for example, should look like the following fragment:

```
conn = ds.getConnection( );
stmt = conn.prepareStatement("SELECT numPets FROM Person WHERE personID = ?");
stmt.setLong(1, 13933L);
rs = stmt.executeQuery( );
if( rs.next( ) ) {
    pets = rs.getInt(1);
    if( rs.wasNull( ) ) {
        pets = -1; // Java has no concept of null for numerics!
    }
}
```

General Database

You can do only so much in Java and JDBC. In the end, your application is at the mercy of the database supporting it. Many best practices are limited to specific database engines. A solid best practice as a database architect is to become intimately familiar with the strengths and quirks of your database of choice. With that in mind, however, I will close this chapter by providing some general best practices for approaching any database engine.

Always Optimize SQL Before Other Optimizations

The natural tendency in JDBC programming is to tweak your Java code. The truth is you will get the most bang for your buck in SQL optimizations. Small things such as indexing the columns in your WHERE clauses will do more for your application performance than anything you can do in Java. A good way to find out what is happening with your SQL code is to use your database engine's command-line utility and run the SQL through the EXPLAIN SELECT command.

The information the EXPLAIN SELECT command provides is database-dependent. Whatever your database, it should tell you some basic things about how it is trying to execute your query. Is the query utilizing indexes fully, or is it doing multiple table scans for what should be a simple query?

Do Not Store Binary Data in Database

Databases are horrible places for binary data. The database engine ends up being a nasty middleman for pulling large chunks of data. Furthermore, it is not particularly optimized for the unique needs of binary data. Unfortunately, moving the data to the filesystem and maintaining pointers to the filesystem in the database puts data integrity at risk. What if someone deletes the file, but the record pointing to the file remains in the database?

For most applications, the data integrity issue is not a huge problem. Digital asset collections, however, can become unmanageable when you store the binary data on the filesystem. These specialized applications should instead use a digital asset management system to manage the binary data.

Normalize First, Denormalize Later

This principle is the database equivalent of design first and optimize later. Unfortunately, many Java programmers who follow the design-first-and-optimize-later strategy fail to normalize first and denormalize later. Instead, the tendency is not to spend much time on the data model at all and just use what works with the current object model.

In data modeling, you will see the best results from taking your design to at least the third normal form until the model is complete. Only when you have a solid data model is it safe to begin denormalizing in places where overnormalization severely impacts performance.

Do Not Use Primary Keys with Real-World Meaning

We spent a lot of time earlier in the chapter discussing a scheme for generating unique identifiers. You would not have to go to all that trouble if you used something natural such as a social security number or an email address. The use of such identifiers as primary keys, however, is a spectacularly bad idea, and is therefore our final best practice.

A primary key identifier should identify something about the thing it represents that can never change. Email addresses and even social security numbers can change. In fact, just about anything with real-world meaning can one day change. The fact that social security numbers rarely change is irrelevant. If the attribute can ever change—even under the most remote of circumstances—it makes a poor primary key.

The best thing for an application to use is otherwise meaningless numeric identifiers as primary key identifiers. Because their sole raison d'être is to identify a row in a specific database, such identifiers will never need to feel the pressure to change. Better yet, by using meaningless numbers, you can pick a data type that will work best in your database as a key. In relational databases, the best data type for a unique identifier is a numeric type. I recommend the use of 64-bit numbers to avoid running out of identifier space.

CHAPTER 5

XML Best Practices

Brett McLaughlin

It's almost impossible for programmers not to use XML in modern enterprise applications. In fact, programmers are finding it increasingly common to read and write XML, either from other components within the same application or from external sources such as a web service.

In this chapter we'll discuss several types of XML-based best practices. First, we'll discuss several ways you can better structure your XML, regardless of the API you choose to use. From there, we'll look at tips for using three significantly different XML APIs included with a Java 2 Enterprise Edition (J2EE) distribution. We'll also discuss how, in addition to good document authoring, it is important that your XML manipulation code be efficient and well-designed. This chapter examines several best practices that will get you on the right track to effective Java and XML programming, and keep you sleeping at night.[*]

XML Authoring

Today's Java programmers frequently see a wealth of tips and tricks on the Internet to improve their use of APIs such as SAX, DOM, and JAXP. While I'll address each of these in turn in the second part of this chapter, all the good coding in the world won't make up for poor document authoring. In this section I'll present a few ideas that can make your documents cleaner and less error-prone.

Use Entity References

An *entity reference* (also called an *entity declaration* in some circles) is one of those topics in XML that seems a little obscure. However, just think of an entity reference

---

[*] Some of the concepts throughout this chapter are based on tips I wrote that were originally published online at the *IBM DeveloperWorks* site (*http://www.ibm.com/developer*). My thanks to IBM for allowing their modification and reuse.

as a variable in XML. That variable has a declared value, and every time the variable occurs, the parser substitutes that value in the XML output. In that regard, an entity reference is like a `static final` variable in Java in that it cannot alter its value from an initial value defined in a Document Type Definition (DTD).

An entity reference often refers to an online resource (you'll see examples of this later in the "SAX" section), but it can also have a value defined in a DTD, such as the following:

```
<!ENTITY phoneNumber "800-775-7731">
```

Instead of typing the phone number for O'Reilly several times in your XML document, and possibly introducing typographical errors, you can just refer to the value through its reference:

```
<content>O'Reilly's phone number is &phoneNumber;.</content>
```

Of course, this seems pretty trivial, so let's look at a more realistic example. Example 5-1 shows a simple XML document fragment intended for display on a web page.

Example 5-1. Sample document without entity references

```
<page>
  <title>O'Reilly Java Enterprise Best Practices</title>
  <content type="html">
    <center><h1>O'Reilly Java Enterprise Best Practices</h1></center>
    <p>
      Welcome to the website for <i>O'Reilly Java Enterprise Best
      Practices</i>. This book was written by O'Reilly's Java
      authors for Java Enterprise professionals. And so on and
      so on, ad infinitum.
    </p>
  </content>
</page>
```

Notice that the title "O'Reilly Java Enterprise Best Practices" was repeated three times. Not only does this introduce room for error, but it also makes it a pain to change all occurrences. After all, there might be 10 or 15 more instances of this title in this and related documents in the future! Criteria such as these make the title a good candidate for an entity reference. First, add the following definition in your DTD:

```
<!ENTITY bookTitle "O'Reilly Java Enterprise Best Practices">
```

Then, change the XML to look like this:

```
<page>
  <title>&bookTitle;</title>
  <content type="html">
    <center><h1>&bookTitle;</h1></center>
```

```
<p>
   Welcome to the website for <i>&bookTitle;</i>. This book was
   written by O'Reilly's Java authors for Java Enterprise
   professionals. And so on and so on, ad infinitum.
</p>
   </content>
  </page>
```

Now, by simply changing the entity reference's value, you can change all references in the XML document to the new value.

Use Parameter Entities

The natural extension of using entity references in an XML document is using *parameter entities* in a DTD. A parameter entity looks very much like an entity reference:

```
<!ENTITY % common.attributes
     'id        ID    #IMPLIED
      account   CDATA #REQUIRED'
  >
```

Here, a more strict textual replacement occurs. In this case, the `common.attributes` definition can be used to specify two attributes that most elements in a constraint set should have. You can then define those elements in the DTD, as shown in Example 5-2.

Example 5-2. Sample DTD with parameter entities

```
<!ELEMENT purchaseOrder (item+, manufacturer, purchaser, purchaseInfo)>
<!ATTLIST purchaseOrder %common.attributes;>

<!ELEMENT item (price, quantity)>
<!ATTLIST item %common.attributes;>

<!ELEMENT manufacturer (#PCDATA)>
<!ATTLIST manufacturer %common.attributes;>

<!ELEMENT purchaser (#PCDATA)>
<!ATTLIST purchaser %common.attributes;>

<!ELEMENT purchaseInfo (creditCard | check | cash)>
```

In Example 5-2, each element uses the `common.attributes` parameter entity, which will be converted into the string in the example (including the `id` and `account` attributes). This is done for each attribute list. And, like entity references, changing the value of the parameter entity changes the definitions for all elements. Again, this technique can be used to clean up the organization of your DTDs.

Use Elements Sparingly, Attributes Excessively

After giving you two recommendations about organization, I will now make what might seem like a counterintuitive suggestion: use elements infrequently and, instead, use attributes whenever possible.

To get a better idea of what I'm talking about, take a look at the XML fragment in Example 5-3.

Example 5-3. An element-heavy document fragment

```
<person>
  <firstName>Adam</firstName>
  <lastName>Duritz</lastName>
  <address type="home">
    <street>102 Elizabeth Lane</street>
    <street>Apartment 23</street>
    <city>Los Angeles</city>
    <state>California</state>
    <zipCode>92013</zipCode>
  </address>
</person>
```

To optimize this XML, you should try and convert as much as possible into attributes. The rule of thumb here is that any single-valued content can be turned into an attribute, while multivalued content must stay as elements. So, the firstName and lastName elements can be converted into attributes; each will always have only one value. Hence, the XML can be modified to look as follows:

```
<person firstName="Adam" lastName="Duritz">
  <address type="home">
    <street>102 Elizabeth Lane</street>
    <street>Apartment 23</street>
    <city>Los Angeles</city>
    <state>California</state>
    <zipCode>92013</zipCode>
  </address>
</person>
```

The address element could not be converted to an attribute. First, it has its own content, and second, there could be multiple addresses for the same person (a home address, work address, and so forth). Within that element, you can perform the same checks: street is multivalued, so it stays as an element, but city, state, and zipCode are all single-valued, and can be moved to attributes:

```
<person firstName="Adam" lastName="Duritz">
  <address type="home" city="Los Angeles" state="California" zipCode="92013">
    <street>102 Elizabeth Lane</street>
    <street>Apartment 23</street>
  </address>
</person>
```

To a lot of developers and content authors, this might look a bit odd. However, if you get into the habit of writing your XML in this fashion, it will soon seem completely natural. In fact, you'll soon look at XML with a wealth of elements as the odd bird.

Of course, I have yet to tell you *why* to perform this change; what is worth all this trouble? The reason behind this is in the way that SAX processes elements and attributes.

 Some of you might be thinking that you don't want to use SAX, or that by using DOM or JAXP (or another API such as JAXB or SOAP), you'll get around this issue. However, it's unwise to assume that you will *never* need a specific API. In fact, almost all higher-level APIs such as DOM, SOAP, and JAXB use SAX at the lowest levels. So, while you might not think this practice affects your XML code, it almost certainly will.

Every time the SAX API processes an element, it invokes the startElement( ) callback, with the following signature:

```
public void startElement(String namespaceURI, String localName,
                         String qName, Attribute attributes) throws SAXException;
```

Typically, there is a great deal of decision-processing logic in this method, which goes something like this: if the element is named "this," perform some processing; if it is named "that," do some other processing; if it's named "something else," do something else again. Consequently, every invocation of this method tends to involve numerous string comparisons—which are not particularly fast—as well as several expression evaluations (e.g., if/then/else, etc.).

In addition, for every startElement( ) call, there is an accompanying endElement( ) call. So, if you processed the first XML fragment earlier in the chapter, you would suddenly find yourself staring at the lengthy list of method calls shown in Example 5-4. And that's without even looking at invocations of characters( ) and the like within each element!

Example 5-4. Element-heavy SAX processing

```
startElement( ) // "person"
startElement( ) // "firstName"
endElement( )   // "firstName"
startElement( ) // "lastName"
endElement( )   // "lastName"
startElement( ) // "address
startElement( ) // "street" (1st one)
endElement( )   // "street" (1st one)
startElement( ) // "street" (2nd one)
endElement( )   // "street" (2nd one)
startElement( ) // "city"
endElement( )   // "city"
```

Example 5-4. Element-heavy SAX processing (continued)

```
startElement( ) // "state"
endElement( )   // "state"
startElement( ) // "zipCode"
endElement( )   // "zipCode"
endElement( )   // "address"
endElement( )   // "person"
```

That is a *lot* of processing time! However, with each invocation, the attributes for the element are passed along. This means there is no difference in processing time between an element with several attributes and an element with just one attribute. So, as I mentioned earlier, decreasing the number of single-value elements and instead loading them as attributes onto an element can drastically decrease the parsing time.

Revisiting Example 5-3 and converting most of the elements to attributes, the long list of method calls in Example 5-4 comes out much shorter, as shown in Example 5-5.

Example 5-5. Element-light SAX processing

```
startElement( ) // "person"
startElement( ) // "address"
startElement( ) // "street" (1st one)
endElement( )   // "street" (1st one)
startElement( ) // "street" (2nd one)
endElement( )   // "street" (2nd one)
endElement( )   // "address"
endElement( )   // "person"
```

Eighteen method calls became eight—a change of over 50%.* Add to that the reduction in decision-processing logic in the startElement( ) method because there are fewer elements, and the reduction in characters( ) callback invocations, and this is clearly a good practice to follow.

SAX

At the base of nearly all Java and XML APIs is SAX, the Simple API for XML. The first part of making good decisions with SAX is deciding whether to *use* SAX. Generally, alpha-geek types want to use SAX and nothing else, while everyone else avoids it like the plague. The mystique of using SAX and the complexity that makes it daunting are

---

* This ignores the work to parse the attributes, which may reduce it from 50%.

both poor reasons to decide for or against using SAX. Better criteria are presented in the following questions:

- Am I only reading and not writing or outputting XML?
- Is speed my primary concern (over usability, for example)?
- Do I need to work with only portions of the input XML?
- Are elements and attributes in the input XML independent (no one part of the document depends on or references another part of the document)?

If you can answer "yes" to *all* these questions, SAX is well-suited for your application. If you cannot, you might want to think about using DOM, as detailed later in this chapter.

Use the InputSource Class Correctly

When using the SAX API, all input begins with the org.xml.sax.InputSource class. This is a class that allows the specification of an input (e.g., a file or I/O stream), as well as a public and system ID. SAX then extracts this information from the InputSource at parse time and is able to resolve external entities and other document source-specific resources.

In fact, SAX uses the InputSource class even when you do not. Consider the code fragment in Example 5-6, which uses JAXP to initiate a SAX parse.

Example 5-6. Using JAXP to initiate a SAX parse

```
import java.io.*;
import java.xml.parsers.*;

File myFile = ...
DefaultHandler myHandler = ...

SAXParserFactory spf = SAXParserFactory.newInstance( );
SAXParser parser = spf.newSAXParser( );

parser.parse(myFile, myHandler);
```

Even though a java.io.File is passed in to the SAXParser parse( ) method, this is converted to a SAX InputSource before being handed off to the underlying SAX implementation. That's because this JAXP code will eventually hand off its unparsed data to the org.xml.sax.XMLReader class, which offers only the following two signatures for its parse( ) method:

```
public void parse(InputSource inputSource);
public void parse(String systemID);
```

You might think the second method is easier, but most SAX implementations actually turn around and convert the string-based system ID into an InputSource and recall the first parse( ) method. Put succinctly, all roads lead to the parse( ) method that takes an InputSource.

Because of this, it is better to create an InputSource yourself than to allow a JAXP or SAX implementation to do it for you. In fact, an implementation will often use internal code such as the following to construct the InputSource instance:

```
InputSource inputSource = new InputSource( );

// Might be a null parameter
inputSource.setByteStream(inputStream);

// Might be a null parameter
inputSource.setCharacterStream(reader);

// Might be a null parameter
inputSource.setSystemId(systemId);

// Might be a null parameter
inputSource.setPublicId(publicId);

// Derived parameter
inputSource.setEncoding(encoding);
```

However, many implementations pass these methods null parameters. And while this might not take a lot of time, every second in an XML parsing application can be critical. By constructing an InputSource yourself, you can cut this down to one or two method invocations:

```
InputSource inputSource = new InputSource(myInputStream);
inputSource.setSystemId("http://www.oreilly.com");

// Note that if you use an input stream in the InputSource
// constructor above, this step is not necessary.

inputSource.setEncoding(myEncoding);
```

Note that you should also always use the setEncoding( ) method to tell the SAX parser which encoding to use; this is critical in XML applications in which internationalization is a concern or in which you are using multibyte character sets. Because this is generally the case when XML is being used in the first place, this should always be a consideration. Unfortunately, it's quite common to see the encoding manually set to a character encoding that is different from that of the supplied input stream (via a java.io.InputStream or a java.io.Reader). This can cause all sorts of nasty parsing problems! To avoid this, you should always create your InputSource with an InputStream rather than a Reader or String system ID. When you take this approach, the SAX implementation will wrap the stream in an `InputStreamReader` and will automatically detect the correct character encoding from the stream.[*]

Understand How SAX Handles Entity Resolution

Another basic building block of the SAX API is the process of entity resolution. This process is handled through the `org.xml.sax.EntityResolver` interface. Like the aforementioned `InputSource`, the `EntityResolver` interface is often overlooked and ignored by SAX developers. However, through the use of a solid `EntityResolver` implementation, XML parsing speed can be dramatically enhanced.

At its simplest, an `EntityResolver` tells a SAX parser implementation how to look up resources specified in an XML document (such as entity references). For example, take a look at the following XML document fragment:

```
<entityContainer>
  <entity>&reference;</entity>
</entityContainer>
```

This document fragment illustrates an entity reference named reference. When a parser runs across this entity reference, it begins the process of resolving that entity. The parser will first consult the document's DTD or XML schema for a definition, like this:

```
<!ENTITY reference
    PUBLIC " -//O'Reilly//TEXT Best Practices Reference//EN"
    "reference.xml"
>
```

From this, it gains both the public ID (`-//O'Reilly//TEXT Best Practices Reference// EN`) and system ID (`reference.xml`) of the entity reference. At this point, the parser checks to see if an implementation of the `EntityResolver` interface has been registered with the `setEntityResolver()` method on an `XMLReader` instance. If one has been registered, the parser invokes the `resolveEntity()` method with the public and system IDs extracted from the DTD or schema. Example 5-7 shows an `EntityResolver` implementation at its simplest.

Example 5-7. The simplest EntityResolver

```
import java.io.IOException;

import org.xml.sax.SAXException;
import org.xml.sax.EntityResolver;
import org.xml.sax.InputSource;
```

[*] To be completely accurate, I should say that all SAX parser implementations I have ever come across perform this step. It would be rare to find a parser that does not wrap an `InputStream` in an `InputStreamReader` because the parser allows for automatic encoding detection.

Example 5-7. The simplest EntityResolver (continued)

```java
public class SimpleEntityResolver implements EntityResolver {

    public InputSource resolveEntity(String publicId, String systemId)
      throws SAXException, IOException {

      // Returning null means use normal resolution.
        return null;
    }
}
```

The method in Example 5-7 does nothing except return null, which signifies to the parser that normal resolution should occur. This means that the public ID and then the system ID (if needed) are looked up using the Internet or local filesystem, as specified by the IDs of the reference.

The problem is that looking up resources on the Internet is time-consuming. One common practice is to download all required references and resources to a local filesystem. However, to ensure that these are used instead of the online resources, developers typically change the DTD or schema of the XML, pointing the system ID of the reference to a local copy of a file or resource. Such an approach is problematic because it forces a change in the constraint model of the document, and it ties the reference to a specific file, on a specific filesystem, in a specific location.

A much better solution is to leave the DTD and schema alone, and to package any needed resources in a JAR file with the XML document and Java classes doing the parsing. This does not affect the XML document or its constraints, and is also independent of the filesystem. Furthermore, it makes deployment very simple, as all required resources are in the JAR file. This archive should then be added to the Java classpath. The final step is to register an entity resolver that looks up named resources (the system ID of the reference, specifically) on the current classpath. Example 5-8 shows just such a resolver.

Example 5-8. Resolving entities through the classpath

```java
import java.io.InputStream;
import java.io.IOException;

import org.xml.sax.SAXException;
import org.xml.sax.EntityResolver;
import org.xml.sax.InputSource;

public class ClassPathEntityResolver implements EntityResolver {

    public InputSource resolveEntity(String publicId, String systemId)
        throws SAXException, IOException {

        InputSource inputSource = null;
```

Example 5-8. Resolving entities through the classpath (continued)

```
    try {
        InputStream inputStream =
            EntityResolver.class.getResourceAsStream(
                systemId);
        inputSource = new InputSource(inputStream);
    } catch (Exception e) {
        // No action; just let the null InputSource pass through
    }

    // If nothing found, null is returned, for normal processing
    return inputSource;
    }
}
```

So, if the system ID of your XML reference is *reference.xml*, you simply place a resource file at the top level of your JAR file, and ensure that it is named *reference.xml*.

Consider Using Partial Validation

Another cornerstone of SAX-based programming is *validation*. Of course, in standard XML parlance, validation means ensuring that an XML document conforms to a set of constraints, usually specified by a DTD or XML schema.* I state the obvious definition here, though, to challenge it.

Certainly, this traditional type of validation has its place. If you are receiving XML documents from an untrusted source, or if you allow manual editing of XML documents, it is probably a good idea to validate these documents to ensure that nothing unexpected has occurred and that your applications don't crater on invalid XML.†

Validation is achieved in SAX through the setFeature( ) method of the XMLReader object:

```
    XMLReader reader = XMLReaderFactory.createXMLReader( );
    reader.setFeature("http://xml.org/sax/features/validation", true);

    reader.parse(myInputSource);
```

If you're using SAX through the JAXP wrapper layer, this would change to:

```
    SAXParserFactory spf = SAXParserFactory.newInstance( );
    spf.setValidating(true);

    SAXParser parser = spf.newSAXParser( );
    parser.parse(myInputSource, myDefaultHandler);
```

---

* Although I should say that alternate constraint models such as Relax NG are looking very promising.

† Of course, you don't really know if you can trust the doctype in an untrusted XML document, but that's another problem.

The problem with this blanket validation is that it is *extremely* process-intensive. Validating every element, every attribute, the content within elements, the resolved content of entity references, and more can take a great deal of time. While you can certainly try to validate in development and avoid validation in production, this is impossible if XML is dynamically generated or passed around and, therefore, prone to errors. The typical case is that validation must be left on in production, and all the penalties associated with it remain.

A much better solution is to put some customized validation in place. This approach allows you to assign business rules to your validation. To get a better idea of this, consider the following fragment from a DTD:

```
<!ELEMENT purchaseOrder (item+, billTo, shipTo, payment)>
<!ATTLIST purchaseOrder
        id         CDATA    #REQUIRED
        tellerID   CDATA    #REQUIRED
        orderDate  CDATA    #REQUIRED
>
```

With traditional validation, when a purchaseOrder element is processed, the parser must ensure it has at least one child item, as well as a billTo, shipTo, and payment child. Validation also ensures that the purchaseOrder element has an id, tellerID, and orderDate attribute. On its face, this sounds great. These are all required, so there should be no problem. However, all this data would rarely be used in the same business component. In one application component, you might need to know the ID of the teller who input the order and the date it was input—this would be common in an audit of employee transactions. In another, such as order fulfillment, you might need the element children but none of the attributes.

In both cases, only *partial validation* is really required. In other words, only a subset of the complete set of constraints needs to be checked. If you handle this partial validation yourself, and turn off validation on the parser, you can achieve some drastic performance improvements. For example, if you need to ensure that the id and tellerID attributes are present, you could turn off validation:

```
reader.setFeature("http://xml.org/sax/features/validation", false);
```

You could then implement the following logic in the SAX startElement() callback, which would handle this custom, partial validation, as shown in Example 5-9.

Example 5-9. Handling partial validation with SAX

```
public startElement(String namespaceURI, String localName,
                    String qName, Attributes attributes)
    throws SAXException {

    // Handle custom validation.
    if (localName.equals("purchaseOrder")) {
        if (attributes.getIndex("tellerID") < 0) {
            throw new SAXException("Error: purchaseOrder elements must contain " +
                "a tellerID attribute.");
```

Example 5-9. Handling partial validation with SAX (continued)

```
        }
        if (attributes.getIndex("orderDate") < 0) {
            throw new SAXException("Error: purchaseOrder elements must contain " +
                "an orderDate attribute.");
        }
    }

    // Normal XML processing
}
```

This might seem overly simple; however, by implementing this instead of a complete validation, you will see tremendous performance improvements in your applications. Additionally, you get the benefit of some self-documentation in your code; through this code fragment, it is simple to see which business rules must be followed in your XML.

DOM

DOM, the Document Object Model, is a far better understood API than SAX. This is largely because it operates using more familiar Java principles: the XML input document is represented as a set of Java objects, output is performed via DOM serializers, and the ability to make significant programming errors is greatly lessened compared to SAX. However, DOM still presents more than its fair share of pitfalls to the unprepared developer.

When deciding to use DOM, you should always begin by first determining if you can use SAX. While SAX programming is generally more complex than DOM programming, it is almost always faster. However, if you were unable to answer "yes" to all the questions in the "SAX" section, DOM might be a better solution for you.

In particular, there are two things that DOM excels at:

- Providing an object model of an XML document
- Providing access to all parts of an XML document at one time

These two aspects of DOM are interesting in that they both are significantly appealing to Java developers. On the whole, today's developers prefer using an object-oriented programming model and having an entire business unit (whether it be an XML document or some other construct) available for random access at all times. SAX forces a more procedural and generally unfamiliar programming model, while DOM's model seems more natural.

Of course, you pay performance and memory penalties for these features—keeping an entire document in memory and representing that document as objects expends both time and resources. That being said, DOM can be very powerful once you learn to account for its shortcomings. The following tips can help you use DOM as effectively as possible, decreasing performance penalties when possible.

Bootstrap DOM Correctly

One of the most misunderstood and abused aspects of using DOM is getting an initial DOM implementation for programming. This is typically referred to as *bootstrapping*, and it is often done incorrectly. There are two different approaches, depending on which version of the DOM specification your implementation adheres to.

DOM Levels 1 and 2

In DOM Levels 1 and 2, the process of getting a DOM implementation to work is difficult. Before I explain why, though, you should understand why you need a DOM implementation in the first place.

 If you are reading in an XML document (e.g., from an existing file or input stream), this entire section is not applicable. In these cases, the `reader.getDocument()` method will return a DOM `Document` object, and you can then operate on that DOM tree without any problem. I'm also assuming that you've chosen not to use JAXP. If you are using JAXP, these issues are taken care of for you. In many cases, however, JAXP either is not available or you have software restrictions that make it a nonoption in your application or organization.

The end goal of bootstrapping is to get a vendor's implementation of the `org.w3c.dom.Document` interface. Most developers' instincts, therefore, are to write this line of code:

```
Document doc = new org.apache.xerces.dom.DocumentImpl();
```

The obvious problem here is that your code is now tied to Xerces, and can't work with another parser without modification. In fact, it often won't function with a different version of the *same* parser you are using. In addition to obtaining a `Document`, using this approach will force you to configure additional vendor-specific details to obtain implementations of the `org.w3c.dom.DocumentType` interface. However, this is not the proper way to access a DOM-creating mechanism in the first place.

Instead, you should always use the `org.w3c.dom.DOMImplementation` class, which acts as a factory for both interfaces. Instead of directly instantiating a DOM `Document` implementation, use this approach:

```
DOMImplementation domImpl = new org.apache.xerces.dom.DOMImplementationImpl();
DocumentType docType = domImpl.createDocumentType("rootElementName", "public ID",
                                                  "system ID");
Document doc = domImpl.createDocument("", "rootElementName", docType);
```

Now, while this is a better approach, it is by no means a great solution. The code is still tied to a vendor-specific class! You can get around that, however, by using a system property, set either in the code through a resource file or at application startup (through the -D flag to the java interpreter). I prefer naming the property org.w3c.dom.DOMImplementationClass. In this case, the value of this property would be the Xerces implementation class: org.apache.xerces.dom.DOMImplementationImpl.

You can then use the simple helper class shown in Example 5-10 to handle creation of the needed DOM types.

Example 5-10. The DOMFactory helper class

```
package com.oreilly.xml;

import org.w3c.dom.Document;
import org.w3c.dom.DocumentType;
import org.w3c.dom.DOMImplementation;

public class DOMFactory {

    /** System property name */
    private static final String IMPL_PROPERTY_NAME =
        "org.w3c.dom.DOMImplementationClass";

    /** Initialization flag */
    private static boolean initialized = false;

    /** The DOMImplementation to use */
    private static DOMImplementation domImpl;

    private static void initialize() throws Exception {
        domImpl =
            (DOMImplementation)Class.forName(
                System.getProperty(IMPL_PROPERTY_NAME)).newInstance();
        initialized = true;
    }

    public static Document newDocument(String namespaceURI,
            String rootQName, DocumentType docType)
        throws Exception {

        if (!initialized) {
            initialize();
        }

        return domImpl.createDocument(namespaceURI, rootQName, docType);
    }

    public static DocumentType newDocumentType(String rootQName,
            String publicId, String systemId)
        throws Exception {
```

Example 5-10. The DOMFactory helper class (continued)

```
        if (!initialized) {
            initialize( );
        }

        return domImpl.createDocumentType(rootQName, publicId, systemId);
    }
}
```

Just add this class to your classpath, along with whatever parser JAR file you need, and set the system property before parsing. You'll be able to obtain DOM types without even dipping into vendor-specific code.

Note that I left the exception handling fairly vague; it's generally not a good idea to just throw `Exception`. Instead, it's preferable to use a more specific exception subclass. However, you should generally use an application exception here. I'll let you replace the generic `Exception` with your more specific one. Other than that, the class is ready to go as is.

DOM Level 3

DOM Level 3 introduced a new means of bootstrapping, one that avoids the nasty vendor-specific problems discussed in the last section. It also avoids the need for a helper class. Through the introduction of a new DOM class, `org.w3c.dom.DOMImplementationRegistry`, it is possible to obtain a DOM implementation in a vendor-neutral way.

First, you or your parser vendor needs to set the system property `org.w3c.dom.DOMImplementationSourceList`. This property's value must consist of a space-separated list of class names that implement the `org.w3c.dom.DOMImplementationSource` interface. This is the key mechanism for DOM-implementing parsers.

Example 5-11 shows how the Apache Xerces parser might implement this interface.

Example 5-11. Apache Xerces implementation of DOMImplementationSource

```
package org.apache.xerces.dom;

import org.w3c.dom.DOMImplementationSource;

public class XercesDOMImplementationSource implements DOMImplementationSource {

    public DOMImplementation getDOMImplementation(String features) {
        return new DOMImplementationImpl( );
    }
}
```

 This is not the actual Xerces implementation class. In reality, the `getDOMImplementation( )` method would need to verify the feature string, ensure that the Xerces implementation was sufficient, and perform other error checking before returning a `DOMImplementation`.

The system property could then be set to the value org.apache.xerces.dom. XercesDOMImplementationSource. Typically, this property is set through the parser's own code, or at startup of your application through a batch file or shell script:

```
java -Dorg.w3c.dom.DOMImplementationSourceList\
=org.apache.xerces.dom.XercesDOMImplementationSource \
  some.application.class
```

With this machinery in place, you can then easily bootstrap a DOM implementation using the following line of code:

```
DOMImplementation domImpl =
    DOMImplementationRegistry.getDOMImplementation("XML 1.0");
```

From here, it is simple to create a new DOM tree and perform other standard DOM operations. Because the system property handles the loading of parser- and vendor-specific details, your code remains free of vendor-specific idioms.

 While this is a nice solution to the problems outlined earlier, it is important to realize that at print time, DOM Level 3 was still a bit off in the future. Some parsers include only a few DOM Level 3 features, while some include almost all of them…and some include none at all. As of this writing, I wasn't able to get this code working flawlessly with any of the major parser projects and products. However, getting this right should be just a matter of time, and as a Java Enterprise developer, you should know how to utilize these features as soon as they become available.

Don't Be Afraid to Use Helper Classes

This is more of a general tip for working with DOM, but it still certainly belongs in the category of best practices. When working with the DOM, you should *always* write yourself a suite of helper classes, or at least look around for existing suites.

I have several versions of helper classes floating around my development environments at any given time, usually with names such as DOMHelper, DOMUtil, or some other permutation. I've omitted many of these from this chapter, as the methods in those classes are specific to the kinds of DOM manipulation I perform, which are likely different from the kinds of DOM manipulation you will perform. If, for example, you often need to walk trees, you may want a method such as the one shown in Example 5-12 to easily obtain the text of a node.

Example 5-12. Helper class for walking DOM trees

```
// Get the text of a node without the extra TEXT node steps.

public static String getText(Node node) {

    // Make sure this is an element.
```

Example 5-12. Helper class for walking DOM trees (continued)

```
    if (node instanceof Element) {

        // Make sure there are children.

        if (node.hasChildNodes()) {

            StringBuffer text = new StringBuffer();
            NodeList children = node.getChildNodes();
            for (int i=0; i<children.getLength(); i++) {
                Node child = children.item(i);
                if (child.getNodeType() == Node.TEXT_NODE) {
                    text.append(child.getNodeValue());
                }
            }
            return text.toString();
        } else {
            return null;
        }
    } else {
        return null;
    }
}
```

This is one of two types of methods that retrieve the text of an element. This variety retrieves *all* top-level text nodes, even if there are also nested elements. Here is a sample in which you might not get what you expect from such a method:

```
<p>Here is some <i>emphasized</i> text.</p>
```

In this case, getText() would return "Here is some text." Other varieties return only the *first* text node, which with the same example would return only "Here is some."

In any case, these sorts of methods can be grouped into toolboxes of DOM utilities that greatly simplify your programming. In short, you shouldn't be afraid to add your own ideas and tricks to the specification and API. There certainly isn't anything wrong with that, especially when the API as it stands is admittedly shallow in terms of convenience methods.

Avoid Class Comparisons

If you've worked with DOM, you know that one of the most common operations is *tree walking*. In fact, the last best practice showed a helper method to aid in this by walking a node's children to get its textual content. This tree walking is generally accomplished through the org.w3c.dom.Node interface, as all DOM structures implement (actually, they extend, and your parser provides implementations of those interfaces) this base interface.

The problem is that there are several methods for determining a node's type, and then reacting to that type. Most Java developers familiar with polymorphism and inheritance would immediately use the methods provided around the Java Class class. Using that approach, you might end up with code such as that in Example 5-13.

Example 5-13. Using Java class comparison

```
NodeList children = rootNode.getChildNodes();

// Figure out which node type you have and work with it.
for (int i=0; i<children.getLength(); i++) {
    Node child = children.item(i);

    if (child.getClass().equals(org.w3c.dom.Element.class)) {
        Element element = (Element)child;
        // Do something with the element.
    } else if (child.getClass().equals(org.w3c.dom.Text.class)) {
        Text text = (Text)child;
        // Do something with the text node.
    } else if (child.getClass().equals(org.w3c.dom.Comment.class)) {
        Comment comment = (Comment)child;
        // Do something with the comment.
    } // etc...
}
```

In a similar vein, I've also seen code that looks similar to Example 5-14.

Example 5-14. Using string comparisons for class names

```
NodeList children = rootNode.getChildNodes();

// Figure out which node type you have and work with it.
for (int i=0; i<children.getLength(); i++) {
    Node child = children.item(i);

    if (child.getClass().getName().equals("org.w3c.dom.Element")) {
        Element element = (Element)child;
        // Do something with the element.
    } else if (child.getClass().getName().equals("org.w3c.dom.Text")) {
        Text text = (Text)child;
        // Do something with the text node.
    } else if (child.getClass().getName().equals("org.w3c.dom.Comment")) {
        Comment comment = (Comment)child;
        // Do something with the comment.
    } // etc...
}
```

Before explaining why this doesn't work in relation to DOM, I should warn you that the second code fragment is a terrible idea. One of the slowest sets of operations within Java is String comparison; using the equals() method like this, over and over again, is a sure way to bog down your programs.

These might still look pretty innocuous, especially the first example. However, these code samples forget that DOM is a purely interface-based API. In other words, every concrete class in a DOM program is actually the implementation, provided by a parser project, of a DOM-standardized API. For example, you won't find in any program a concrete class called org.w3c.dom.Element, org.w3c.dom.Comment, org.w3c.dom.Text, or any other DOM construct. Instead, you will find classes such as org.apache.xerces.dom.ElementNSImpl and org.apache.xerces.dom.CommentImpl. These classes are the actual implementations of the DOM interfaces.

The point here is that using the class-specific operations will always fail. You will inevitably be comparing a vendor's implementation class with a DOM interface (which is never a concrete class, can never be instantiated, and will never be on the left side of an object comparison). Instead of these class operations, you need to use the instanceof operator, as shown in Example 5-15.

Example 5-15. Using the instanceof operator

```
NodeList children = rootNode.getChildNodes( );

// Figure out which node type you have and work with it.
for (int i=0; i<children.getLength( ); i++) {
    Node child = children.item(i);

    if (child instanceof org.w3c.dom.Element) {
        Element element = (Element)child;
        // Do something with the element.
    } else if (child instanceof org.w3c.dom.Text) {
        Text text = (Text)child;
        // Do something with the text node.
    } else if (child instanceof org.w3c.dom.Comment) {
        Comment comment = (Comment)child;
        // Do something with the comment.
    } // etc...
}
```

Here, instanceof returns true if the class is the same as, is a subclass of, or is an implementation of the item on the righthand side of the equation.

Of course, you can also use the getNodeType( ) method on the org.w3c.dom.Node interface and perform integer comparisons, as shown in Example 5-16.

Example 5-16. Using integer comparisons

```
NodeList children = rootNode.getChildNodes( );

// Figure out which node type you have and work with it.
for (int i=0; i<children.getLength( ); i++) {
    Node child = children.item(i);
```

Example 5-16. Using integer comparisons (continued)

```
    if (child.getNodeType() == Node.ELEMENT_NODE) {
        Element element = (Element)child;
        // Do something with the element.
    } else if (child.getNodeType() == Node.TEXT_NODE) {
        Text text = (Text)child;
        // Do something with the text node.
    } else if (child.getNodeType() == Node.COMMENT_NODE) {
        Comment comment = (Comment)child;
        // Do something with the comment.
    } // etc...
}
```

This turns out to be a more efficient way to do things. Comparison of numbers will always be a computer's strong suit. (You can also use a switch/case statement here to speed things up slightly.) Consider the case in which you have an implementation class—for example, com.oreilly.dom.DeferredElementImpl. That particular class extends com.oreilly.dom.NamespacedElementImpl, which extends com.oreilly.dom.ElementImpl, which finally implements org.w3c.dom.Element. Using the instanceof approach would cause the Java Virtual Machine (JVM) to perform four class comparisons and chase an inheritance tree, all in lieu of comparing a numerical constant such as "4" to another numerical constant. It should be pretty obvious, then, that getClass() doesn't work, instanceof works but performs poorly, and getNodeType() is the proper way to do node type discovery.

JAXP

The next API on the list is one which readers should realize is not a parser, or even an API for parsing XML. JAXP is the Java API for XML Processing and is simply an abstraction layer, a thin shim that sits on top of the SAX and DOM APIs. JAXP performs no XML parsing itself, but instead defers this task to the underlying SAX and DOM APIs. The same thing is true for JAXP's XML transformation processing capabilities.

You should always attempt to use JAXP in a J2EE application. With the release of JAXP 1.1[*] and support for SAX 2.0 and DOM Level 2, JAXP provides the baseline tool support required for solid Java and XML programming. You'll be able to migrate applications more easily and change parser and processor vendors at will—with minimal impact on your applications. JAXP also has shown no adverse performance effects, so there is no reason to avoid using JAXP.

---

[*] JAXP 1.2 offers even more, such as support for XML schema. However, the SAX 2.0 and DOM Level 2 compliance is of much greater import, so I recommend using JAXP 1.1 as a minimum requirement rather than Version 1.2.

At times, you will decide you need to use vendor-specific extensions to a parser or processor. In these cases, JAXP will obviously not suffice. However, I still recommend using JAXP, except in the specific portions of your code that reference these vendor-specific features.

Don't Be Afraid to Use Format Transformations

Here, we will discuss a core feature of JAXP that is underused: conversion from one API format (SAX, a stream, or DOM) to another. While this has always been one of the basic features of JAXP, it is rarely used, probably due to a lack of understanding of JAXP's Transformation API for XML, or TRaX.

An example is the best way to illustrate this sort of format transformation. Example 5-17 shows a helper class that will perform these conversions for you, so you don't have to constantly deal with new `Transformer` instances and the JAXP `TransformerFactory`.

Example 5-17. Format conversion helper class

```
package com.oreilly.xml;

import javax.xml.transform.Transformer;
import javax.xml.transform.TransformerException;
import javax.xml.transform.TransformerFactory;
import javax.xml.transform.sax.SAXResult;
import javax.xml.transform.sax.SAXSource;
import javax.xml.transform.dom.DOMResult;
import javax.xml.transform.dom.DOMSource;
import javax.xml.transform.stream.StreamResult;
import javax.xml.transform.stream.StreamSource;

public class FormatConverter {

    private static boolean initialized = false;

    private static Transformer transformer;

    private static void initialize() throws TransformerException {
        TransformerFactory factory = TransformerFactory.newInstance();
        transformer = factory.newTransformer();
        initialized = true;
    }

    public static void convert(StreamSource source, SAXResult result)
        throws TransformerException {

        transformer.transform(source, result);
    }

    public static void convert(StreamSource source, DOMResult result)
        throws TransformerException {
```

Example 5-17. Format conversion helper class (continued)

```
        transformer.transform(source, result);
    }

    public static void convert(SAXSource source, DOMResult result)
        throws TransformerException {

        transformer.transform(source, result);
    }

    public static void convert(SAXSource source, StreamResult result)
        throws TransformerException {

        transformer.transform(source, result);
    }

    public static void convert(DOMSource source, StreamResult result)
        throws TransformerException {

        transformer.transform(source, result);
    }

    public static void convert(DOMSource source, SAXResult result)
        throws TransformerException {

        transformer.transform(source, result);
    }
    static {initialize();}
}
```

This example takes in the various types of TrAX (JAXP) sources and outputs to the
various TrAX outputs through the Result interface. While this is a pretty trivial class,
it actually contains quite a bit of power. If you've used DOM before, you're probably aware that the process of serializing a DOM tree to a file, or to any other kind of
stream, is typically vendor-specific. It moves your vendor-neutral DOM code to
something dependent on some project or implementation. However, the
FormatConverter class takes care of this handily:

```
// Get your DOM tree built up, manipulated, and ready for serialization.
Document doc = getDOMTreeSomehow( );

// Set up input and output.
javax.xml.transform.dom.DOMSource domSource=
    new javax.xml.transform.dom.DOMSource(doc);
javax.xml.transform.stream.StreamResult streamResult =
    new javax.xml.transform.stream.StreamResult("output.xml");

// Serialize.
FormatConverter.convert(domSource, streamResult);
```

Through this transformation, often called the *identity transformation*, serialization
becomes trivial and requires no vendor-specific code at all. You can use the same

---

method with different parameters as input to transform an input source (StreamSource) to a DOM tree (DOMResult), or convert from SAX (SAXSource) to a file (StreamResult) or a DOM tree (DOMResult). Just to be sure you get the idea, here's another sample, which reads in a file and converts it to a DOM tree:

```
StreamSource source = new StreamSource("person.xml");
DOMResult result = new DOMResult();

// Convert (essentially, parse).
FormatConverter.convert(source, result);

// Now get the DOM Document object and work with it.
Document doc = (Document)result.getNode();
```

You might have noticed something amiss about the FormatConverter class as it stands: it can actually be simplified quite a bit, as all the TrAX Source classes implement a common interface, and all the TrAX Result classes implement another interface. Now that you have an idea about what is behind the format conversion, you can simplify your helper class to that shown in Example 5-18.

Example 5-18. Simplified version of FormatConverter

```
package com.oreilly.xml;

import javax.xml.transform.Result;
import javax.xml.transform.Source;
import javax.xml.transform.Transformer;
import javax.xml.transform.TransformerException;
import javax.xml.transform.TransformerFactory;

public class FormatConverter {

    private static boolean initialized = false;

    private static Transformer transformer;

    private static void initialize() throws TransformerException {
        TransformerFactory factory = TransformerFactory.newInstance();
        transformer = factory.newTransformer();
        initialized = true;
    }

    public static void convert(Source source, Result result)
        throws TransformerException {

        transformer.transform(source, result);
    }
    static {initialize();}
}
```

This approach is much simpler and keeps things brief.

CHAPTER 6

RMI Best Practices

William Grosso

Java's Remote Method Invocation (RMI) framework is a powerful, easy-to-use, and robust framework for building distributed applications. It's ideal for a wide variety of mid-range applications that don't fit into the Enterprise JavaBean (EJB) model, don't require the cross-language capabilities of either CORBA or web services, and don't use a web browser for a client.

RMI's ease of use is legendary. But ease of use gets you only so far. In this chapter, I will outline a number of best practices that will enable you to take an ordinary RMI application and turn it into one that performs well, is easy to maintain, and will be useful for years to come.

Because of space considerations, I've chosen to focus on three basic areas: marshalling and unmarshalling objects, making applications more robust, and improving application performance.[*]

Marshalling and Unmarshalling Objects

Marshalling is a generic term for gathering data from one process and converting it into a format that can be used either for storage or for transmission to another process (correspondingly, *unmarshalling* involves taking the converted data and recreating the objects). In RMI, marshalling is done either via serialization or externalization. Marshalling and unmarshalling occupy a strange role in designing a distributed application. On the one hand, the means by which you perform marshalling and unmarshalling is a technical detail: once you've decided to send information to another process, how you do so shouldn't be a primary design consideration. On the other hand, it's a very important technical detail, and the way you do it can often make or break an application.

---

[*] Neither "using exceptions effectively" nor "versioning an application" made the cut.

Use Value Objects to Separate Marshalling Code from Your Application Logic

Value objects are objects that contain data and very little behavior, aside from a few constructors that are convenient. They are encapsulations of information intended solely for communication between processes (they are more like structs in C or C++ than full-fledged objects). The idea behind using value objects is that by specifying remote interfaces, and then using data objects that play no further computational role, you separate the protocol definition (e.g., how the processes communicate) from the computational class structures (e.g., the objects and classes that the client or server needs to use to function effectively).

Building separate objects for data transmission might seem oppositional to standard object-oriented practices. And, to some extent, it is. But it's not as contrary as you might think. Consider writing a stock-trading application. Your stock-trading application probably has an idea for a purchase order. But it's not a single class—each part of the application deals with different aspects of the purchase order:

- The client wants to help the customer enter data and verify the purchase order.
- The networking infrastructure wants to send as little data as possible, in as efficient and robust a way as possible, to the server.
- The server needs to validate the purchase order, execute it, and then store information in a database for auditing.

These are all aspects of the "purchase order idea." But they're very different, and each layer of the application deals with only one of them. Even object-oriented purists might find using three different classes to represent "purchase orders" a resonable design decision. Defining value objects gives you five main benefits:

- It makes it easier to define the process boundaries. Using value objects helps you think in terms of "information flow." Doing so is often beneficial at early stages of program development.
- It makes your program easier to write. Conceptually, separating the information flow from the computational tasks makes it easier to define interfaces and helps you "lock down" a crucial part of your codebase. Practically, if you tweak the server's purchase order implementation, you don't want to have to recompile and redeploy the client during development.
- It helps with versioning your codebase. One of the biggest headaches in distributed computing is deploying a new version of an application. Frequently, the requirement is for total backward compatibility (for example, if a machine doesn't have the upgraded client application, everything should still work transparently). If the remote interfaces and the objects that are passed over the wire don't change often, this becomes easier.

- It helps with security. If all calls to the server go through a translation layer (even if it's as simple as calling the constructor of the server's "purchase order class"), you've gained two things: you have a place in your code to perform validity checks, and you can avoid some of the more serious side effects of serialization's famous "extralinguistic constructor."

 The phrase "extralinguistic constructor" was coined by Josh Bloch in *Effective Java* (Addison-Wesley). The basic point is that the deserialization algorithm doesn't actually call a constructor in your class; it creates the objects without calling any local constructors (the no-argument constructor in the superclass is still called). This means that when you decide to make an object serializable, you need to know whether an instance was created without calling a constructor. We'll discuss more side effects of the extralinguistic constructor later in the chapter. For more on the basics of serialization's extralinguistic constructor, see Item 54 of *Effective Java*.

Use Flat Hierarchies When Designing Value Objects

The first rule of thumb when designing a suite of value objects is this: avoid inheritance. There are two basic reasons for this. The first is efficiency. When you send an instance of a class over the wire, you also send information about the class hierarchy. If you run Example 6-1, you'll see that in Java Development Kit (JDK) 1.4 the cost of one extra level of inheritance is 44 bytes (regardless of whether you use serialization or externalization).

Example 6-1. FlatHierarchies.java

```java
public class FlatHierarchies {
    public static void main(String[] args) {
        try {
            System.out.println("An instance of A takes " + getSize(new A()));
            System.out.println("An instance of B takes " + getSize(new B()));
            System.out.println("An instance of C takes " + getSize(new C()));
            System.out.println("An instance of D takes " + getSize(new D()));
        }
        catch(Exception e) {
            e.printStackTrace();
        }
    }

    private static int getSize(Object arg) throws IOException {
        ByteArrayOutputStream byteArrayOutputStream = new ByteArrayOutputStream();
        ObjectOutputStream oos = new ObjectOutputStream(byteArrayOutputStream);
        oos.writeObject(arg);
        oos.close();
        byte[] bytes = byteArrayOutputStream.toByteArray();
        return bytes.length;
    }
```

Example 6-1. FlatHierarchies.java (continued)

```java
    protected static class A implements Serializable {
    }

    protected static class B extends A {
    }

    protected static class C implements Externalizable {
        public void readExternal(ObjectInput oi) {}
        public void writeExternal(ObjectOutput oo) {}
    }

    protected static class D extends C {
        public void readExternal(ObjectInput oi) {}
        public void writeExternal(ObjectOutput oo) {}
    }
}
```

Forty-four bytes (and the extra CPU time to marshal and demarshal them) might not seem significant. But this overhead happens with every single remote call, and the cumulative effects *are* significant.

The second reason for avoiding inheritance hierarchies is simple: inheritance hierarchies rarely mix well with any form of object persistence. It's just too easy to get confused, or not account for all the information in the hierarchy. The deeper the hierarchy is, the more likely you will run into problems.

Be Aware of How Externalization and Serialization Differ with Respect to Superclasses

One of the biggest differences between externalization and serialization involves how they handle superclass state. If a class implements `Serializable` but not `Externalizable` and is a subclass of another class that implements `Serializable`, the subclass is only responsible for marshalling and demarshalling locally declared fields (either a method code in the superclass or the default serialization algorithm will be called to handle the fields declared in the superclass).

If, on the other hand, a class implements `Externalizable`, it is responsible for marshalling and demarshalling all object state, including fields defined in any and all superclasses. This behavior can be very convenient if you want to override a superclass's marshalling code (for example, this lets you repair broken marshalling code in a library). Implementing `Externalizable` will let you do so quite easily.

But externalization's requirement that you explicitly marshal and demarshal superclass state doesn't really mesh well with inheritance. Either you break encapsulation and let the subclass handle the superclass's state, or the subclass has to call a superclass method to marshal and demarshal the superclass state. Both options can lead to error-prone code. In the first case, if you add or remove a field in the superclass, you then have to remember to modify the subclass. In the second case, you have to rely on programmer discipline to call the superclass method; the compiler doesn't enforce this at all (and forgetting to call the superclass method can be a source of subtle bugs).

And finally, there's one related problem in the way externalization is defined. Consider the following code:

```java
public  class A implements Externalizable {
    // Some class state is declared.
    public A() {
    }
    public void writeExternal(ObjectOutput oo) throws IOException{
    // Correct implementation
    }
    public void readExternal(ObjectInput oi) throws IOException,
ClassNotFoundException{
    // Correct implementation
    }
}

protected static class B extends A {
    // New state variables are defined,
    // but methods from Externalizable are not implemented.
}
```

This code will compile. And instances of B can be marshalled and demarshalled. The only problem is that the only state that will be written out is defined in A. B has the public methods the Externalizable interface requires; it's just that implementations are inherited from A.

Don't Marshal Inner Classes

Inner classes aren't as simple as they appear. When an inner class is compiled it gains at least one new variable, which is a reference to the outer class, and it can potentially gain many more, depending on which local variables are accessed and whether they're declared as final. For example, consider the following class definition which declares an inner class inside the test method:

```java
public class InnerClasses {
    public static void main(String[] args) {
        new InnerClasses().test("hello");
    }

    public void test(final String string) {
        class StringPrinter {
            public void print() {
                System.out.println(string);
                System.exit(0);
            }
        }
```

```
        new StringPrinter().print();
    }
}
```

When you compile this, and then decompile the resulting inner class,* you find the following:

```
class InnerClasses$1$StringPrinter {
    private final String val$string;
    private final InnerClasses this$0;

    InnerClasses$1$StringPrinter(InnerClasses p0, String p1) { }
    public void print() { }
}
```

The inner class has two "additional" fields. Having automatically generated fields (with automatically generated names) in a class you will marshal is a recipe for disaster—if you don't know the variable names or types in advance, all you can do is rely on default serialization and hope everything works out. What makes it even worse in this case is that the names of the fields aren't part of the Java specification (the names of the fields depend on the compiler).

Always Explicitly Initialize Transient Fields Inside Marshalling Methods

The transient keyword is very useful when you're writing marshalling code. Very often, a first pass at making an object implement the Serializable interface consists of the following two steps:

1. Declare that the object implements the Serializable interface.

2. Declare all the fields you don't want to be serialized to be transient variables.

Many programmers will look at this and wonder if it's efficient enough. But very few will wonder whether it's correct. And the sad truth is that it is often incorrect. The reason is that the transient keyword really means "Serialization shouldn't pay attention to this field at all."† And that has serious consequences when you combine it with the notion of serialization's extralinguistic constructor (as discussed earlier). If you implement the Serializable interface by following the previous two methods, here's what will happen when your object is deserialized:

1. The instance will be created using the extralinguistic constructor (and hence, none of the initialization code in your constructors will be executed).

2. The serialization algorithm will completely ignore your transient fields.

---

* The full name of the resulting inner class isn't specified either. On my system (JDK 1.4, standard compiler), it's InnerClasses1StringPrinter.class.

† The transient keyword has no effect if you're using externalization and writing all the marshalling code yourself.

The net result is that none of the transient fields will be initialized. This is rarely the expected outcome, and can result in bugs that are subtle and hard to track down.

The SerializationTest class illustrates the problem in detail. It has four integers (a, b, c, and d), which are initialized in various ways. Of these integers, only a is not declared as a transient variable. When an instance of SerializationTest is serialized and then deserialized, only a will have the "correct" value. b, c, and d will all be set to 0 (which is the default value for integers in the Java language specification):

```
public class SerializationTest implements Serializable {
    private int a = 17;            // Value is preserved by serialization
    private transient int b = 9;   // Value is not preserved by serialization
    private transient int c;
    private transient int d;

    {   // Initialization blocks are ignored by the deserialization algorithm.
        c = 12;
    }

    private SerializationTest( )  { // Won't be called by the deserialization
                                    // algorithm
        d = 421;
    }

    public void printState( ) {
        System.out.println("a is " + a);
        System.out.println("b is " + b);
        System.out.println("c is " + c);
        System.out.println("d is " + d);
    }
}
```

Always Set the serialVersionUID

serialVersionUID is a class invariant that the RMI runtime uses to validate that the classes on both sides of the wire are the same. Here's how it works: the first process marshals an object and sends it over the wire. As part of the marshalling process, the serialVersionUID of all relevant classes is also sent. The receiving process compares the serialVersionUIDs that were sent with the serialVersionUIDs of the local classes. If they aren't equal, the RMI runtime will throw an instance of UnmarshalException (and the method call will never even reach your code on the server side).

If you don't specify serialVersionUID, you will run into two problems. The first is that the system's value for serialVersionUID is generated at runtime (not at compile time), and generating it can be expensive. The second, more serious problem is that the automatically generated values of serialVersionUID are created by hashing together all the fields and methods of the class and are therefore extraordinarily sensitive to minor changes. For these reasons, whenever you define a class that will be marshalled, you should always set the serialVersionUID, as in the following example:

```
public class ClassWhichWillBeMarshalled  implements Externalizable{
    public static final long serialVersionUID = 1L;
    // ...
}
```

Set Version Numbers Independently of serialVersionUID

serialVersionUID is a very coarse-grained versioning control. If one Java Virtual Machine (JVM) is using a class with a serialVersionUID that has been set to 1, and the other JVM is using a later version of the class with a serialVersionUID that has been set to 2, the call never reaches your server code because the RMI runtime in the server's JVM will throw an instance of UnmarshalException (as demonstrated earlier).

This level of protection is often overkill. Instead of having the RMI runtime reject the call, you should have your code look at the data that was sent over the wire, realize that there is a versioning problem, and behave appropriately. The following scenario illustrates the problem:

> Bob, a busy executive, has been traveling around Europe. While in Europe, he occasionally plugs his laptop into a local Internet connection and attempts to use a corporate application. However, the latest version of the server has been rolled out, and his client is out-of-date. The application fails completely because serialVersionUIDs have been updated, and the RMI runtime throws instances of UnmarshalException with every remote call. Bob has to live without the application for the remainder of his sales trip, use the web-based version of the application (which has a much poorer user interface), or install the new version of the client application himself.
>
> Bob would really prefer that the application just worked.

This problem is easy to solve: simply use a second static variable to indicate the "actual version" of the class, and then use it to implement a robust versioning scheme, as in the following code:

```
public class ClassWhichWillBeMarshalled  implements Externalizable{
    public static final long serialVersionUID = 1L;
    public static final int actualVersion = 1;
    // ...
}
```

Never Use Default Serialization

The serialization algorithm is a very simple and robust algorithm. In pseudocode, it consists of the following five steps:

1. Check to see that the class implements Serializable. If not, throw an instance of NotSerializableException.

2. Get the class for the instance. If the class description hasn't been written out to the stream, write it out immediately.

---

3. If the class implements `Externalizable`, call the `writeExternal( )` method.

4. Otherwise, see if the class implements the `writeObject` method. If it does, call the `writeObject( )` method.

5. Otherwise, use reflection to iterate through all the fields. For each field, write out a description of the field followed by its value.

This last step is often referred to as *default serialization*. It's what you get if you do nothing beyond adding the words "implements `Serializable`" to your class definition. And it's such a bad idea that you should never use it.*

The problem is that default serialization encodes the exact structure of your class, down to the names of the fields, into the output stream, and it does so in a way that completely prevents any form of versioning. Suppose you want to change the internal representation of your data inside the object, but you still want to maintain some level of backward compatibility. For example, "instances serialized with the old program can still be read in with the new program." If you just use default serialization, this is actually quite hard to achieve.

Suppose, on the other hand, you implement a very simple versioning scheme such as the one in the following code snippet:

```
public class ClassWhichWillBeMarshalled  implements Serializable {
    public static final long serialVersionUID = 1L;
    public static final int actualVersion = 1;
    // ...
    private void writeObject(java.io.ObjectOutputStream out) throws IOException {
        out.writeInt(actualVersion);
        out.defaultWriteObject( );
    }

    private void readObject(java.io.ObjectInputStream in)  throws IOException {
        in.readInt( );
        in.defaultReadObject( );
    }
}
```

This actually does use the default serialization algorithm. But before it invokes the default serialization algorithm, it handles the reading and writing of a version number (which is actually a class-level static variable). And the nice thing is that when you version the object, it becomes quite easy to read everything in and handle the data appropriately. The code to do so looks a lot like the following:

```
private void readObject(java.io.ObjectInputStream in)  throws IOException {
    int version  = in.readInt( );
    switch (version) {
        case 1:
```

---

* That's *never*, as in "not ever." Not in RMI and not in any other application that uses serialization.

```
        handleVersionOne(in);
    // ...
}
```

There is one slight fly in the ointment here. Suppose version two is grossly incompatible with version one. For example, suppose you renamed all the variables to conform to a new corporate variable naming standard (or switched from being Serializable to Externalizable). The solution is simple: you can use the readFields() method on ObjectInputStream to read in the name/value pairs for your original fields (and then handle setting the values yourself). The following code example shows you how to read in the serialization information using this technique:

```
private static class A implements Serializable {

    private static final int DEFAULT_VALUE_FOR_A = 14;
    private int a = DEFAULT_VALUE_FOR_A;

    private void readObject(java.io.ObjectInputStream in) throws IOException,
ClassNotFoundException {
        ObjectInputStream.GetField getFields = in.readFields();
        a = getFields.get("a", DEFAULT_VALUE_FOR_A);
    }
}
```

Many books advocate thinking through the "serialized form" of your classes in a much more thorough and principled way. There's nothing wrong with doing that, of course (in general, thinking more improves the quality of your code). But my experience has been that spending a lot of time thinking about serialized forms is often a waste of time. If you include enough information to version data later on, you're doing fine (and you can spend your time solving other, more pressing problems).

You might be forced to think more about the serialized form eventually, but by then you'll have a lot more information about how your class will be used (and whether marshalling and demarshalling it is a performance bottleneck).

Always Unit-Test Marshalling Code

Because marshalling in RMI is always based on streams, it's very easy to write unit tests for your marshalling code. And doing so can save you a lot of headaches as you modify your codebase. All you need to do is use streams that map to byte arrays in memory. For example, the following code creates a deep copy of an object and then makes sure the deep copy is equal to the original instance:

```
public static boolean testSerialization(Serializable object) throws Exception {
    Object secondObject = makeDeepCopy(object);
    boolean hashCodeComparison = (object.hashCode() == secondObject.hashCode());
    boolean equalsComparison = object.equals(secondObject);
    return hashCodeComparison && equalsComparison;
}
```

```
private static object makeDeepCopy(Serializable object) throws Exception{
    ByteArrayOutputStream byteArrayOutputStream = new ByteArrayOutputStream( );
    ObjectOutputStream objectOutputStream = new
        ObjectOutputStream(byteArrayOutputStream);
    objectOutputStream.writeObject(object);
    objectOutputStream.flush( );
    byte[] bytes = byteArrayOutputStream.toByteArray( );
    ByteArrayInputStream byteArrayInputStream= new ByteArrayInputStream(bytes);
    ObjectInputStream objectInputStream = new
        ObjectInputStream(byteArrayInputStream);
    SerializationTest deepCopy = (SerializationTest) objectInputStream.readObject( );
    return deepCopy;
}
```

If you insert tests for each value object in your codebase, and then run them occasionally (for example, as unit tests in either Cactus or JUnit), you'll catch errors as they occur (and before they cost you significant time and energy).

Profile Before Customizing

From an engineering perspective, any project contains two very different types of costs: *people costs* and *performance costs*. People costs are what working on a particular piece of code implies for the development team; they're measured in terms of features not implemented, extra testing that might be required, and (in the long term) maintenance overhead. Performance costs deal with the runtime overhead of a program; they're measured in terms of application performance, network overhead, and machine resource utilization.

The rule of thumb for getting projects in on time is very simple: don't write bad code. But don't trade people costs for performance costs unless you have to.

Following this rule doesn't guarantee that your project will finish on time. But if you willfully ignore it, I guarantee that your project won't. Thus, whenever you're tempted to customize a working piece of code, some variant of the following scenario should play inside your head:

> **You:** Hmmm. Maybe I'll customize our marshalling code. I bet I can save a bunch of network and process overhead by optimizing it.
>
> **Your Internal Product Manager:** Don't you have some business logic to write?

This applies to marshalling and demarshalling in a very straightforward way. You should always make sure you can version your marshalled objects because it's very hard to retrofit versioning into your codebase (therefore, not doing so is bad code). And you should write unit tests because they're immediately valuable and will save you time even in the short term. But you shouldn't customize your code any more than that. Use either serialization or externalization (whichever is appropriate), and use defaultWriteObject( ) and defaultReadObject( ) until it's absolutely clear that you have to perform further customization. Unless your marshalling code is wedging the network or the CPU, you probably won't need to do either of these things, which should make your Internal Product Manager very happy.

Consider Using Byte Arrays to Store Marshalling Results

Marshalling converts an object graph into a set of bytes. The bytes are usually simply pushed into a stream and sent over a wire (or to a file or database). But there's no reason why another level of indirection can't be inserted into the process, as in the following code example:

```
public class SerializeIntoBytes implements Externalizable {
    private byte[] _bytes;
    public void writeExternal(ObjectOutput out) throws IOException {
        if (null == _bytes) {
            createByteArray();
        }
        out.writeInt(_bytes.length);
        out.write(_bytes);
    }

    public void readExternal(ObjectInput in) throws IOException,
ClassNotFoundException {
        int byteArrayLength = in.readInt();
        _bytes = new byte[byteArrayLength];
        in.read(_bytes);
        restoreStateFromByteArray();
    }

    protected void createByteArray()  {
    // The "real" marshalling goes on in here.
    }

    protected void restoreStateFromByteArray() {
    // The "real" demarshalling goes on in here.
    }
}
```

The first thing this idiom does is enable you to reuse the end result of marshalling an object more than once. Consider, for example, the following scenario:

> A client application makes a remote method call to an authentication server and receives an authentication key which will expire in two hours. For the next two hours, whenever the client application makes a call to a back-end server, it passes in the authentication key to prove that it is authorized to make the method call.

The authentication key in this scenario has two crucial features: it's being sent over the wire many times, and it doesn't change. Session keys have similar properties. And distributed event systems frequently have objects that aren't as long-lived but are sent to many recipients. In cases such as these, the savings that result from not having to marshal the object repeatedly can often be significant.

Using byte arrays can be very difficult if you're also using RMI's dynamic classloading facility. RMI actually uses subclasses of both ObjectInputStream and ObjectOutputStream to make dynamic class-loading possible. The subclass of ObjectOutputStream adds in the codebase URL to the class description during the marshalling process. The subclass of ObjectInputStream reads in the instance data and downloads the classes from the codebase URL if necessary.

If you're using dynamic classloading, you probably need to use the RMI infrastructure (including the RMI Classloader).

Another scenario in which byte arrays can be useful is when you want to postpone demarshalling for a while. Suppose we change the previous code a little by removing restoreStateFromByteArray( ) from the demarshalling process. The new version of readExternal looks like the following:

```
public void readExternal(ObjectInput in) throws IOException, ClassNotFoundException {
    int byteArrayLength = in.readInt( );
    _bytes = new byte[byteArrayLength];
    in.read(_bytes);
}
```

This new class isn't very useful as is; it requires some other instance, somewhere, to call readStateFromByteArray before it can be said to be fully demarshalled. In essence, you've decoupled the "interpretation" of the bytes from the "transmission" of the bytes.

This type of decoupling can be useful in two distinct scenarios. The first scenario involves asynchronous messaging. If the client application doesn't need a return value, and doesn't need to find out about demarshalling errors, an RMI call can return a little faster because it won't have to wait for demarshalling to complete before returning. And the server can postpone interpreting the bytes until it needs to handle the fully demarshalled object (or it can perform demarshalling in a background thread).

But, to be honest, supporting asynchronous messaging, while important for certain classes of applications, is not a major reason for postponing interpretation. The major reason for postponing interpretation is that interpreting the bytes might involve loading classes that aren't available in the local process. When you interpret the bytes, you're creating instances of classes. If you don't have those classes in the process that's interpreting the bytes, instances of ClassNotFoundException will be thrown.

Let's consider a distributed event service again. Suppose you've built an event service based on a publish/subscribe metaphor using event channels. The event service is a server that lives on your network and is available on a 24/7 basis. Client applications register for certain types of events (based on an event channel), and server applications drop off events in a particular channel.

For any given event, the following processing sequence occurs:

1. A server creates an event object and makes an RMI call to the event service, passing in the event object on a channel.

2. The event service logs the event, and information about it, in a transaction log.

3. The event service attempts to deliver the event to every client application that's registered for this particular channel.

There are two important points here. The first is that the event service doesn't change the event object at all. In which case, repeatedly marshalling the object (each time it's sent to another client) is just painful; you should avoid that performance hit, and that means a piece of infrastructure such as an event service should use byte arrays to avoid performance problems.

The second point is that the event service might have been written two years ago, and might not actually have most of the event objects on its classpath. This is perfectly OK: the event service doesn't need to know about those objects to deliver the events.

If you were actually building an event service, you might consider creating an envelope class. The envelope class would contain information about the event (that helps the event service deliver the event) and has a byte array with event-specific information that the recipient will demarshal. Using an envelope class makes the interface a little cleaner but doesn't alter the main idea (that explicitly storing and handling the byte array and controlling when the "interpretation step" happens can be useful).

 Envelope classes are actually fairly widely used. For example, if you look at RMI's activation daemon, you'll see that it uses the MarshalledObject class for exactly the same reason: passing around instances of MarshalledObject (which contains a byte array) helps the activation daemon avoid knowing about application-specific classes.

Making Applications More Robust

The first set of practices in this chapter dealt with how to encode objects that will be sent to another process. This section is very different; it contains practices for making an application more robust. The practices in this section aren't really about "design" in the classic sense. Nothing in these practices will help you determine the object composition for your business logic or write a better remote interface. Instead, they mostly deal with two related topics: *connection maintenance* and *failure handling*.

Connection maintenance refers to practices that make sure the programs in a distributed application can connect with each other and send method calls. Failure handling refers to practices that enable an application to recover as gracefully as possible from a connection failure; you might think there's not a lot you can do when an application crashes (or starts performing badly), but there are a few simple practices that will help you diagnose problems and provide end users with a better experience.

Include Logic for Retrying Remote Calls

Everyone knows that networks fail. Failures can range from small-scale and transient to massive and persistent. Obviously, in the case of massive and persistent network failures, a distributed application will not work. But your application can be built to survive small-scale and transient network failures.

One of the best things you can do to make your application more robust is implement a retry strategy. That is, whenever you make a remote call, wrap it in a loop based on catching RemoteException, as in the following code snippet:

```java
public void wrapRemoteCallInRetryLoop( ) {
    int numberOfTries = 0;
    while (numberOfTries < MAXIMUM_NUMBER_OF_TRIES) {
        numberOfTries++;
        try {
            doActualWork( );
            break;
        }
        catch (RemoteException exceptionThrownByRMIInfrastructure) {
            reportRemoteException(exceptionThrownByRMIInfrastructure);
            try {
                Thread.sleep(REMOTE_CALL_RETRY_DELAY);
            }
            catch (InterruptedException ignored) {}
        }
    }
}
```

This method is simply an encapsulation of a loop. It relies on two other methods, doActualWork( ) and reportRemoteException( ), to make the remote method call and to report failures in communicating with the remote server, respectively. This code also assumes that RemoteException indicates a network failure, and that retrying the method call a small (and fixed) number of times is a reasonable strategy when the RMI infrastructure throws an instance of RemoteException.

Note that in some cases this is not the correct behavior. For example, if the failure is a timeout, this could lead to a very bad user experience—no user wants to wait through a single timeout, much less three consecutive timeouts. And there are exceptions, such as NoSuchObjectException, which subclass RemoteException and for which retrying the method call is usually pointless. (NoSuchObjectException usually indicates that the client has a stub for a server that no longer exists. In which case, using the same stub and trying the call again makes no sense.) I'll address all these objections in later practices.

Associate Unique Identifiers with Requests

Once you decide to implement retry logic, you need to worry about partial failures. For example, consider the following scenario:

1. The client makes a remote method call.
2. The server receives the call, handles it, and returns the appropriate answer.
3. The network hiccups.
4. The client gets a RemoteException and tries again.

Sometimes this is harmless. For example, clients frequently fetch information from a server to display to a user. As long as the request doesn't change any state on the server, it's OK to simply make the request twice. If, however, the request changes state on the server (for example, depositing money to an account), it's usually important that the request not be processed twice. That is, the client needs to make the request a second time, and the server needs to return the correct answer. But the server shouldn't actually perform the requested action twice.

In complicated cases, the client application might need to use a distributed transaction manager to actually make sure that a set of related calls to the server will succeed or fail atomically.[*] But in many cases, it simply suffices to associate a unique identifier to the method call. For example, the following code uses the VMID class (from the java.rmi.dgc package) to define a RequestIdentifier class:

```
public final class RequestIdentifier implements Serializable {

    public static synchronized RequestIdentifier getRequestIdentifier() {
        return new RequestIdentifier();
    }

    public boolean equals(Object object) {
        if  (!(object instanceof RequestIdentifier) ){
            return false;
        }
        RequestIdentifier otherRequestIdentifier = (RequestIdentifier) object;
        if (_requestNumber != otherRequestIdentifier._requestNumber) {
            return false;
        }
        return _sourceVM.equals(otherRequestIdentifier._sourceVM);
    }

    public int hashCode() {
        return _sourceVM.hashCode() * 31 + _requestNumber;
    }

    private static int REQUEST_NUMBER_COUNTER;
    private static VMID THE_VM = new VMID();
```

---

[*] Although, in such cases, you should use a server-side proxy to handle the transaction.

```
        private int _requestNumber;
        private VMID _sourceVM;

        private RequestIdentifier( ) {
            _requestNumber=REQUEST_NUMBER_COUNTER++;
            _sourceVM = THE_VM;

        }
    }
```

If the remote calls include an instance of `RequestIdentifier` as an additional argument, the retry loop is much safer: the server can simply check whether it has already handled this request and respond appropriately.

Performance costs are associated with the use of request identifiers. Some are obvious—for example, the instance of `RequestIdentifier` must be created on the client side and sent over the wire to the server. But some are more subtle. The server probably can't store a hashtable of all requests it has ever handled in memory. And the performance costs associated with checking against a database for each remote method call are probably intolerable (especially given that retries will be rare).

The usual strategy, one which is more than good enough for most cases, is for the server to track *recent requests* and assume that if a request identifier isn't stored in the recent requests, it hasn't been handled yet. For example, servers can usually store the last 30 minutes of request identifiers in an in-memory data structure.[*]

 If you find you need more assurances than tracking recent requests provides, you probably should be using a message queueing system and not RMI.

Distinguish Between Network Lag Time and Server Load

When servers are busy, requests take a longer time to handle. Most of the time, the client simply waits longer. But sometimes, when servers are very busy, a request will simply time out, and an instance of `RemoteException` will be thrown. In this latter case, retry logic turns out to be fairly painful: if the server is too busy and cannot handle additional requests, the last thing in the world the client should do is send the request again, especially if the request isn't very important, or can wait awhile.

One way to deal with this is to use what I call the *bouncer pattern*. The idea is to define a new subclass of `Exception`, called `ServerIsBusy`, add it to all the remote methods, and then throw instances of `ServerIsBusy` whenever the server is too busy to handle additional requests.

[*] I recommend using a hashbelt. See the data experation articles I wrote for *www. onjava.com* for more details.

In the simplest implementation, the server simply keeps track of the number of pending requests and throws an instance of ServerIsBusy whenever there are too many pending requests, as in the following implementation of the Bouncer class:

```
public class Bouncer {
    private static final int MAX_NUMBER_OF_REQUESTS = 73;
    private static in CURRENT_NUMBER_OF_REQUESTS;
    private static ServerIsBusy REUSABLE_EXCEPTION = new ServerIsBusy();
    public synchronized static void checkNumberOfRequestsLimit throws ServerIsBusy {
        if (MAX_NUMBER_OF_REQUESTS == CURRENT_NUMBER_OF_REQUESTS ) {
            throw REUSABLE_EXCEPTION;
        }
        CURRENT_NUMBER_OF_REQUESTS++;
    }
    public synchronized static void decrementNumberOfActiveRequests() {
        CURRENT_NUMBER_OF_REQUESTS--;
    }
}
```

Once you've defined a bouncer class, you need to implement the check in all your remote methods. The code transformation is simple. A method such as:

```
public foo (arguments) throws exception-list {
    method body
}
```

is rewritten as:

```
public foo(arguments) throws exception-list, ServerIsBusy{
    Bouncer.checkNumberOfRequestsLimit();
    try {
        method body
    }
    finally {
        Bouncer.decrementNumberOfActiveRequests();
    }
}
```

Adding this check to your server code has two main benefits. The first is that it enables the client application to distinguish between network failures and when the server is simply too busy. And the second is that it enables you to implement much friendlier client applications. In the simplest case, putting up a dialog box saying "The server is very busy right now, and as a result, this application won't perform very well" will save users a fair amount of frustration. More complicated clients might switch to a secondary server.

 It might seem tedious to implement this logic inside every single method that can be called remotely. That's because it *is* tedious. It's also error-prone. The best solution to this problem is to use aspects to insert this code at the appropriate places. To learn more about aspects, see the AspectJ web site at *http://www.aspectj.org*.

Wrap RMI Calls in Command Objects

Suppose you're wrapping each remote method call in a retry loop, distinguishing the different types of remote exceptions, and stamping remote requests with identifiers. Then simple remote method invocations such as `server.performAction( )`, in which `server` is a stub associated with some remote object, balloon to 20 or 30 lines of code, most of which simply deal with the complexities of failure handling. This is bad for two reasons. The first is that a simple and easy-to-read line of business logic has become cluttered with extraneous things. And the second is that a lot of code is being written over and over again (the failure-handling code is boilerplate code).

The solution to both of these problems is to encapsulate all the code you've been adding inside a single class. For example, you could define a new class called `SpecificCallToServer` which encapsulates all this code. And then `server.performAction( )` becomes:

```
(new SpecificCallToServer(...))..makeRemoteCall( )
```

This is a little less readable than the original code, but it's still very readable. And all the logic dealing with the network infrastructure has been neatly encapsulated into a single class, `SpecificCallToServer`. If `SpecificCallToServer` simply extends an abstract base class (named something like `RemoteMethodCall`), you've made the client application more readable, and only written the code that deals with the complexities of making the remote method call once.

 For more information on how to design and implement a command object framework, see the series of command object articles I wrote for onjava.com.

Wrapping remote calls in command objects also facilitates many of the other practices in this chapter. For example, using command objects makes it easier for the client to use a remote stub cache.

Consider Using a Naming Service

A naming service, such as the RMI registry or a JNDI service provider, provides a very simple piece of functionality: it lets a client application pass in a logical name (such as "BankAccountServer") and get back a stub to the requested server.

This level of indirection is incredibly useful. It makes writing the client code much simpler, it means that you don't have to figure out another way to get stubs to the servers (which isn't so hard: `RemoteStub` does implement `Serializable`), and it allows you to easily move servers to different machines.

In short, using a naming service makes it much easier to write and deploy applications.

Using a naming service also makes it possible to use the `Unreferenced` interface reliably. We'll talk more about this later in the chapter.

Don't Throw RemoteException in Your Server Code

The javadocs for `RemoteException` say the following:

> A RemoteException is the common superclass for a number of communication-related exceptions that may occur during the execution of a remote method call. Each method of a remote interface, an interface that extends java.rmi.Remote, must list RemoteException in its throws clause.

This might make it seem like it's OK, and maybe even a good thing, for your server-side code to throw instances of `RemoteException`. It's certainly easy, if you're working on a server and discover a new exceptional condition, to add a line of code such as the following:

```
throw new RemoteException("You can't deposit a negative amount of money");
```

It might even seem like good programming practice—after all, the client code already catches `RemoteException`. But it's a very bad idea to use `RemoteException` in this way.

To understand why, you need to understand what `RemoteException` really means. The real meaning of `RemoteException` is that something has gone wrong between your client code and server code. That is, your client made a method call on a stub. Your server code is expecting to receive a method invocation via its skeleton. If something goes wrong between that call to the stub and the resulting invocation made by the skeleton, it will be signalled by an instance of `RemoteException`. Exceptions that happen within the server should be signalled by instances of some other exception class that doesn't extend `RemoteException`. There are two reasons for this. The practical one is that it's too easy for a client to misunderstand a `RemoteException`. For example, the retry loop shown earlier would try to invoke the remote method again. And the more abstract reason is that you should really be declaring the types of exceptions the server is throwing so that the client can react appropriately. Throwing generic exceptions is almost always a bad idea.

Distinguish Between Different Types of Remote Exceptions

Almost all RMI exceptions extend `RemoteException`. This can be very convenient because it makes generic code easier to write; you can simply catch `RemoteException` and be confident that you've caught all RMI-related exceptions. But it can also lead to programmer sloppiness. The different subclasses of `RemoteException` have very different meanings, and treating them generically is often a mistake.

Every `RemoteException` can be classified using four major attributes: what code throws it, when it will be thrown, why it will be thrown, and what this indicates about your application. Consider the following list, which classifies the nine most common remote exceptions along these axes.

AccessException

Where thrown:	In the RMI infrastructure on the client side.
When thrown:	As part of the standard distributed communication between client and server, before the remote call is even attempted.
Why thrown:	The client code doesn't have permission to open a socket to the server.
What it means:	This indicates a client configuration problem (e.g., a problem in deploying the application). This exception is consistently thrown; it will not "spontaneously heal" if you try the call again.

AlreadyBoundException

Where thrown:	By the RMI registry.
When thrown:	Usually during launching, when the launch code attempts to bind the server into the registry.
Why thrown:	The server code used bind( ) and the name was already taken.
What it means:	This usually indicates a configuration error, that an instance of the server was already running, or a coding mistake (you meant to use rebind( )). In any of these cases, you probably need to clean out the registry.

ConnectException

Where thrown:	In the RMI infrastructure on the client side.
When thrown:	As part of the standard distributed communication between client and server. The client has tried to connect with the server but has been unable to establish a connection.
Why thrown:	This is thrown by the RMI infrastructure on the client when a call fails. A ConnectException means the server object never got the method call at all.
What it means:	If the network is working (e.g., if you can ping the server machine from the client machine), this exception usually means that the server isn't running (e.g., it crashed or was never started). Otherwise, it indicates a network failure.

MarshalException

Where thrown:	In the RMI infrastructure on the client side.
When thrown:	As part of the standard distributed communication between client and server. This is thrown after the client establishes a connection to the server (e.g., when a stream has already been created).
Why thrown:	You tried to send an object that didn't implement either Serializable or Externalizable.
What it means:	You must send an object that implements either Serializable or Externalizable.

NoSuchObjectException

Where thrown:	In the RMI infrastructure on the server side.
When thrown:	As part of the standard distributed communication between client and server. This is thrown after the RMI infrastructure on the server has already demarshalled the arguments and is trying to actually call a method on your code.
Why thrown:	Every remote method call contains an `ObjID`, which uniquely identifies the object on which the method call is being made. The RMI infrastructure maintains a hashtable of instances of `ObjID` to `RemoteServers`. This error indicates that the `ObjID` passed over the wire was not a key in this table.
What it means:	This usually occurs when a client has a stub to a server that no longer is running in the server process. This is a strange exception to encounter because stubs try to maintain leases on servers (which usually prevents a server from being shut down). As such, this exception usually indicates a failure in the distributed garbage collector (it doesn't indicate that the server process crashed; if the server process crashed, an instance of `ConnectException` would have been thrown instead).

NotBoundException

Where thrown:	By the RMI registry.
When thrown:	As part of a `lookup( )` call.
Why thrown:	The registry's hashtable of objects doesn't have any stub bound under the specified name.
What it means:	This usually indicates that there is a transaction issue (a server was unbound while the client was interacting with the registry), or that the registry was restarted and not all the servers bound themselves in again.

StubNotFoundException

Where thrown:	In the RMI Infrastructure on the server side.
When thrown:	When an attempt is made to export an instance of `RemoteServer` that does not have an associated stub.
Why thrown:	Stubs are necessary for RMI to function properly. The right point in time to signal this error is when the server is starting up (or just being exported), not when the stub is actually required.
What it means:	This usually means you forgot to run rmic (or that you made a mistake when deploying your server).

UnknownHostException

Where thrown:	In the RMI Infrastructure on the client side.
When thrown:	When a particular stub is used for the first time.
Why thrown:	The client is unable to resolve the server name using DNS.
What it means:	The client and the server are on different subnets of your network, and somebody in IT configured DNS incorrectly.

`UnmarshalException`

Where thrown:	In the RMI infrastructure on the server side.
When thrown:	While attempting to unmarshal the arguments from a remote method call.
Why thrown:	The server either cannot find the class referenced, or has an incompatible version of it.
What it means:	The client and the server have different, and incompatible, versions of the codebase.

You shouldn't panic when you look at this list. It's not that complicated, and once you actually start thinking about the different types of `RemoteExceptions`, most of the information here will become second nature to you. The important point here is that these nine exceptions cover about 95% of the instances of `RemoteException` thrown in practice. And they are all thrown at different times, for very different reasons. If you write code that simply catches instances of `RemoteException`, you might be missing an opportunity to make your code more robust, better at reporting urgent problems to someone who can fix them, and more user-friendly.

 Note that other exceptions are also thrown during the course of RMI calls. For example, `java.net.BindException` is sometimes thrown on the server side (if a specified port is already in use), and `java.lang.ClassNotFoundException` can be thrown on either the client or the server (it's usually thrown on the client side, when the stub classes haven't been deployed correctly).

Use the Unreferenced Interface to Clean Up Allocated Server State

The distributed garbage collector is a wonderful piece of code. It works in a very straightforward manner: a client gets a *lease* on a particular server object. The lease has a specific duration, and the client is responsible for renewing the lease before it expires. If the lease expires, and the client hasn't renewed the lease, the server JVM is allowed to garbage-collect the server object (as long as no other clients have leases against that particular object).

If a server implements the `Unreferenced` interface—which contains a single method, `unreferenced( )`—the server will be notified via a call to `unreferenced( )` that there are no valid leases against the server.

It's important to note that any active instance of a stub, in any JVM, will automatically try to connect to the server and maintain a lease. This means that, for example, if the server is bound into the RMI registry, the registry will keep the server alive. (The RMI registry basically stores the stub in a hashtable. The stub keeps renewing its lease.)

In turn, this means that if you're using a naming service to get instances of stubs, no other process can actually get a stub to a server if unreferenced has been called (unreferenced will be called only if the server is no longer bound into any naming services).

All of this makes the unreferenced method an ideal place to release server-side resources and shut down the server object gracefully.

Always Configure the Distributed Garbage Collector

By default, a lease should last 10 minutes, and clients should renew every 5 minutes (clients attempt to renew when a lease is halfway expired). The problem is that, in a wide variety of production scenarios, the default values don't work very well. Using JDK 1.3, I've experienced intermittent distributed garbage-collection failures (in which a client has a stub to a server that's been garbage-collected) when the network is congested or starts losing packets.

Fortunately, you can change the duration of a lease by setting the value of java.rmi. dgc.leaseValue. This parameter, which is set on the server, specifies the duration of a typical lease. The trade-off is simple: smaller values for java.rmi.dgc.leaseValue mean shorter lease durations, and hence quicker notification when a server becomes unreferenced.

But smaller values also mean a greater chance of a false positive: if a client has trouble renewing a lease, giving the client a larger window in which to renew the lease (for example, before the client's lease is expired and unreferenced is called) is often helpful. In particular, larger values of java.rmi.dgc.leaseValue will make your system more robust when the network is flaky. I tend to use at least 30 minutes for java.rmi.dgc.leaseValue.

You might also think that longer leases result in less network traffic (because there are fewer renewals). This is true, but the amount of bandwidth you save is so small that it's really not worth thinking about.

Improving Application Performance

The practices outlined in this section focus on client performance. That is, we assume there is a client application, probably being used by an end user, which talks to a server using RMI. The goal of these practices is to improve both the performance and the perceived performance of the client application.

Perceived performance is a strange thing. The goal in improving perceived performance is improving application responsiveness. That is, when the user clicks a button, the application does the right thing, and it does the right thing *quickly*. Most practices that improve performance also improve perceived performance. But the converse is not true—improving application responsiveness can actually degrade overall performance, or at least cause the server to work harder. But that's often a price worth paying if it means the end user is happier.

 This section isn't as RMI-specific as the previous two sections because, when you get right down to it, all enterprise applications have a fairly similar structure, and a lot of optimization practices are fairly general.

Cache Stubs to Remote Servers

One of the practices in "Making Applications More Robust" was entitled "Always Use a Naming Service." This is sound advice—it does make the application more robust. When followed naïvely, it also makes the application much slower. If you simply replace a remote method call (to a server) with two remote method calls (one to the naming service and then one to the server), you deserve whatever criticism comes your way.

A much better solution is to implement a centralized cache for stubs for remote servers. This cache should meet the following requirements:

- It takes logical arguments, such as server names, and returns a stub. As much as possible, the rest of the code should not know about the structure of the application or the location of individual servers. Code is much more robust, and much easier to read, when knowledge about the application topology is encapsulated.

- If the cache doesn't have a stub already, it fetches the stub (and does so in a way that's transparent to the rest of the application).

- The cache expires stubs that haven't been used in a while. Otherwise, the cache will keep remote server stubs until the client application shuts down. Because having a live stub counts as a reference to the distributed garbage collector, holding on to stubs for long periods of time effectively prevents the server JVM from cleaning up unused resources.

- It has a way for you to flush bad stubs (e.g., stubs to servers that no longer exist). When you discover that a stub is bad (e.g., attempting to make a remote call on the associated server consistently throws an instance of RemoteException), you should remove the stub from the cache right away, instead of waiting for it to expire.

If you implement a stub cache that meets these four criteria, remote method call invocations will look like the following code snippet (assuming that your implementation of a cache has get and remove methods):

```
try {
    MyServer stubToRemoteServer = (MyServer) cache.get(LOGICAL_NAME_FOR_SERVER);
    stubToRemoteServer.performMethod(...);
}
```

```
catch {RemoteException remoteException) {
    cache.remove(LOGICAL_NAME_FOR_SERVER);
}
```

This has many benefits. For one, it's clear code. If the cache has the stub (e.g., if any part of the application has already talked to the server in question), the naming service is bypassed. And if the stub points to a server that is no longer running, the stub is immediately removed.

The next step in using a stub cache is to integrate it with the retry loop discussed earlier. Here's a very simple integration to illustrate the idea:

```
public void wrapRemoteCallInRetryLoop( ) {
    int numberOfTries = 0;
    while (numberOfTries < MAXIMUM_NUMBER_OF_TRIES) {
        numberOfTries++;
        try {
            MyServer stubToRemoteServer = (MyServer)
                                            cache.get(LOGICAL_NAME_FOR_SERVER);
            doActualWork(stubToRemoteServer);
            break;
        }
        catch (RemoteException exceptionThrownByRMIInfrastructure) {
            cache.remove(LOGICAL_NAME_FOR_SERVER);
            reportRemoteException(exceptionThrownByRMIInfrastructure);
            try {
                Thread.sleep(REMOTE_CALL_RETRY_DELAY);
            }
            catch (InterruptedException ignored) {}
        }
    }
}
```

This attempts to get the stub and then makes the remote call. If the call fails, the stub is flushed and, on the second try, a new stub is fetched from the naming service. This is good. In most cases, the cache has the stub, and the overhead of the cache is strictly local. In return for the overhead of maintaining a local cache, you've eliminated most of the calls to the naming service.

Using a stub cache inside the retry loop also lets you gracefully handle the cases when a server is restarted or migrated. In these cases, the stubs in the cache won't work, and attempting to use them will cause instances of RemoteException to be thrown. Logically, the client performs the following sequence of operations:

1. The client fetches the stub from the cache and attempts to make a remote method call.

2. The call fails because the server the stub references is no longer running.

3. The client removes the stub from the cache.

4. The retry loop kicks in, and the client tries again.

5. Because the cache is empty, the cache fetches a new stub from the naming service.

6. Because the new stub points to the new server, everything succeeds.

Combining a stub cache with a retry loop is both efficient and robust!

Consider Caching Return Values from Distributed Calls

At one company for which I worked, my first task was described in the following way: "This call is too slow. See if you can make it faster."

I looked at the call. It was slow. It involved 18 separate modules on the server and implicitly depended on about 40,000 lines of code, and all I could think was, "Oh yeah. I'll optimize this in my first week on the job."

Because the task was impossible, I decided to cheat. I thought, "Hmmm. If I can't make the call faster, I can at least use a cache to try and make the call less often." This turned out to be good enough for the application in question, and is often good enough in distributed applications.

The benefits of caching return values on the client side are:

Faster performance for a given sequence of operations
> Instead of making a call to the server, which involves network and marshalling overhead, you retrieve the value from an in-process cache. Unless you're doing something truly stupid, this should be faster.

More reliable and predictable performance for a given sequence of operations
> In addition to the performance benefit, looking in a local data structure is more reliable than calling a remote server, and it has a predictable level of overhead (unlike a remote method call, which can take more time if the network is busy).

Lower bandwidth
> Bandwidth is the scarcest resource for distributed applications because it is shared by all distributed applications, and because upgrading a network is a lot harder than upgrading a single server. If you don't make a remote call, you aren't using the bandwidth necessary to make the remote call.

Lower server load
> If you don't call the server, the server doesn't have to handle the call, which means you've lowered the effective load on the server.

On the other hand, caching does have some major drawbacks. The two most significant are:

Potentially inaccurate data
> Whenever you cache data, you run the risk of the cached values being incorrect. Sometimes this isn't very important. Sometimes it is. Generally speaking, the more important a piece of information is, or the more time-sensitive it is, the less likely you are to cache it.

The cost of maintaining the cache

Within a given sequence of operations (for example, responding when a user clicks a button), a cache improves performance. But caches have to be maintained: data has to be checked for consistency and occasionally thrown out.

Cache maintenance is usually done in a background thread so that a main thread doesn't take the hit of maintaining the cache (otherwise, perceived performance would suffer, and the "more predictable" item listed as an advantage would be false). But nonetheless, if you're not accessing data that's been cached very often, the client-side cache might very well be a net loss in performance.

 This last item is somewhat paradoxical in that, even if the cache winds up costing you more processing time than it saves, it still might be viewed as a performance improvement. This is because the cost occurs in a background thread, but the performance improvements occur in a main thread (where performance improvements are likely to be noticed).

Caching is a subtle and tricky subject. One reference worth looking at is the series of data expiration articles I wrote for onjava.com. In addition, if you're interested in the subject, you might want to keep an eye on JSR-107, the "Java Temporary Caching API," at *http://jcp.org.jsr/detail/107.jsp*.

Use Batch Methods to Group Related Method Calls

I once had lunch with a group of programmers who were visiting my company from Germany. They were from a company that was partnering with the company I was working for. We were supposed to use CORBA to handle the method calls from their system to ours. But there was a problem.

"CORBA," they confided to me, "doesn't work. It's much too expensive. It doesn't scale very well at all." I was a little surprised by this. I'd been using CORBA for a couple of years at that point, and I'd never run into scalability problems (at least, not at the scale we were talking about).

It turned out that their idea of "building a distributed application" was to "build a single-process application using standard object-oriented techniques and then stick the network in." Their testing had revealed that if an instance of Person is on one machine, and the user interface displaying information about the person is on another machine, a sequence of fine-grained calls such as getFirstName( ), getLastName( ), and getSSN( ) to get the values to display on the screen has performance problems.

Once I figured out what they were complaining about, I had a solution: "Don't do that." The object decompositions that make sense in a single-process application often don't make as much sense in a distributed application. Instead, you need to carefully look at the intent behind sequences of calls and see if you can encapsulate a sequence of calls in one bigger method call (which I refer to as a batch method).

In the previous example, the sequence getFirstName( ), getLastName( ), getSSN( ),... should really have been a call to a new method called getDisplayData( ). Of course, getDisplayData( ) shouldn't exist for a single-process implementation of the Person class (it completely breaks encapsulation). But it has to be there for the distributed application to perform well, and that's the point of this practice.

How do you spot a potential batch method? There's no cut-and-dried way to do so (that I know of). But here are four rules of thumb for when batch methods are appropriate:

- The methods you want to include in a batch method must be called in a sequence fairly often. Batch methods are an optimization and they shouldn't be created for uncommon cases.

- If the methods are all for data access (with no side effects), a batch method is more likely to be appropriate.

- The methods should all block the same task (and not distinct tasks). If all the method calls are associated with the same set of client-side conceptual tasks, and none of the tasks can continue until the client gets all the return values, a batch method is almost certainly appropriate.

- The methods have a predetermined outcome. That is, the client will make a sequence of calls. If the client doesn't know all the arguments (for all the calls) at the time the first call is made, or if the return values for all the calls can't be computed at the time when the first call is made, the methods can't be grouped into a batch method.

Use a Server-Side Proxy to Manage Transactions Across Servers

Sometimes a client will make a series of calls to a server, and these calls, while conceptually a transaction, aren't easily batched, or don't feel like a batch method. A classic example of this is transferring money between two bank accounts.

If you have two distinct servers (one for each account), this involves the following four steps:

1. Opening a transaction (presumably using a transaction management server)
2. Withdrawing money from one server
3. Depositing the money in another server
4. Committing the transaction

This sequence of calls should not be executed from a client application for two reasons. The first is that client applications are often deployed across a WAN, which is slow (especially compared to a datacenter managed by IT personnel). Making four concurrent remote method calls under those conditions could lead to significant performance problems.

The second reason is that logic about transactions will most likely change. Even something as simple as "We've decided to log all money transfers from now on" would force you to redeploy a new version of the client that would call a logging method on a server somewhere, which is very bizarre in and of itself.

The solution is to use a server-side proxy for the client. A server-side proxy is a server, running "near" the other servers, which is client-specific and whose sole role is to manage complex transactions for the client. If you're using a server-side proxy, the previous calling sequence turns into a single call to the proxy's transferMoney method. The proxy still has to perform the four remote method calls, but it does so on a LAN inside a well-managed environment. Figure 6-1 illustrates the trade-off.

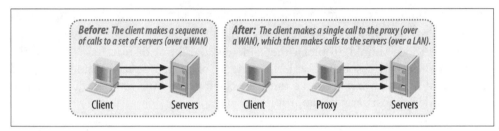

Figure 6-1. Using a server-side proxy

Use Asynchronous Messaging Wherever Possible

Most remote method calls are synchronous: the calling thread stops and waits for a response from the server. An asynchronous method call is one in which the caller doesn't wait for a response, or even wait to know if the call succeeded. Instead, the calling thread continues processing.

RMI doesn't directly support asynchronous calls. Instead, you have to use a background thread to make the call. In Example 6-2, the calling thread creates a command object and drops it off in a background queue for execution. This leaves the calling thread free to immediately resume processing, instead of waiting for a response, as in the following code snippet:

```
BackgroundCallQueue _backgroundQueue = new BackgroundCallQueueImpl();
// ...
_backgroundQueue.addCall(new SpecificCallToServer(...));
```

Example 6-2 is a sample implementation of BackgroundCallQueue and BackgroundCallQueueImpl.

Example 6-2. BackgroundCallQueue.java and BackgroundCallQueueImpl.java

```
public interface BackgroundCallQueue {
    public void addCall(RemoteMethodCall callToAdd);
}
```

Example 6-2. BackgroundCallQueue.java and BackgroundCallQueueImpl.java (continued)

```java
public class BackgroundCallQueueImpl implements BackgroundCallQueue {

    private LinkedList _pendingCalls;
    private thread _dispatchThread;

    public BackgroundCallQueueImpl () {
        _stopAcceptingRequests = false;
        _pendingCalls = new LinkedList();
        _dispatchThread = new Thread(this, "Background Call Queue Dispatch Thread");
        _dispatchThread;.start();
    }

    public synchronized void addCall(RemoteMethodCall callToAdd) {
        _pendingCalls.addCall();
        notify();
    }

    public void run() {
        while (true) {
            RemoteMethodCall call = waitForCall();
            if (null!=call ) {
                executeCall(call);
            }
        }
    }

    private synchronized RemoteMethodCall waitForCall() {
        while (0== _pendingCalls.size()) {
            wait();
        }
        return (RemoteMethodCall) _pendingCalls.removeFirst();
    }

    private void executeCall(RemoteMethodCall call) {
        // ...
    }
}
```

This isn't very complicated code, but it does offer two very significant advantages over synchronous method calls. The first is that it decreases the time a main thread spends sending remote messages. Imagine, for example, that a user clicks on a button, and, as a result of that click, the server needs to be told something. If you use a synchronous method call, the button processing time (and, hence, the perceived performance of the application) will include the time spent sending the remote method call (and the time the server spends processing the call). If you can make the call asynchronously, in a background thread, the application isn't any faster or more efficient, but the user thinks it is.

The second reason is that, once you've moved to a model where requests are dropped off into a queue, you can tweak the queue and make performance improvements without altering most of the client code. For example, if you are making a lot of calls to a single method on a server, you can group these calls and make them in a single call. For example, instead of 100 calls to:

```
server.patientGivenMedication(Patient patient, Medication medication, long time,
HealthCareProvider medicationSource);
```

you might have 1 call to:

```
server.patientsGivenMedication(ArrayList medicationEvents);
```

Because each remote method call contains information about all the relevant classes involved, this will dramatically reduce both marshalling time and bandwidth. Instead of marshalling and sending information about the `Patient` class 100 times, you will send it only once.

There are two major downsides to putting messages in a background queue. The first is that your code will be harder to debug. Decoupling the source of the remote method call from the time the remote call is made makes it harder to trace the source of logical errors. For example, if a command object has the wrong value for an argument, it's harder to track down the source of the error.

The second problem with putting messages in a background queue is that it's harder to report failures (and harder to respond to them). If a user clicks a button and therefore thinks of an operation as "done," it can be disconcerting for him to find out later on that the operation failed.

Given all this, the question is: when should you use asynchronous messaging? Here are three indicators that a method can be put safely into a background queue:

- If the method returns void and throws no exceptions (other than `RemoteException`). Methods with this sort of signature tend to be information-sending methods rather than information-retrieval methods or methods that are requesting an action. And, hence, they can be safely postponed and performed in the background.

- If there is an associated method to find out the status of an operation at a later time. For example, consider a method to submit a print request to a print server. It might have a boolean return value, and it might throw all sorts of interesting exceptions. But having clicked on the Print button, the user really wants to be able to continue with his work, not wait until the method call transfers the entire file to the print server, and he wants a status view so that he can see where his document is in the print queue.

- If the server can call the client back with a return value (or an exceptional condition). Certain requests aren't particularly urgent and can be performed in the background. But the user would like to know if he succeeded. Consider email, for example. When he clicks on the Send button, the user is really saying, "This can go off into the email cloud now." Whether it is sent now or three minutes from now is not really an issue. But he is assuming that if it can't be sent, he will be told.

Printing documents is also a case when callbacks can improve the user interface. A callback to let a user know that his document has been printed is a nice feature.

Using callbacks to let the user know the outcome of an event could incur some additional overhead. It replaces one bidirectional socket connection (the method call and then the return value) with two unidirectional connections (the method call is sent and then, in a later connection, the response is sent). Breaking apart messages like this is a useful technique for optimizing perceived performance, but it almost always incurs some extra overhead.

Further Reading

- *Java RMI* by William Grosso (O'Reilly & Associates, 2002).
- *Effective Java* by Joshua Bloch (Addison-Wesley Professional, 2001).
- AspectJ web site at *http://www.aspectj.org*.
- Command object articles. These are a series of articles I wrote for onjava.com. The first of the articles is at *http://www.onjava.com/pub/a/onjava/2002/10/17/rmi.html*.
- Data expiration articles. These are a series of articles I wrote for onjava.com. The first of the articles is at *http://www.onjava.com/pub/a/onjava/2002/01/09/dataexp1.html*.
- JSR 107 at *http://jcp.org/detail/107.jsp*.

CHAPTER 7

Java Management Extensions

J. Steven Perry

Enterprise Java's management technology is called Java Management Extensions (JMX). JMX provides patterns, APIs, and architecture for managing any application resource, including queues and connection pools. The patterns are used to encapsulate your application resources as managed beans (MBeans) by defining the management interface for each resource. The APIs are then used to register the MBeans with the MBean server, which acts not only as a registry for MBeans, but also as a communications bus for management applications to obtain information about registered MBeans. The JMX architecture defines how MBeans, the MBean server, and management applications interact.

In this chapter we will take a look at some best practices for MBean naming and instrumentation. Each section presents a problem or issue, some possible approaches to addressing it, and the practice or pattern that best solves it.

Naming

JMX provides a great deal of flexibility in how you can name your MBeans. With only a few exceptions imposed by the specification, the sky is the limit. However, with this flexibility comes a potential hazard: collisions between names. You should make every effort to give your MBeans unique names. There are two components of an MBean object name: the domain name and the key property list. In this section, we will look at how to use these two components of the object name to mitigate the risk of MBean naming collisions.

 In this section, the term "object name" is used to refer to the string representation of the ObjectName instance required to register an MBean with the MBean server.

Name MBean Domains Just Like Packages

The domain name is part of the object name of an MBean and serves as a namespace mechanism for MBeans. The JMX specification imposes a few limitations on how you can name the domain of an MBean. For instance, you can't use wildcard characters (? and *) or a comma, colon, or equals sign. You also cannot use the JMImplementation string as a domain name because it is reserved for the particular JMX implementation you're using.

Other than that, there are no further restrictions on naming the domain of your MBeans. But as I said, with this freedom comes a potential problem: object name collisions. If the domain name you choose for your MBean is the same as an object name that is already registered, the MBean server will not allow you to register your MBean!

It's necessary, therefore, to take great care when choosing a naming idiom because you want to ensure that your MBeans can coexist with MBeans named by other developers from your team, company, and even the industry. As a developer, I understand the tendency to create new idioms to solve naming problems. For example, I could use my application's name as the domain name for all of my MBeans. However, this could lead to problems when integrating with other applications. Imagine if you have a great deal of investment in a particular domain naming idiom, only to find out that none of your MBeans can be registered as a result of collisions with MBeans from another vendor!

Java uses packages as its namespace mechanism, separating a parent package from its immediate child by a period ("dot"), its child by a dot, and so on. Because the domain name serves as a namespace mechanism for MBeans, it seems reasonable, then, to use the same idiom. The generally accepted idiom for naming packages is:

```
org-type.org-name.application-name[.subsystem-name]
```

Use this same idiom for naming domains. Here are a few examples:

```
org.apache.xerces
com.alltel.framework.logging
com.acme.accounting.payable
```

Of course, there is no guarantee that all developers will follow this idiom, but naming domains like packages significantly reduces the likelihood of object name collisions.

Use the Key Property List to Help Avoid Collisions

The domain name is only part of what makes up the object name of an MBean. The key property list, which makes up the rest, is an unordered set of key/value pairs. The specification imposes no explicit restrictions on how you can assign key properties, other than requiring that there be at least one key property, and that all are in the following format:

```
property1=value1[,propertyN=valueN]
```

The specification makes it clear that the key property list enables uniqueness among MBean names within a given domain (and within a given MBean server instance). It is logical, then, to establish some guidelines for naming key properties. For the purposes of this example, assume that we are talking about MBeans within the same domain. Here are some recommendations.

First, define a key property called name and use that property to establish uniqueness within a given domain. The value of this property should be the same as the Java class (unqualified) of the MBean. For example, suppose you have a payroll system with a queue resource for processing vendor payments called VendorQueue within the com.acme.accounting.payable domain. You could define a key property called name that would take the form:

```
name=VendorQueue
```

The resulting object name would be:

```
com.acme.accounting.payable:name=VendorQueue
```

If you want to register multiple instances of the same MBean class in the same domain, define a key property called instanceId that contains a unique identifier that is determined at runtime.

One approach is to use the string representation of the MBean instance's hash code as the value of the key property:

```
VendorQueue v = new VendorQueue();
String domain = "com.acme.accounting.payable";
String keyPropertyList = "name=VendorQueue,instanceId=" +
    Integer.toString(v.hashCode());
```

However, this approach won't work if you don't have access to the MBean object reference. Here are some other approaches to take:

- Use the system time just prior to registering the MBean (via a call to System.currentTimeMillis()) as the instanceId. Even for two MBeans whose creation/registration are relatively close within a given code path, it is unlikely that the second call to System.currentTimeMillis() will yield the same value due to the amount of processing required by the MBean server to act as an MBean registry.

- Use a sequence number obtained from a facility you provide as instanceId. This facility could be as simple as a singleton object that provides access to an int value that is increased each time an access method is called.

- If you know at development time the number of MBeans of a particular class that will be registered, and if they are all registered by the same agent, an agent-dependent sequence number can be applied when each MBean is registered.

The approach you choose for distinguishing between instances of the same MBean class depends on your application needs. The point is that no two MBeans registered within the same MBean server can have the same combination of domain name and key property list.

Instrumentation

Instrumentation is the layer of the JMX architecture closest to the MBean resource. The purpose of instrumentation is to define the management interface for an MBean so that an operator looking at a management console can see what is happening with the resource (via the MBean's attributes), control it as necessary (through the MBean's operations), and be sent events (via the MBean's notifications) should a condition with the resource require attention.

Avoid Overinstrumentation

An MBean should have "just the right amount" of instrumentation. But what does that mean, exactly? Well, it depends on who will be looking at the information provided by the management interface of your MBean. Will it be a developer, or an operator at a management console? The answer is important. Because management is focused on the health of a resource, an MBean should contain the *minimum* amount of information necessary to ensure that the resource is functioning within normal parameters. It is up to you to define these parameters. Remember, there is overhead associated with management, so use it carefully.

At a fundamental level, management consists of three aspects:

Monitoring
> The current state of what's going on in the system. It consists of an MBean's attributes.

Controlling
> How to impose control on the system. It consists of an MBean's operations.

Events
> Notification of something potentially harmful happening in the system. It is an MBean notification.

Let's put this in a context to which most of us can relate: an automobile. An automobile is a system that can be monitored and controlled, and can send events to its operator. Here are some examples of each of these aspects of management:

Monitoring
> To monitor what is happening in cars, manufacturers provide gauges that measure speed, fuel, the rate of rotation of revolving shafts, oil pressure, battery power, and engine temperature. These enable drivers to monitor the current state of their cars to better manage their operation.

Controlling

> To control cars, manufacturers provide control points such as the ignition switch, steering wheel, accelerator, brake and clutch pedals, shift lever, and headlamp switch.

Events

> Car manufacturers provide warning lights to tell drivers if something is happening with the car's systems that they need to know about. For instance, warning lights indicate when the fuel level is low, the engine temperature is too high, a door is ajar, or the emergency brake is engaged. And when the ignition is turned off, cars even have a warning bell that sounds when the driver has left the lights on or the keys in the ignition switch.

Here is a simple questionnaire that can help you decide what to include in the management interface of a management-focused MBean.

Monitoring (attributes)

A resource's management attributes make up its state, which gives an operator cues regarding its health. When identifying management attributes, ask:

- Does the value of this attribute convey information to an operator that is related to the health of the underlying MBean resource? If the answer is yes, include the attribute on the management interface.

  For example, the fuel gauge in your car tells you the health of your car's fuel supply. Without this information you would have to guess how much fuel is in the tank based on when you last refueled and how far you've driven in the meantime.

- Does the value of this attribute convey information to the operator that, within a given operational context, one or more control points should be activated to keep the system healthy? If yes, include the attribute on the management interface.

  For example, if you notice that your car's speedometer indicates that you are exceeding the speed limit, you need to let off of the accelerator pedal (and maybe even press the brake pedal) so that you can slow the car's speed. However, in a different part of town where the speed limit is higher (the operational context), that same speed might be just fine.

Controlling (operations)

This really boils down to one question: what actions must be performed on the resource to ensure the health of the system? Here are some examples using the automobile scenario:

- The car must be accelerated (accelerator pedal).
- The car must be slowed (brake pedal).
- The car must be steered (steering wheel).

In this example, as the operator of your car, you must have these control points to keep the system (and you along with it) healthy.

However, not all MBean resources need to have management operations. It is possible that resources in your application will require no control at all. Simply accessing their attribute values and receiving their notifications is sufficient for that resource type. For other resources, it will be necessary for an operator to exert control over the resource to keep the system healthy.

Events (notifications)

An event results in an unsolicited notification to the operator that the event has occurred. To identify the events associated with a resource, look at the management attributes and the range of possible values the attribute can have. Ask:

- What is the "normal" range (or set) of values for this attribute?
- Is there a low or high threshold value?

An event signals some condition regarding the state of the resource; usually the management attribute currently has a value that requires attention from the operator. For example, the low fuel warning light in your car comes on whenever the fuel level drops below some predefined level set by your car's manufacturer. When the fuel level drops below the predefined value (the event), the light comes on (the notification) and is a cue for you to check the fuel gauge (the management attribute), indicating that you need to find a gas station.

Once you have identified the possible events, ask a simple question: must this event be reported to the operator for the system to remain healthy? If the answer is yes, a notification type should be created for the event.

Implement MBeanRegistration

Sometimes a JMX agent is an MBean and might need to use the services provided by the MBean server to interact with other MBeans that are registered in the same MBean server. To do so, the agent needs a reference to the MBean server. In addition, a mechanism is needed for MBeans to provide their own object names when the agent is generic or is provided by another vendor. Finally, MBeans that are using system resources such as connections need to release these resources when the MBeans are no longer needed by the application.

The MBeanRegistration interface provides the ability to handle all these situations. It defines four methods:

```
public interface MBeanRegistration {
  public ObjectName preRegister (MBeanServer server, ObjectName name)
    throws java.lang.Exception;
  public void postRegister (Boolean registrationDone);
```

```
    public void preDeregister() throws java.lang.Exception;
    public void postDeregister();
}
```

The MBean server invokes these methods on MBeans that implement this interface. You can probably guess, based on the names of the methods when they are called during the process of registering and unregistering your MBean. There are several advantages to implementing this interface:

- The MBean gets the opportunity to store a reference to the MBean server in which it is registered. Using this reference, the MBean can now interact with other MBeans, using the MBean server as a communications bus.

- The MBean gets a chance to provide its own object name if the `ObjectName` passed to `preRegister()` is `null`. This can be useful for generic agents that simply know how to register MBeans but are not responsible for naming them.

- This interface can be used to allocate (in `pre/postRegister()`) and free (in `pre/postDeregister()`) system resources such as a JDBC connection or a socket. This is an important advantage of MBeans that is not available to straight Java classes because it is not known when a Java class will be garbage-collected once it becomes eligible.

- The MBean can perform application-specific processing related to its lifetime as a managed resource.

Use Dynamic MBeans

Dynamic MBeans provide significant benefits over standard MBeans for MBean resources that are deployed in production systems. As opposed to standard MBeans, whose metadata is created and maintained by the JMX implementation, the MBean developer creates dynamic MBean metadata. Therein lies the key to the power and flexibility of dynamic MBeans. However, with this power and flexibility comes a clear trade-off: complexity. Dynamic MBeans are not trivial to implement. But don't worry, at the end of this section I will provide a few recommendations that will make life easier when implementing dynamic MBeans.

The JMX specification defines an interface called `DynamicMBean` and three types of dynamic MBeans that implement it:

Dynamic MBeans
> The root type of dynamic MBean—an implementation of the `DynamicMBean` interface and nothing more.

Open MBeans
> MBeans that are described using flexible, open MBean metadata types, allowing a management application to manipulate MBeans whose attribute values are user-defined types, without having to access the bytecode for those types.

Model MBeans

MBeans that are described using special model MBean metadata classes. Each JMX implementation is required to provide a concrete model MBean implementation called `RequiredModelMBean`.

The significant benefits of dynamic MBeans over standard MBeans are:

- Each MBean feature can have a description.
- You, as the MBean developer, have control over the creation of the metadata that describes the management interface an operator sees.
- The management interface can change dynamically.
- There are fewer source files to maintain.

Let's look at each benefit in more detail.

Each MBean feature can have a description

An MBean feature is a constructor, a parameter, an attribute, an operation, or a notification. Metadata about standard MBean features is created by the JMX implementation; you are not given a way to specify a description. And while it is possible to create dynamic MBean feature metadata without providing descriptions, *you should never do so*. These descriptions can be critical for an operator to understand how to properly interpret what he is looking at in the management console (and to decide whether to page you at 2:00 A.M.!). Here are some categories you should keep in mind when describing MBean features:

Constructors

The purpose of the constructor, including any special consequences of using one constructor versus another (if more than one constructor is provided).

Parameters

The valid values, which can be a range of minimum to maximum values, or discrete values, which allow the operator to safely (i.e., without exceptions being thrown) invoke a management operation or constructor.

Attributes

The piece of management information the attribute represents, along with the "safe" values of the attribute, which can be a range of values or discrete values. This information can help the operator determine whether the attribute value is within acceptable limits and might even include a procedure for restoring the attribute value to an acceptable value.

Operations

A description of what the operation does and any consequences that might occur as a result of invoking the operation.

Notifications

A description of the notification type,* the conditions under which the notification will be sent, and a possible list of steps that might be taken to resolve the condition that resulted in the notification.

You, as the MBean developer, have control over the creation of the metadata...

It is entirely up to you to make sure that the management interface advertised by the getMBeanInfo( ) method of DynamicMBean maps correctly to the underlying implementation. Because you create the metadata, MBean features can have intuitive names displayed to the operator, regardless of the names of those features in the underlying implementation. Ideally, the name of the underlying feature is the same as it appears on the management interface. However, if you have a compelling reason to make the feature name of the underlying resource different from the name you want the operator to see as part of the MBean metadata (say, the source code for the underlying resource is out of your control), you can do so.

In addition, it is unclear how standard MBeans that emit notifications have that information communicated to a management console. Because the specification provides no standard mechanism for the MBean server to determine what notifications an MBean emits (it can only check to see if the MBean class implements NotificationBroadcaster), the JMX implementation cannot create metadata for notifications emitted by standard MBeans.

The management interface can change dynamically

The management interface of a standard MBean is static. Any changes to the management interface require a recompile/redeploy step. However, the management interface of a dynamic MBean can change at runtime. This can be a useful feature for keeping the management interface as slim as possible: only those features that are required based on the current state of the MBean are added to the management interface of the MBean. Let's look at an example.

Suppose you have an MBean that represents a queue with a management operation that allows the operator to suspend activity in the queue with a method called suspend( ). When this operation is invoked, no more items can be added or removed from the queue. It then makes sense that there should be a management operation called resume( ) that allows activity to resume. However, this operation is not necessary when the queue is not suspended. In the implementation of suspend( ), you can

---

* The MBeanNotificationInfo metadata object actually contains an array of notification types, but I recommend using a single MBeanNotificationInfo object for each notification type that is emitted by the MBean.

write code to dynamically add the resume() method to the management interface, as shown in Example 7-1.

Example 7-1. Queue MBean with suspend capability

```java
import javax.management.*;

public class Queue implements javax.management.DynamicMBean {
// ...
  private MBeanInfo _mbi;
  public MBeanInfo getMBeanInfo() {
    return _mbi;
  }
// ...
  public synchronized void suspend() {
    _isSuspended = true; // Set member variable.
    MBeanInfo mbi = this.getMBeanInfo();
    MBeanOperationInfo[] ops = mbi.getOperations();
    MBeanOperationInfo[] newOps = new MBeanOperationInfo[ops.length];
    for (int aa = 0; aa < newOps.length; aa++) {
      MBeanOperationInfo op = ops[aa];
      // Replace "suspend" with "resume".
      if (op.getName().equals("suspend")) {
        newOps[aa] = new MBeanOperationInfo(
          "resume",                        // Name
          "Resumes activity in the queue.", // Description
          new MBeanParameterInfo[0],        // Operation signature
          Void.TYPE.getName(),              // Return type
          MBeanOperationInfo.ACTION         // Impact
        );
      } else {
        newOps[aa] = ops[aa];
      }
    }
    // MBeanInfo is immutable, so create new one.
    MBeanInfo newMbi = new MBeanInfo(
      mbi.getClassName(),
      mbi.getDescription(),
      mbi.getAttributes(),
      mbi.getConstructors(),
      newOps,
      mbi.getNotifications()
    );
    _mbi = newMbi;
    notifyAll();
  }
// ...
}
```

Essentially, all you need to do is search the MBeanOperationInfo array for the suspend() method's metadata. Once you find it, simply create a new MBeanOperationInfo metadata object for the resume() method and place it in the array at the same location. All other operation metadata is used as is. Because MBeanInfo is immutable, you must create a new instance of it.

You also replace resume( ) with suspend( ) when resume( ) is invoked and switch out the operation metadata in a similar fashion. Example 7-2 shows this.

Example 7-2. MBean with suspend() replacing resume ()

```
import javax.management.*;

public class Queue implements javax.management.DynamicMBean {
// ...
  private MBeanInfo _mbi;
  public MBeanInfo getMBeanInfo( ) {
    return _mbi;
  }
// ...
  public synchronized void resume( ) {
    _isSuspended = false; // Set member variable.
    MBeanInfo mbi = this.getMBeanInfo( );
    MBeanOperationInfo[ ] ops = mbi.getOperations( );
    MBeanOperationInfo[ ] newOps = new MBeanOperationInfo[ops.length];
    for (int aa = 0; aa < newOps.length; aa++) {
      MBeanOperationInfo op = ops[aa];
      // Replace "resume" with "suspend".
      if (op.getName( ).equals("resume")) {
        newOps[aa] = new MBeanOperationInfo(
          "suspend",                         // Name
          "Suspends activity in the queue.", // Description
          new MBeanParameterInfo[0],         // Operation signature
          Void.TYPE.getName( ),              // Return type
          MBeanOperationInfo.ACTION          // Impact
        );
      } else {
        newOps[aa] = ops[aa];
      }
    }
    // MBeanInfo is immutable, so create new one.
    MBeanInfo newMbi = new MBeanInfo(
      mbi.getClassName( ),
      mbi.getDescription( ),
      mbi.getAttributes( ),
      mbi.getConstructors( ),
      newOps,
      mbi.getNotifications( )
    );
    _mbi = newMbi;
    notifyAll( );
  }
//...
}
```

When the queue is not suspended, the only action the operator can take is to suspend the queue because this is the only operation available. By the same token, when the queue is suspended, the only allowable action is to resume processing. This behavior is similar to how a graphical user interface application might add or remove items from a menu based on the state of the application.

A well-designed MBean should have the ability to alter its management interface to match those attributes, operations, and notifications that are appropriate to its current state.

There are fewer source files to maintain

Every time the management interface of an MBean changes, you must change two source files: the MBean interface and the class that implements it. This means that by using dynamic MBeans, you cut in half the number of MBean-related source files that have to be maintained!

Use a Dynamic MBean Façade Pattern

Much of the code for a dynamic MBean is similar from one dynamic MBean to another. Hence, there are two primary tasks on which to focus:

- Creating metadata to describe each feature of the MBean
- Implementing the DynamicMBean interface

Dynamic MBean metadata classes are immutable, so the only way to set their various properties is to use a constructor. In addition, a metadata class must be created—and code written—for every feature on the management interface of a resource, resulting in lots of code that basically looks the same. A simplified approach to creating dynamic MBean metadata would help to reduce code clutter (and hence, readability). Here is an example of how to create a dynamic MBean metadata class for an attribute called MyAttribute of type Integer that is read-only:

```
MBeanAttributeInfo attribute = new MBeanAttributeInfo(
    "MyAttribute",              // Name
    Integer.class.getName(),    // Type
    "My very own attribute.",   // Description
    true,                       // Is Readable?
    false,                      // Is Writeable?
    false);                     // isIs (i.e., is boolean?)
```

Of course, you could have squeezed all the parameters onto one line of code, but that would sacrifice readability (and could introduce errors). For example, JMX will allow you to create incorrect metadata for the attribute we just looked at:

```
MBeanAttributeInfo attribute = new MBeanAttributeInfo(
    "MyAttribute",              // Name
    Long.class.getName(),       // Type
    "My very own attribute.",   // Description
```

```
    true,                        // Is Readable?
    false,                       // Is Writeable?
    false);                      // isIs (i.e., is boolean?)
```

In this example, this attribute is incorrectly described as a java.lang.Long instead of its correct type, java.lang.Integer. This mistake will not be caught until runtime, and can lead to hours of needless debugging to fix. The reverse situation could also occur if the data type of the attribute changes (as a result of, say, maintenance to the resource class), but you forget to modify the metadata to match the attribute's new type. Again, this could lead to wasted hours of debugging.

Much of the code for the second task, to implement the DynamicMBean interface, is similar from implementation to implementation. For example, the getAttribute( ) method is passed the name of an attribute and retrieves its value. Suppose MBean A has an attribute A, and MBean B has an attribute B. MBean A's implementation of getAttribute( ) might look like this:

```
public class MBeanA implements DynamicMBean {
  // ...
  public Object getAttribute(String name) throws // Some exceptions {
    try {
      if (name.equals("A") {
        return this.getA( );
      }
    } catch (Exception e) {
      // Handle...
    }
  }
}
```

while MBean B's implementation might look like this:

```
public class MBeanB implements DynamicMBean {
  // ...
  public Object getAttribute(String name) throws // Some exceptions {
    try {
      if (name.equals("B") {
        return this.getB( );
      }
    } catch (Exception e) {
      // Handle...
    }
  }
}
```

In this extremely simple example, only the highlighted lines of code are different, and all they do is figure out if the requested attribute is supported and delegate to the appropriate getter. Suppose you introduce a class called DynamicMBeanFacade, which looks similar to the class shown in Example 7-3.

Example 7-3. DynamicMBeanFacade

```
public class DynamicMBeanFacade implements DynamicMBean {
  public DynamicMBeanFacade(Object managedResource) {
```

Example 7-3. DynamicMBeanFacade (continued)

```
    // ...
  }
  public void addAttribute(String name, String description) {
    // ...
  }
  public void removeAttribute(String name) {
    // ...
  }
  public void addOperation(String name, String description) {
    // ...
  }
  public void removeOperation(String name) {
    // ...
  }
  public void addNotification(String type, String description) {
    // ...
  }
  public void removeNotification(String type) {
    // ...
  }
  // DynamicMBean interface implementation here...
}
```

There is a method that adds and removes each feature to be defined on the management interface of the resource. For example, to add the MyAttribute attribute that we saw earlier, the agent code looks like this:

```
public void someAgentMethod( ) {
  try {
    MBeanServer mbs = /* Obtain somehow. */
    DynamicMBeanFacade resource =
      (DynamicMBeanFacade) mbs.instantiate("MyClass");
    resource.addAttribute("MyAttribute", "My very own attribute");
    // ...
  } catch (Exception e) {
    // Handle...
  }
}
```

This pattern describes the use of a façade over these two tasks and provides three key benefits:

- Metadata creation is hidden behind the façade, resulting in cleaner, more readable code.

- Metadata creation is less error-prone for attributes and operations because the reflection API is used to introspect the managed resource class to ensure correct data types.

- The number of lines of code to be maintained in your application is reduced because the DynamicMBean implementation is hidden behind the façade class and can be reused for every MBean in your application.

Here's how it works. The agent creates an instance of DynamicMBeanFacade and invokes the appropriate methods to describe the attributes, operations, and notifications (i.e., the features) that will be part of the management interface of the managed resource. The agent is only required to pass the name and description of the feature. DynamicMBeanFacade uses Java's reflection API to introspect the managed resource and discover data type information for attributes. For operations, DynamicMBeanFacade determines the return type and any parameter names and their types. Only those attributes and operations that actually exist on the underlying resource can be added to the management interface, which presupposes some knowledge of the underlying resource on the part of the agent.

In the following sections, we will take a quick look at some of the methods of DynamicMBeanFacade and how they can be implemented for each MBean feature type, which should give you an idea of how an implementation of DynamicMBeanFacade might look. For a complete source listing of the DynamicMBeanFacade, refer to *http://www.oreilly.com/catalog/javaebp* for information on how to download the sample application code for this chapter.

You can employ two strategies when using this pattern:

- The managed resource class is a subclass of the DynamicMBeanFacade class.
- The managed resource is already a subclass of some other class and uses DynamicMBeanFacade via containment.

For the sake of brevity, the examples in this section will use the first strategy because it is slightly easier to implement. However, the implementations are remarkably similar, and I will briefly describe the differences at the end of this section.

To implement the addAttribute( ) and addOperation( ) methods of DynamicMBeanFacade, follow these steps:

1. Search the metadata for the specified feature. If it's not found, throw an exception.
2. Set various properties of the feature. For attributes, these include whether the attribute is readable and writeable, and its type. For operations, these properties indicate the return type and information about the operation's parameters.
3. Create dynamic MBean metadata specific to that feature. For attributes, the metadata class is MBeanAttributeInfo, and for operations, it is MBeanOperationInfo (and MBeanParameterInfo for the operation's parameters).
4. Add the newly created metadata to the MBeanInfo object that describes the management interface of the managed resource.

Attributes

For each attribute in the managed resource, the agent calls addAttribute( ), passing the name and description of the attribute. Based on the JMX design patterns, DynamicMBeanFacade is expecting the name of the attribute to be preceded by get or is

---

for readable attributes and/or set for writeable attributes. If the attribute is called MyAttribute, the implementation of addAttribute( ) will introspect the managed resource for getMyAttribute( ) and/or setMyAttribute( ) (isMyAttribute( ) is allowed as a getter for boolean attribute types).

As you saw earlier, describing the management interface is very simple. Of course, the trade-off is that the bulk of the work falls to the implementation of DynamicMBeanFacade. Even still, it's not terribly complicated. Let's look at a very simple implementation of the addAttribute( ) method, as shown in Example 7-4.

Example 7-4. Implementation of the addAttribute() method

```
public class DynamicMBeanFacade implements DynamicMBean {
// ...
  public synchronized void addAttribute(String name, String description)
    throws DynamicMBeanFacadeException {


    Class current = this.getClass( );
    boolean isReadable = false;
    boolean isWriteable = false;
    boolean isIs = false;
    String type = null;
    Method[ ] methods = current.getMethods( );
    for (int aa = 0; aa < methods.length; aa++) {
      String methodName = methods[aa].getName( );
      if (methodName.equals("get" + name)) {
        isReadable = true;
        type = methods[aa].getReturnType( ).getName( );
      } else if (methodName.equals("set" + name)) {
        Class[ ] parmTypes = methods[aa].getParameterTypes( );
        if (parmTypes.length > 1) {
          continue;
        }
        else {
          isWriteable = true;
          type = parmTypes[0].getName( );
        }
      } else if (methodName.equals("is" + name)) {
        type = methods[aa].getReturnType( ).getName( );
        if (type.equals(Boolean.TYPE.getName( ))) {
          isReadable = true;
          isIs = true;
        } else type = null;
      }
    }

    if (!isReadable && !isWriteable)
      throw new DynamicMBeanFacadeException("Attribute not found.");
```

Example 7-4. Implementation of the addAttribute() method (continued)

```
MBeanAttributeInfo attribute = new MBeanAttributeInfo(
  name, type, description, isReadable, isWriteable, isIs);
// Recreate MBeanInfo using new attribute metadata.


 }
}
```

This method searches all the public methods of the managed resource class for a getter and/or setter for the specified attribute. If the attribute is found, an MBeanAttributeInfo metadata object for the attribute is created and added to the existing attribute metadata by recreating the MBeanAttributeInfo array. The MBeanInfo object that describes the management interface is recreated (because MBeanInfo instances are immutable) using this new attribute metadata array.

When an agent wishes to remove an attribute from the management interface, it invokes the removeAttribute( ) method, passing the name of the attribute to remove. In this case, DynamicMBeanFacade does not need to introspect the managed resource class; it only needs to search the metadata that describes the attributes of the management interface and remove the metadata describing the specified attribute.

Operations

When the agent wishes to add an operation to the management interface, it invokes the addOperation( ) method, passing the name and description of the operation. The implementation of addOperation( ) must then introspect the managed resource to ensure that the operation actually exists and create the necessary metadata to describe the operation, including metadata for any parameters to the operation. The metadata is then added to the MBeanOperationInfo array that is part of the MBeanInfo object that describes the management interface, as shown in Example 7-5.

Example 7-5. DynamicMBeanFacade using metadata

```
public class DynamicMBeanFacade implements DynamicMBean {
// ...
  public synchronized void addOperation(String name, String description)
    throws DynamicMBeanFacadeException {


    Class current = this.getClass();
    StringreturnType = null;
    Method[] methods = current.getMethods();
    Method theMethod = null;
    for (int aa = 0; aa < methods.length; aa++) {
      if (methods[aa].getName().equals(name)) {
        theMethod = methods[aa];
        break;  // Take only the first one encountered.
      }
    }
```

BUSINESS REPLY MAIL
FIRST CLASS MAIL   PERMIT NO. 80   SEBASTOPOL, CA

Postage will be paid by addressee

O'Reilly & Associates, Inc.
BOOK REGISTRATION
1005 GRAVENSTEIN HIGHWAY NORTH
SEBASTOPOL, CA 95472-9910

O'REILLY BOOK REGISTRATION

Register your book with O'Reilly by completing this card and receive a **FREE** copy of our latest catalog. Or register online at **register.oreilly.com** and, in addition to our catalog, we'll send you email notification of new editions of this book, information about new titles, and special offers available only to registered O'Reilly customers.

Which book(s) are you registering? Please include title and ISBN # (above bar code on back cover)

Title _____ ISBN # _____

Title _____ ISBN # _____

Title _____ ISBN # _____

Name _____ Company/Organization _____

Address _____

City _____ State _____ Zip/Postal Code _____ Country _____

Telephone _____ Email address _____

Example 7-5. DynamicMBeanFacade using metadata (continued)

```
    if (theMethod == null)
      throw new DynamicMBeanFacadeException("Operation not found.");

    MBeanOperationInfo newOp =
      new MBeanOperationInfo(description, theMethod);
    // Recreate MBeanInfo using new operation metadata.
  }
// ...
}
```

The algorithm used to create the operation metadata, adding it to the operation metadata array, and recreating the MBeanInfo object should look familiar: this process is almost identical to addAttribute( ). In Example 7-5, I have used an alternate constructor of MBeanOperationInfo that takes a java.reflect.Method object. This constructor will perform further introspection and create the necessary metadata to describe the operation's parameters.

When an agent wishes to remove an operation from the management interface, it invokes the removeOperation( ) method, passing the name of the operation to remove. In this case, DynamicMBeanFacade does not need to introspect the managed resource class; it only needs to search the metadata that describes the operations of the management interface and remove the metadata describing the specified operation.

Notifications

When the agent wishes to add a notification emitted by a managed resource to the resource's management interface, it invokes the addNotification( ) method, passing the type (i.e., name) of the notification and a description of the notification. Unlike attributes and operations, there is really no way for DynamicMBeanFacade to introspect the managed resource class to see if the notifications exist because it is entirely up to the managed resource to define and emit JMX notifications and communicate this information to the agent developer a priori through, say, documentation. Assume that the managed resource implements the NotificationBroadcaster interface, as shown in Example 7-6.

Example 7-6. Implementing the NotificationBroadcaster interface

```
public class DynamicMBeanFacade implements DynamicMBean {
// ...
  public synchronized void addNotification(String type,
    String description) throws DynamicMBeanFacadeException {

    MBeanNotificationInfo notif = new MBeanNotificationInfo(
      new String[ ] {type},
      "javax.management.Notification", description);
```

```
    MBeanNotificationInfo[ ] notifs = _mbi.getNotifications( );
    MBeanNotificationInfo[ ] newNotifs =
      new MBeanNotificationInfo[notifs.length + 1];
    System.arraycopy(notifs, 0, newNotifs, 0, notifs.length);
    newNotifs[notifs.length] = notif;

    // Recreate MBeanInfo with new notification metadata array.

  }
// ...
}
```

When an agent wishes to remove a notification from the management interface, it invokes removeNotification( ), passing the notification type.

DynamicMBean implementation

Implementing the DynamicMBean interface is actually very straightforward, as you'll see. Example 7-7 shows how to implement invoke( ), which you can use as the implementation backbone of all the other methods of DynamicMBean.

Example 7-7. Implementing the DynamicMBean invoke( ) method

```
public class DynamicMBeanFacade implements DynamicMBean {
// ...
  public Object invoke(String actionName, Object[ ] params, String[ ] signature)
    throws javax.management.MBeanException, javax.management.ReflectionException {
    Object ret = null; // Return code
    try {
      Class[ ] sig = new Class[signature.length];
      for (int bb = 0; bb < signature.length; bb++)
        sig[bb] = this.getClassFromClassName(signature[bb]);
      Class mr = this.getClass( );
      Method method = mr.getMethod(actionName, sig);
      ret = method.invoke(_managedResource, params);
    } catch (Exception e) {
      throw new ReflectionException(e);
    }
    return ret;
  } // ...
}
```

This is not the most robust implementation possible, but even this simple implementation does a lot in remarkably few lines of code. This method creates the array of Class objects that represents the method signature, uses this signature to obtain a Method object from the reflection API, and invokes the method. Any exceptions that arise will be caught and rethrown in the form of a javax.management.ReflectionException.

Externalize the Description of an MBean's Management Interface

The purpose of a management interface is to define the contract between an operator and the resources in your application. JMX defines patterns and an API for defining the management interfaces for your MBeans. A standard MBean's management interface is static because it is defined using a Java interface. As a result, you are required to code the instrumentation necessary to support the definition of the management interface according to JMX MBean design patterns. A dynamic MBean's management interface is described programmatically through the use of metadata classes. The necessary instrumentation to support the definition of the management interface is a combination of your implementation of DynamicMBean and the methods in the underlying MBean resource. Regardless of the type of MBean strategy you choose, the definition of the management interface is internalized, or internal to the MBean resource code.

The main issue with instrumenting and defining a resource's management interface entirely in source code is that only a Java programmer can change it. Should the management interface need to be altered at deployment time, for example, the deployer needs to have Java programming skills, or access to a Java programmer.

This is not a new concern and is one that has been addressed in a number of ways. The Enterprise JavaBeans (EJB) specification provides a mechanism to handle deployment-time modifications to the runtime behavior of Enterprise beans through the env-entry element of the ejb-jar file deployment descriptor. The bean provider offers an enterprise bean with more flexibility by externalizing certain control points specific to the deployment environment.

Externalizing the definition of the management interface of an MBean has similar benefits, allowing you to move the definition of an MBean's management interface outside your code base. You still have to write code for operations, send notifications, and sense and maintain attribute values. But the description of the management interface will be maintained outside the code base. You cannot use this best practice if your MBeans are standard MBeans because a standard MBean's management interface definition is in a Java interface.[*]

The benefits of this best practice are:

- The management interface is maintained outside the code base, allowing the management interface to be configured at deployment time.
- Different MBean configurations can be stored, retrieved, and versioned, allowing different configurations to be deployed more quickly.

---

[*] OK, strictly speaking you can, but it would involve reading the external definition of the management interface, creating a Java interface on the fly, and invoking the Java compiler to compile the interface into your code base before starting your application.

There are many ways to maintain the external representation of an MBean interface such as a text file, relational database, or LDAP. Regardless of the medium, the language used to express the definition will be XML. In the example implementation in this section we will use an XML document that resides on the local filesystem. The XML grammar used will be sufficient to describe management attributes, operations, and notifications. The XML document will be validated using a DTD.

In a generic sense, the agent must:

- Instantiate the managed resource.
- Read and parse the XML definition for the managed resource. Some mechanism must be defined to tie the resource with the correct tags in the XML document.
- Create a dynamic MBean implementation for the managed resource and register it with the MBean server.

In the implementation we will look at, the agent instantiates the managed resource, reads the XML definition for the management interface definition that corresponds to the managed resource class, and creates a DynamicMBeanFacade (which we looked at earlier in this chapter) to use as the MBean for the managed resource. The DTD that defines the structure of valid XML documents for this example is defined as:

```
<!ELEMENT application (mbean+)>

<!ELEMENT mbean (description?, (attribute | operation | notification)+)>
<!ATTLIST mbean className CDATA #REQUIRED>

<!ELEMENT description (#PCDATA)>

<!ELEMENT attribute (#PCDATA)>
<!ATTLIST attribute name CDATA #REQUIRED>

<!ELEMENT operation (#PCDATA)>
<!ATTLIST operation name CDATA #REQUIRED>

<!ELEMENT notification (#PCDATA)>
<!ATTLIST notification type CDATA #REQUIRED>
```

That's about as simple as it gets. This DTD defines XML documents that describe one or more MBeans. For each MBean, there is an optional description for the MBean, and there must be at least one attribute, operation, or notification. Attributes and operations must have an attribute called name, and notifications must have an attribute called type. The description of an attribute, operation, or notification is provided optionally as the value of that element.

Example 7-8 shows an MBean called Queue that has the following features:

AddWaitTime *(Attribute)*

The total time (in milliseconds) that all supplier threads have waited to add items to the queue because it was full.

NumberOfItemsProcessed *(Attribute)*

The number of items that have been removed from the queue.

QueueEmpty *(Attribute)*

Will be true if the queue is currently empty.

QueueFull *(Attribute)*

Will be true if the queue is currently full.

QueueSize *(Attribute)*

The maximum number of items that can coexist in the queue at any one time. Also referred to as the queue depth.

RemoveWaitTime *(Attribute)*

The total amount of time (in milliseconds) that all consumer threads have waited to remove items from the queue because it was empty.

Suspended *(Attribute)*

Will be true if activity in the queue is currently suspended.

TraceOn *(Attribute)*

Will be true if trace-level logging is currently enabled.

disableTracing *(Operation)*

Disables logging of trace-level information.

enableTracing *(Operation)*

Enables logging of trace-level information to provide more detailed runtime diagnostic information.

resume *(Operation)*

Resumes activity in the queue. All previously blocked threads are notified that they can become eligible for scheduling.

suspend *(Operation)*

Suspends activity in the queue. All threads are blocked until the resume operation is invoked.

sample.Queue.queueStalled *(Notification)*

This notification is sent when logic internal to the queue has determined that the queue is stalled in some way. This generally means that no processing has occurred for more than 10,000 milliseconds (10 seconds) and that other attributes of this class need to be investigated to resolve the problem.

Information such as this is communicated to the deployer, who does not necessarily have access to the source code. Let's suppose that all the deployer knows are the available attributes, operations, and notifications that can be defined on the management interface through the use of an XML file whose structure is dictated by the

DTD we looked at earlier. Example 7-8 shows how such an XML definition of the management interface for the Queue class might look.

Example 7-8. XML definition of the management interface for Queue

```
<?xml version="1.0" encoding="UTF-8"?>
<!DOCTYPE application SYSTEM "mbean.dtd">
<!-- Root element: application -->
<application>


<!--==========================-->
<!-- Queue MBean definition -->
<!--==========================-->
<mbean className="jmxbp.Queue">
<description>This MBean is a managed queue to which one or more supplier threads is adding
items (objects) and one or more consumer threads is removing them.</description>


<!-- ********** -->
<!-- Attributes -->
<!-- ********** -->
<attribute name="NumberOfItemsProcessed"> The number of items that have been removed from
the queue.</attribute>

<attribute name="AddWaitTime"> The total time (in milliseconds) all supplier threads have
waited to add items to the queue because it was full.</attribute>

<attribute name="Suspended">Will be true if the queue is currently suspended.</attribute>

<attribute name="QueueFull">Will be true if the queue is currently full.</attribute>

<attribute name="QueueEmpty">Will be true if the queue is currently empty.</attribute>

<attribute name="RemoveWaitTime"> The total amount of time (in milliseconds) that all
consumer threads have waited to remove items from the queue because it was empty.
</attribute>

<attribute name="QueueSize"> The maximum number of items that can coexist in the queue at
any one instant. Also referred to as the queue depth.</attribute>


<!-- ********** -->
<!-- Operations -->
<!-- ********** -->
<operation name="suspend"> Suspends activity in the queue. All threads are blocked until
the resume operation is invoked.</operation>

<operation name="resume"> Resumes activity in the queue. All previously blocked threads
are notified that they might become eligible for scheduling.</operation>

<operation name="enableTracing">Enables logging of trace-level information to provide more
detailed runtime diagnostic information.</operation>

<operation name="disableTracing">Disables logging of trace-level information.</operation>
```

Example 7-8. XML definition of the management interface for Queue (continued)

```
<!-- ************* -->
<!-- Notifications -->
<!-- ************* -->
<notification type="sample.Queue.queueStalled"> This notification is sent when logic
internal to the queue has determined that the queue is stalled in some way. This generally
means that no processing has occurred for more than 10000 ms (10 seconds) and that other
attributes of this class need to be investigated to resolve the problem.</notification>

</mbean>

</application>
```

In this simple example, only the jmxbp.Queue class is defined as an MBean. When the application is started, the agent reads in the XML document describing the management interface for jmxbp.Queue and uses the DynamicMBeanFacade from earlier in the chapter. In this example, JAXP is used to process the XML file and is included in the example download for this chapter. This is a working example with some of the details elided for simplicity. The following code comments show the major steps involved:

```
try {
  DynamicMBeanFacade mbean = null;
  String className = "jmxbp.Queue";
  Queue queue = (Queue)mbs.instantiate(className);

  // Set up the XML parser.
  DocumentBuilderFactory dbf = DocumentBuilderFactory.newInstance( );
  dbf.setValidating(true);
  DocumentBuilder db = dbf.newDocumentBuilder( );
  Document config = db.parse(new File("c:\\home\\myapp.xml"));

  // Look through document for element nodes called "mbean".
  NodeList nodes = n.getChildNodes( );
  for (int aa = 0; aa < nodes.getLength( ); aa++) {
    Node node = nodes.item(aa);
    if (node.getNodeType( ) == Node.ELEMENT_NODE &&
        node.getNodeName( ).equals("mbean")) {
      NamedNodeMap atts = node.getAttributes( );

      // If "className" attribute equals className, read all MBean attributes,
      // operations, and notifications.
      Node att = atts.getNamedItem("className");
      if (att.getNodeValue( ).equals(className)) {
        String mbeanDesc = this.getElementText(node);
        mbean = new DynamicMBeanFacade(resource, mbeanDesc);
        NodeList features = node.getChildNodes( );
        for (int cc = 0; cc < features.getLength( ); cc++) {
          Node feature = features.item(cc);
          if (feature.getNodeType( ) == Node.ELEMENT_NODE) {
            NamedNodeMap atts2 = feature.getAttributes( );
```

```
                    // Add attribute, operation, or notification to the management interface,
                    // providing its name and description from the XML document.
                    if (feature.getNodeName( ).equals("attribute")) {
                      Node nameNode = atts2.getNamedItem("name");
                      String attName = nameNode.getNodeValue( );
                      String attDesc = this.getElementText(feature);
                      mbean.addAttribute(attName, attDesc);
                    } else if (feature.getNodeName( ).equals("operation")) {
                      Node nameNode = atts2.getNamedItem("name");
                      String opName = nameNode.getNodeValue( );
                      String opDesc = this.getElementText(feature);
                      mbean.addOperation(opName, opDesc);
                    } else if (feature.getNodeName( ).equals("notification")) {
                      Node nameNode = atts2.getNamedItem("type");
                      String notifName = nameNode.getNodeValue( );
                      String notifDesc = this.getElementText(feature);
                      mbean.addNotification(notifName, notifDesc);
                    }
                  }
              } // for (int cc ...
            } // att.getNodeValue( ).equals(className)
          }
        if (mbean != null)
          break;
      }
  } catch (Exception e) {
    // Handle...
  }
```

Keep in mind that this is only one possible way to implement externalization of the
MBean interface. It is not necessary to define a DTD (or XML schema) to validate the
XML definition, but it makes the agent code simpler to write because the XML
parser can be used to enforce constraints, such as the presence of certain attributes,
for example.

Use createMBean( ) to Create MBeans

One of the purposes of the MBean server is to act as a communications bus for interacting with MBeans. You should never manipulate an MBean through a direct object
reference, for several reasons:

- Only registered MBeans can be manipulated via the MBean server. Part of the
  registration process is an introspection of the MBean to ensure that it conforms
  to the requirements of the JMX specification. Only compliant MBeans should be
  considered manageable.

- Only agents in the same process as an MBean can manipulate it through an
  object reference. This presupposes knowledge of the deployment of the MBean
  relative to the agent and should be avoided to minimize maintenance issues.

- Java Specification Request (JSR) 160, or JMX 1.2 Remoting, specifies security requirements for JMX implementations.[*] Direct manipulations of an MBean through an object reference are not subject to JMX security checks and should be avoided.

- In the same vein, creating MBeans via the Java `new` keyword should also be avoided. The `MBeanServer` interface implemented by the MBean server provides a method (`instantiate( )`) to create instances of MBeans, which return a reference to the newly created MBean object. To register an existing MBean, the agent calls `registerMBean( )`. The `MBeanServer` interface also provides a method called `createMBean( )` that combines these two steps, but never exposes a reference to the MBean object outside the JMX implementation.

[*] At the time of this writing, JMX 1.2 Remoting is due for release by the end of 2002.

CHAPTER 8
Enterprise Internationalization

David Czarnecki and Andy Deitsch

The proliferation of the Internet and the World Wide Web has made access to global markets (especially for software products) easier today than ever before. For companies to capture market share in non-English–speaking countries, it is critical that their software products support languages other than English. Unfortunately, software developers who are not aware of software internationalization issues can build cultural biases into the products they develop. These built-in cultural biases will have a negative impact on the company's ability to localize the software product for foreign markets. Having an understanding of the issues associated with various cultures, languages, and writing systems will minimize or eliminate cultural bias and make the process of delivering localized software to global markets a realizable dream.

Software internationalization is the term used to define the architecture and design of software for which only one set of source and binary code is produced to support all the markets in which the software will be sold. Internationalized applications require planning, forethought, and proper design. Trying to retrofit an application to be internationalization-ready requires much more time and money than designing the application correctly in the first place. Retrofitted applications also usually end up being far more difficult to maintain.

Enterprise applications add yet another layer of complexity to the issue of internationalization. In most cases, enterprise internationalization involves developing multilingual applications. By this we mean that one application, sitting on a server, must simultaneously handle data appropriately for users who might be geographically distributed and who might have a preference for a given language or cultural convention.

Imagine, for a moment, a Pan-European travel agency with travel agents all over Europe. This agency wants to have one enterprise application to support all its offices. Clearly, the agents in France want to be able to interact with the system in French, while the agents in Italy want to interact with the system in Italian, and so on for each office in the other European countries. The enterprise application needs to be designed in such a way that it recognizes the local needs of each agent. This requires that the session be conducted in the correct language and data such as numbers, dates, and currency be formatted appropriately. Also, lists displayed to the user must be collated according to the rules for the given language.

Internationalization and Localization

For the most part, software that has not been internationalized will not work outside the country for which it was originally developed. Why, you ask? To understand why, you need to be aware of only a small subset of issues that face developers who design and write internationalized software:

- Text displayed to a user must be translated to different languages. It must therefore not be hardcoded into the program but externalized and loaded at runtime.

- Many languages use non-Latin writing systems (e.g., Arabic, Chinese, Hebrew, Korean, Russian, Thai, etc.).

- Some writing systems are bidirectional (text flows both left to right and right to left).

- Colors have semantic meaning depending on the region of the world you are in (e.g., red in the Western Hemisphere usually denotes a warning, danger, or stop, while in China red denotes happiness).

- Different languages have different rules for how characters should be sorted. This includes languages that share the same writing system, such as Danish, English, French, and German.

- Numbers can have different shapes depending on the writing system and region of the world you are in.

- Dates are formatted differently in different parts of the world (e.g., 06/10/02 could be June 10th 2002, October 6th 2002, or even October 2nd, 2006!).

This list only scratches the surface of the kinds of issues that must be taken into account when internationalizing software. Take a moment to think about the number of times you have written some code to sort a list of words. If you are like most people, you hardcoded the sort order to that of the English alphabet!* You now know from reading this list that your program wouldn't operate correctly in France.

Internationalization, often referred to as i18n in the software development community, is the process by which software is designed and implemented so it can be easily adapted to specific languages, cultures, and local conventions. The process of adapting the software to a specific region is known as *localization*.

While the task of internationalizing software is the responsibility of software architects and developers, a completely separate team working in conjunction with the

---

* To be more accurate, you probably hardcoded it to the sort order of the ASCII character set.

software development team usually handles the task of localization. A localization project manager who typically oversees a group of translators, technical writers, testers, and, in some cases, programmers leads the localization team. Depending on the core competencies of the company producing the software, the localization team can be either in-house or outsourced.*

In this chapter, we will share with you some best practices for applying software internationalization techniques to the development of Java Enterprise applications. Although the format of this book is to address best practices, we couldn't possibly cover all aspects of Java internationalization here. For a more in-depth discussion on the topic, see our book, *Java Internationalization* (O'Reilly).

The Model-View-Controller Paradigm

Enterprise applications are typically split into three different tiers, or *layers*. They are more commonly referred to as the *presentation layer* (the application's "view"), the *business object layer* (the application's "controller"), and the *data access layer* (the application's "model"). Does any of this seem vaguely familiar to you? In a round-about way, we have described the Model-View-Controller (MVC) paradigm that you have no doubt seen in *Java Swing* or *JavaServer Pages*.

In this chapter, we will present some of the more common issues you are likely to run into, with respect to internationalization and localization, for the various tiers in the MVC paradigm when developing an enterprise application, along with best practices to handle these issues. Our discussion will move from the presentation layer to the business object layer and finally to the data access layer.

Presentation Layer

JavaServer Pages (JSP) technology is the preferred technology for developing user interfaces in the Java 2 Enterprise Edition (J2EE). The technology was developed to separate the presentation of dynamic content from the components responsible for generating the business logic. It also allows for separation of roles between user interface designers and application designers.

Do Not Rely on Browser Settings for Storing Localization Preferences

In designing your presentation layer, you need to be concerned with where you pull localization information to drive the presentation of the user interface. In other

---

* A large number of localization houses exist that will gladly help you with your localization needs. For more information on localization, check out LISA (the Localisation Industry Standards Association) at *http://www.lisa.org*.

words, how are your JSP pages supposed to know that they should present the information for one user in English and information for another user in Hebrew?

The Internet Explorer Language Preference dialog, as shown in Figure 8-1, allows the user to configure the languages he would like to see in order of preference. A setting such as this will affect certain HTTP headers such as the `Accept-Language` header. You might think this is great for you as an application developer; you no longer have to be concerned about where to pull a user's preferred localization information. Simply grab that information from the request headers and use it to drive your user interface.

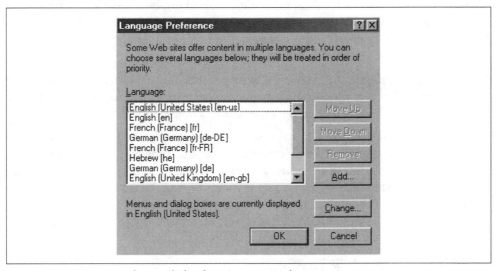

Figure 8-1. Language preference dialog from Internet Explorer

There are a number of reasons why relying on a browser's settings or, for that matter, the user's ability to configure these settings will get you into trouble:

- The browser's settings are outside the scope of your application. Although most browsers on the market today do offer the ability to configure language preference settings, it is not a requirement and therefore might not be present in the configuration. If this is the case, you must drive the localization preference from another setting.

- The fewer configuration settings a user has to manage or remember to use your application, the better. It's not that a user of web-based applications is not savvy enough to adjust the browser's language settings appropriately, but she might not want to use your application if she has to change browser settings each time.

- The user might configure localization settings that are not supported by your application. That is, she might configure the browser for Russian when in fact your application supports only English, Italian, and Spanish. However, in this case, an application can be proactive in notifying the user that a particular localization is not supported by the application (but now the user has to readjust her browser settings again.)

- The browser's settings are typically user-dependent or profile-based. So it can be a hassle to reconfigure a colleague's browser settings if, for example, you are not at your local desktop.

The point here is that the localization settings should not be driven by a browser setting, but instead by a configuration option in the application. The supported localizations for an application can be stored in a user's profile when a user registers or signs onto an application.

How should you proceed? First, you should present only the valid localizations for an application. As mentioned earlier, if your application is localized only for English, Italian, and Spanish, do not offer any other choices to the user.

You'll also need to decide where to store the localization preference. This is often a method that is called on the `User` object defined for your application. For example, you might have a method, `getLocalizationPreference( )`, which returns a `java.util.Locale` object indicating the user's localization preference. This locale object can then be passed to appropriate methods on custom tags in the user interface, to the proper business logic methods in the business object layer, or to the data access layer to retrieve localized data from a back-end datastore.

Another possibility is to store the localization preference as an attribute held in the user's session that would be accessible from JSPs and servlets in your application. For example, the session variable `com.oreilly.bestpractices.j2ee.i18n.USER_PREFERRED_LOCALE` could be used to store the user's localization preference as a `Locale` object. Initially, this object would be set by the application to a default localization preference for the application. Once a user logs into the J2EE application, this variable would be updated to reflect the user's preference. It would also be updated once a user changes his localization preference within the application.

Use JSP Custom Tags or the JSTL for Locale-Specific Data Presentation

No doubt, if you've used the JSP technology in the past, or if you've heard or read discussions on the topic, you can run into trouble by embedding too much Java code in your JSP pages. A reusable and component-based approach to removing Java code from your JSP pages is to use custom tags. As you broaden your scope from the user's language preference, an application will need to present data to the user. Certain data elements such as text, numbers, dates, and times will need to be presented in the most locale-specific manner possible.

A number of tag libraries are available for presenting data in a locale-specific way. The JavaServer Pages Standard Tag Library (JSTL)* falls under Java Specification Request (JSR) 52 and provides you with a common set of tags that you would expect to see when developing J2EE-based applications that use the JSP technology. A number of tags that handle internationalization formatting fall under the JSTL. Chapters 8 and 9 of the JSTL specification discuss all the relevant details of the tags specific to internationalization and localization.

A more formal discussion of JSP custom tags (and developing these tags) is outside the scope of this chapter. However, we would like to cover an example of using the JSTL. Example 8-1 demonstrates the use of the JSTL using Tomcat 4.0.3 running under Java 2 SDK 1.4.0 under Windows 95. You can download the JSTL Reference Implementation and Tomcat from the Jakarta web site (*http://jakarta.apache.org*).

Example 8-1 shows part of the FormatNumber.jsp included with the JSTL demonstration web application. It demonstrates how simple the JSP tags are to use in your JSP pages.

Example 8-1. JSTL demonstration application showing use of internationalization-specific JSTL tags

```
// Above JSP code removed

<li> Format &quot;12345.67&quot; as German currency (given string is
    parsed using &quot;en&quot; locale before it is formatted):<br>
 <fmt:setLocale value="de-DE"/>
 <fmt:formatNumber value="12345.67" type="currency"/>
</ul>

</body>
</html>
```

Figure 8-2 is a rendering of a JSP page that demonstrates locale-specific formatting from the examples shipped with the JSTL. Try changing the language settings in your browser to see how certain tags pull information from the HTTP request to determine which locale to use to display data.

A common feature of web-based applications is the use of forms to collect data from a user. Forms can be relatively straightforward, as shown in Example 8-2.

---

* The specification for the JSTL, or JSR 52, can be found online at *http://jcp.org/aboutJava/communityprocess/first/jsr052/*.

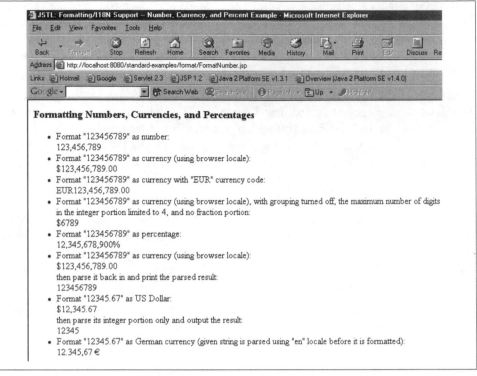

Figure 8-2. Formatting using the JSTL tags

Example 8-2. Simple HTML form

```
<html>

<head>
<title>Simple form page</title>
</head>

<body>

Hi, we'd like to collect some information about you.

<form action="user-information-collector.jsp" name="user_information" method="post">
First name: <input type="text" name="first_name">
Last name: <input type="text" name="last_name">
Checking account balance: <input type="text" name="checking_account_balance">
</form>

</body>

</html>
```

Each form item, when read by a servlet or another JSP page, can contain information that needs to be read in a locale-specific way. Why? The character encoding will differ depending on the user entering the information. For U.S. English, a user entering information into that form will typically have entered the information in the ISO-8859-1 character encoding. However, for Japanese, the character encoding will most likely be Shift-JIS.

What steps can you take to ensure that your forms can be read correctly? The simplest approach is to add a hidden element to the form indicating the character encoding that was used to enter the information in the form. You can get this element from the user's language-preference setting, and it typically looks like this:

```
<input type="hidden" name="input_character_set" value="Shift_JIS">
```

On the server side, the code you use to read the form items will need to use this character set value to convert the data appropriately. This value is passed to the setCharacterEncoding(String encoding) method on the ServletRequest object so that the form parameters can be parsed using the character set of the form.

HTML forms can also be quite complex, performing custom formatting and validation of the data. Among other things, this helps to ensure that certain form elements that are required by an application contain data and that the data in all form elements conforms to a specific type that can introduce locale-specific complexities. This would be necessary if, for example, you have to validate a price field on a form for English, French, and German.

A very comprehensive and freely available tag library for performing locale-specific form validation is available from a company called SQL Technology.* The custom tag library is called PBP. In addition to JSP tags to do formatting, PBP contains a set of tags for generating locale-specific forms containing localized client-side JavaScript for appropriate form validation. Figures 8-3 and 8-4 demonstrate the PBP Custom Tag Library running in English and Italian, respectively.

Notice in Figure 8-4 that the date field is formatted as appropriate for Italian. Attempting to submit the form will also validate the contents of this form item as appropriate for Italian.

Take a Portal-Based Approach to JSP Development

In David's article on Java, "Designing Internationalized User-Interface Components for Web Applications,"† the use of JSP custom tags for the presentation of localized data in JSP pages was discussed. In that article, the InsertText tag not only pulled a specific item from a resource bundle, but it also handled issues with text direction. In certain locales, text can be written from left to right or right to left, or it can be

---

* Information about the SQLT tag library can be found online at *http://www.sqlt.com/taglib.html*.

† The entire text for this article can be found online at *http://java.oreilly.com/news/javaintl_0701.html*.

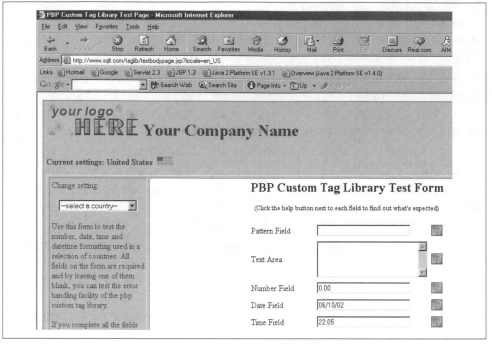

Figure 8-3. The SQLT PBP Custom Tag Library using the American rules for validation

bidirectional. Arabic and Hebrew are the canonical examples of languages that are bidirectional.*

The example usage of the tag in this article did not elucidate the other looming issue you might be faced with·when designing for bidirectional languages. The entire user interface can also be "written" differently. Take Figure 8-5, for example, which shows Microsoft Outlook Express running under a Hebrew version of Windows.

To accommodate such issues in your web-based applications, develop your user interface through a *portal approach*. In a portal approach, you identify potential areas of content that need to be displayed to a user. From Figure 8-5, you can discern four distinct content areas:

1. Menu bar at the top of the screen containing the various menu options and a button bar
2. Folder list containing the various mail folders for the mailbox(es) that have been set up for Outlook Express
3. Address book containing the names of contacts for the given user
4. Content area where information about Outlook Express is displayed, as well as a list of messages and the current message body

---

* In these languages, text is written from right to left, while numbers and currency are written from left to right.

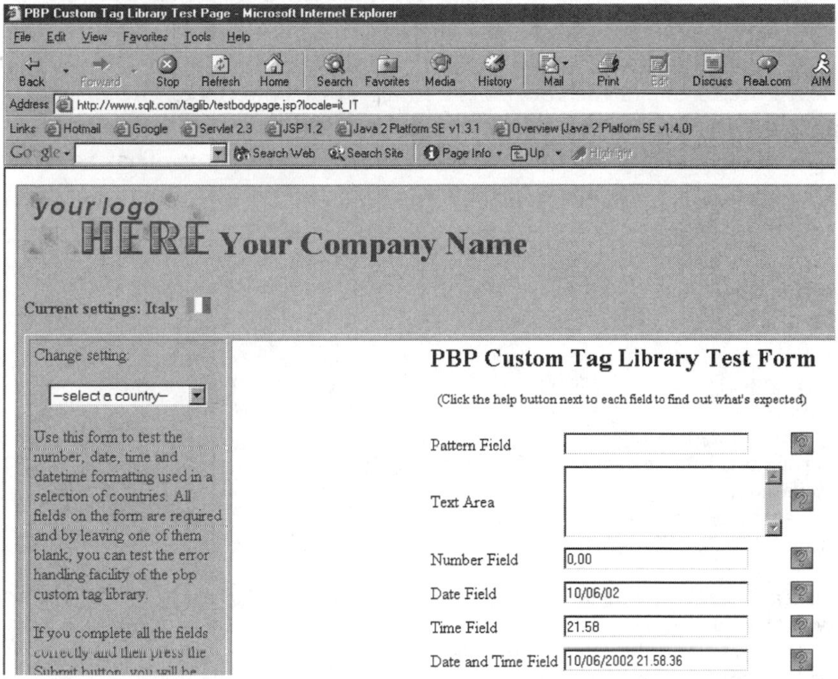

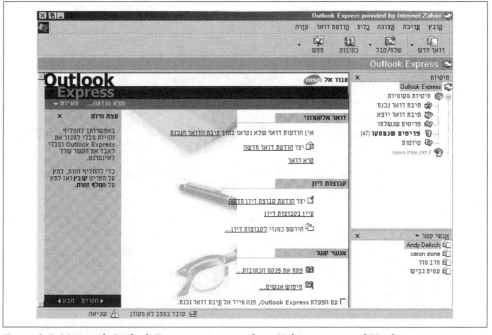

Figure 8-4. The SQLT PBP Custom Tag Library using the Italian rules for validation

Figure 8-5. Microsoft Outlook Express running under a Hebrew version of Windows

In Example 8-3, we have modified the InsertText tag from David's article to implement the LocaleSupport interface (this interface is discussed in the next section). You implement the required getLocale( ) and setLocale( ) methods and initialize the locale attribute to one of the constants defined in this interface. The InsertText custom tag is used to handle the output of localized text from a resource bundle onto a JSP page while taking directionality of the text into account. That is, for certain locales, as in English, the text will be written left to right with the HTML <DIV> tag and its directionality attribute, DIR.

Example 8-3. Adaptation of InsertText JSP custom tag using the LocaleSupport interface

```
package com.ora.i18n.jsptags;

import com.ora.i18n.LocaleSupport;

import javax.servlet.jsp.*;
import javax.servlet.jsp.tagext.TagSupport;
import java.awt.*;
import java.io.IOException;
import java.util.*;

public class InsertText extends TagSupport implements LocaleSupport {
    private Locale locale;
    private String textID;
    private String resourceBundleName;

    private final static String DIV_LTR = "<DIV DIR=\"LTR\">";
    private final static String DIV_RTL = "<DIV DIR=\"RTL\">";
    private final static String CLOSING_DIV = "</DIV>";

    public InsertText( ) {
        locale = LocaleSupport.APPLICATION_DEFAULT_LOCALE;
        textID = null;
        resourceBundleName = null;
    }

    public void setLocale(Locale inLocale) {
        this.locale = inLocale;
    }

    public Locale getLocale( ) {
        return locale;
    }

    public void setTextID(String textID) {
        this.textID = textID;
    }

    public void setResourceBundleName(String resourceBundleName) {
        this.resourceBundleName = resourceBundleName;
    }
```

```java
    public int doStartTag( ) throws JspException {
        JspWriter out = pageContext.getOut( );

        ResourceBundle rb = ResourceBundle.getBundle(resourceBundleName,
                locale);
        try {
            ComponentOrientation co =
                    ComponentOrientation.getOrientation(locale);
            if (co.isLeftToRight( ) ||
                    co.equals(ComponentOrientation.UNKNOWN)) {
                out.print(this.DIV_LTR);
            } else {
                out.print(this.DIV_RTL);
            }
            out.print(rb.getString(textID));
            out.print(this.CLOSING_DIV);
        } catch (IOException ioe) {
            throw new JspTagException(ioe.toString( ));
        } catch (MissingResourceException mre) {
            throw new JspTagException(mre.toString( ));
        }
        return SKIP_BODY;
    }

    public void release( ) {
        super.release( );
        locale = LocaleSupport.APPLICATION_DEFAULT_LOCALE;
        textID = null;
        resourceBundleName = null;
    }
}
```

Example 8-4 is the *taglib.tld* file used in your web application containing the definition of the InsertText tag and the appropriate tag attributes. Notice that the locale attribute is not a required attribute, as it defaults to the value set from the LocaleSupport interface.

Example 8-4. taglib.tld used in your web application

```xml
<?xml version="1.0"?>
<!DOCTYPE taglib PUBLIC "-//Sun Microsystems, Inc.//DTD JSP Tag Library
1.1//EN" "http://java.sun.com/j2ee/dtds/web-jsptaglibrary_1_1.dtd">

<taglib>
    <tlibversion>1.0</tlibversion>
    <jspversion>1.1</jspversion>
    <shortname>oreillytags</shortname>

    <tag>
        <name>InsertText</name>
        <tagclass>com.ora.i18n.jsptags.InsertText</tagclass>
        <bodycontent>JSP</bodycontent>
```

Example 8-4. taglib.tld used in your web application (continued)

```
        <attribute>
            <name>textID</name>
            <required>true</required>
            <rtexprvalue>true</rtexprvalue>
        </attribute>
        <attribute>
            <name>resourceBundleName</name>
            <required>true</required>
            <rtexprvalue>true</rtexprvalue>
        </attribute>
        <attribute>
            <name>locale</name>
            <required>false</required>
            <rtexprvalue>true</rtexprvalue>
        </attribute>
    </tag>

</taglib>
```

In Example 8-5, a simple *web.xml* file is defined, along with the tag library from
Example 8-4.

Example 8-5. web.xml used in your web application

```
<?xml version="1.0" encoding="ISO-8859-1"?>

<!DOCTYPE web-app
    PUBLIC "-//Sun Microsystems, Inc.//DTD Web Application 2.2//EN"
    "http://java.sun.com/j2ee/dtds/web-app_2.2.dtd">

<web-app>

  <taglib>
    <taglib-uri>/oreilly-taglib</taglib-uri>
    <taglib-location>/WEB-INF/META-INF/taglib.tld</taglib-location>
  </taglib>

</web-app>
```

Example 8-6 shows the JSP page that is used to render Figure 8-6. Note that you set
the language locale directly in the user's session.

*Example 8-6. Simple JSP template layout using HTML frames to achieve a left-to-right layout
(English)*

```
<%@ page import="java.util.Locale,
                 com.ora.i18n.LocaleSupport" %>
<%@ page contentType="text/html; charset=UTF-8" %>
<%@ page session="true" %>
<%@ taglib uri="/oreilly-taglib" prefix="oreillytags"%>
<%
```

Example 8-6. Simple JSP template layout using HTML frames to achieve a left-to-right layout (English) (continued)

```
        Locale userLocale = new Locale("en");
        session.setAttribute(LocaleSupport.USER_PREFERRED_LOCALE, userLocale);
%>

<html>

<frameset rows="20%, 80%">
    <frame src="menu_bar.jsp">
    <frameset cols="30%, 70%">
        <frame src="navigation_bar.jsp">
        <frame src="content.jsp">
    </frameset>
</frameset>

</html>
```

Example 8-7 shows the JSP page that is used to render Figure 8-7. The locale set for the language preference differs from that in Example 8-3 in that you use a locale appropriate for Hebrew. Note that you use the same content "areas": the topmost menu bar, the navigation bar, and the content area. However, in this example, you specify a right-to-left layout, which is appropriate for this locale.

Example 8-7. Simple JSP template layout using HTML frames to achieve a right-to-left layout (Hebrew)

```
<%@ page import="java.util.Locale,
                 com.ora.i18n.LocaleSupport"%>
<%@ page contentType="text/html; charset=UTF-8" %>
<%@ page session="true" %>
<%@ taglib uri="/oreilly-taglib" prefix="oreillytags"%>
<%
    Locale userLocale = new Locale("iw");
    session.setAttribute(LocaleSupport.USER_PREFERRED_LOCALE, userLocale);
%>

<html>

<frameset rows="20%, 80%">
    <frame src="menu_bar.jsp">
    <frameset cols="70%, 30%">
        <frame src="content.jsp">
        <frame src="navigation_bar.jsp">
    </frameset>
</frameset>

</html>
```

In Figure 8-6, the content appears in English, and the layout goes from left to right, which is appropriate for this language.

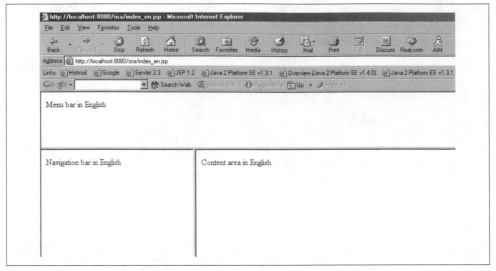

Figure 8-6. Template-based approach to JSP development showing a left-to-right layout

In contrast to Figure 8-6, Figure 8-7 shows how Example 8-7 is rendered. As you can see from Figure 8-7, the content areas run right to left, as does the content with the individual areas.

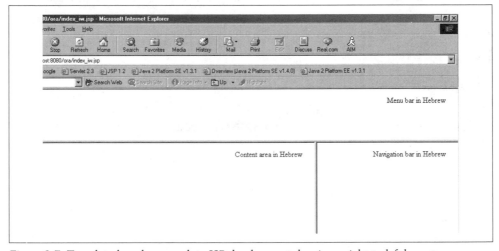

Figure 8-7. Template-based approach to JSP development showing a right-to-left layout

The text resource bundle for English is not given, but Example 8-8 shows, for the sake of simplicity, an untranslated resource bundle used for the Hebrew language. If you were to give a real Hebrew resource bundle, you would of course have the text translated and use the appropriate Unicode characters.

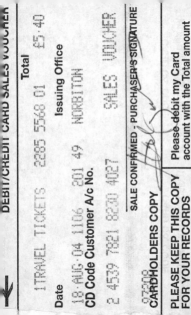

Example 8-8. textresources_iw.properties

```
Menu_Bar_Message=Menu bar in Hebrew
Navigation_Bar_Message=Navigation bar in Hebrew
Content_Area_Message=Content area in Hebrew
```

Customize Localization and Data Manipulation Using XML and XSTL

To say that XML is widely becoming a popular data transport in web applications is an understatement. However, some aspects of XML related to internationalization are not necessarily overstated, but can be overlooked. See Example 8-9.

Example 8-9. Header portion of web.xml

```
<?xml version="1.0" encoding="ISO-8859-1"?>

<!DOCTYPE web-app
    PUBLIC "-//Sun Microsystems, Inc.//DTD Web Application 2.2//EN"
    "http://java.sun.com/j2ee/dtds/web-app_2.2.dtd">

<web-app>
</web-app>
```

At this point, you probably have zeroed in on the encoding attribute of the XML prolog. In this snippet from a *web.xml* document, you can see that you are allowed to define the character encoding for the XML document. Example 8-9 specifies the encoding of the document as ISO-8859-1, or Latin-1. Typically, you will see XML documents with an encoding of UTF-8.

This attribute dictates the encoding of all the data in the XML document. Therefore, it affects how your XML parser treats the data. So, if you are writing your own XML documents, you should output the encoding in the XML prolog that is appropriate for the data within the XML document.

For example, suppose that you are passed data from the business object layer in XML that represents a user's order from an online warehouse. Aside from the encoding, how can you display certain data elements appropriate for the user? Well, remember that the overall document and subsequent elements can be tagged with a locale identifier to dictate how certain data will be displayed. Example 8-10 shows how a sample order might look.

Example 8-10. Simplified XML order data

```
<?xml version="1.0" encoding="UTF-8"?>

<order-summary>
<locale>en_US</locale>
<user-id>czarnecki</user-id>
```

Example 8-10. Simplified XML order data (continued)

```
<order-total-items>3</order-total-items>
<order-total-price>56.78</order-total-price>
</order-summary>
```

The locale can be used to select the appropriate surrounding text for the order from a resource bundle. It can also be used to display numbers, dates, and times appropriate for the given locale. Business rules might also dictate that certain elements must maintain their own locale attribute. For example, a U.S.-based web site might want to display catalog item prices in Japanese Yen for Japanese customers.

If you are dealing with large amounts of XML that you need to turn into another presentation format (e.g., HTML), you might want to investigate the Cocoon web-publishing framework from the Apache project.* Cocoon is a very sophisticated framework that addresses internationalization and localization requirements for applications, in large part through the I18nTransformer class. Cocoon is very easy to set up and use.† We leave further investigation of Cocoon up to you, but we would like to show you some screenshots of the internationalization example included with Cocoon to demonstrate the power and flexibility it offers.

Figure 8-8 shows the simple internationalization example from Cocoon with U.S. English as the selected language.

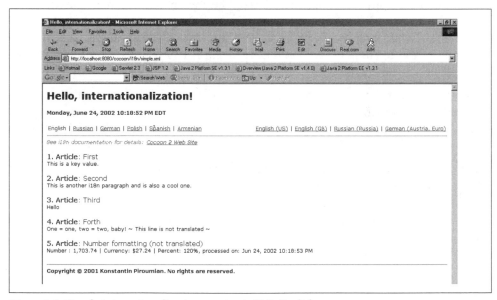

Figure 8-8. Simple internationalization running in U.S. English

---

* Cocoon is available at *http://xml.apache.org*.

† We set up Cocoon 2.0.2 using Tomcat 3.3.1 and the Java 2 SDK 1.3.1_01.

Figure 8-9 shows the sample example, but with UK English as the selected language.

Figure 8-9. Simple internationalization running in UK English

As you can see in Figure 8-9, the date and time at the top of the page are different from those in Figure 8-8. The date, time, and currency at the bottom of the page are also formatted appropriately for UK English.

Business Object Layer

If you're dealing with servlets, standard JavaBeans or web services, or the name du jour for business object components, you should be certain that you design with internationalization in mind. As far as business objects are concerned, you typically need to know the user's preferred locale from which to decode and parse information from an incoming request.

Design Internationalization-Ready Business Objects

The components needed to construct your business object layer are too vast to enumerate or give due treatment in this chapter. When designing for internationalization, however, you must always take into consideration the types of data items that you are working with. In this chapter, we cannot go into all the details of how to use the various internationalization APIs for formatting items such as numbers, dates, and times, but we can say that if you haven't done so already, familiarize yourself with the following Java 2 Standard Edition (J2SE) APIs* when designing various J2EE components (e.g., servlets, standard JavaBeans, Enterprise JavaBeans (EJBs), and web services). Here are some important classes:

`java.text.BreakIterator`
Allows you to break apart text in a locale-specific way.

`java.text.Collator`
Useful if you need to sort a list of data (e.g., strings). The sorting rules will differ per locale.

`java.text.DateFormat`
Appropriate for formatting and parsing date strings in a locale-independent manner.

`java.text.MessageFormat`
Used when you need to construct appropriate messages in a language-independent manner.

`java.text.NumberFormat`
Appropriate for formatting and parsing numeric values in a locale-independent manner.

`java.util.Locale`
As the Java documentation says, "represents a specific geographical, political, or cultural region."

`java.util.ResourceBundle`
Contains locale-specific objects.

This is by far not an exhaustive list of the APIs you will need to be familiar with, but it touches on the major areas for dealing with data in a J2EE application.

If you look through the various internationalization APIs, a common pattern emerges: constructors (direct or factory-based) and methods all take a `java.util.Locale` object when the class handles locale-sensitive operations or when the operation being performed is locale-sensitive. As we mentioned in the previous section, at an application-design level, you need to decide where the user's locale preference is stored. Again, this can be a method accessed from the appropriate `User` object, or it can be an object stored directly in the user's session that is accessed under a certain key.

If you feel as if you're being left in the dark, you're not. As far as the J2EE APIs† are concerned, few J2EE APIs ask for a `Locale` object.‡

---

* These APIs are present in the Java 2 SDK Standard Edition 1.4.0 API, which can be found online at *http:// java.sun.com/j2se/1.4/docs/api/index.html*.

† The current Java 2 SDK Enterprise Edition APIs available at the time of this writing are 1.3.1_02. They can be found online at *http://java.sun.com/j2ee/sdk_1.3/techdocs/api/index.html*.

‡ Actually, we found only 13 methods that explicitly dealt with or returned a `Locale` object.

Although the dot-com revolution has since peaked, e-commerce is not dead. Therefore, there are a number of areas for you to consider when communicating a locale to the business object layer:

- Localization of various product prices
- Currency and tax manipulation
- External communication via email (e.g., order confirmation)

For certain components, such as the InsertText JSP custom tag developed in Example 8-3, your component should have the appropriate methods for retrieving and setting the locale.

Create a Simple Interface for Supporting Localization in Business Objects

The LocaleSupport interface, defined in Example 8-11, is arguably an oversimplified version of an interface for handling locales. However, certain components might need to retrieve and/or set the locale, but other components might just need to know how to "find" a user's preferred locale by looking for a certain key, which in this case is com.ora.bestpractices.j2ee.i18n.USER_PREFERRED_LOCALE.

Example 8-11. LocaleSupport interface

```
package com.ora.i18n;

import java.util.Locale;

public interface LocaleSupport {

    static final String USER_PREFERRED_LOCALE = "com.ora.bestpractices.j2ee.i18n.USER_
PREFERRED_LOCALE";
    static final Locale APPLICATION_DEFAULT_LOCALE = Locale.getDefault( );

    public void setLocale(Locale inLocale);
    public Locale getLocale( );
}
```

The simplicity of this interface underscores the simplicity with which you can start designing your business components to take a locale as appropriate.

Take the Locale into Consideration in the Application Controller

You've already seen LocaleSupport used in a JSP custom tag, but what about a business component such as a servlet? Its use in this scenario might be appropriate if you're designing an application controller to route users to locale-specific JSP pages.

As with the LocaleSupport interface, this is not meant to be an exhaustive component, but a starting point for your own development.

The essence of how this business component can use LocaleSupport is as follows:

- Look for the user's preferred locale attribute from the name defined in the LocaleSupport interface.
- If the user's preferred locale is not set, fall back to the application's default locale defined in the LocaleSupport interface.
- Identify the requested page and form an appropriate page name by tacking on the preferred locale to the page and adding the appropriate extension.
- Forward the user to the proper locale-s
- pecific JSP page.

Example 8-12 shows one such application controller.

Example 8-12. Servlet controller that helps route to locale-specific JSP pages

```
package com.ora.i18n.servlets;

import com.ora.i18n.LocaleSupport;

import javax.servlet.RequestDispatcher;
import javax.servlet.ServletException;
import javax.servlet.http.*;
import java.io.IOException;
import java.util.Locale;

public class LocalePageServlet extends HttpServlet {

    private final static String DEFAULT_PAGE = "index";
    private final static String PAGE_ID_PARAMETER = "pageID";
    private final static String JSP_EXTENSION = ".jsp";

    public LocalePageServlet( ) {
    }

    protected void doPost(HttpServletRequest httpServletRequest, HttpServletResponse
httpServletResponse) throws ServletException, IOException {
        Locale pageLocale;
        pageLocale = (Locale) httpServletRequest.getSession( ).getAttribute(LocaleSupport.
USER_PREFERRED_LOCALE);
        if (pageLocale == null) {
            pageLocale = LocaleSupport.APPLICATION_DEFAULT_LOCALE;
        }

        String requestedPage = httpServletRequest.getParameter(PAGE_ID_PARAMETER);
        if (requestedPage == null) {
            requestedPage = DEFAULT_PAGE;
        }
        requestedPage += "_";
```

Example 8-12. Servlet controller that helps route to locale-specific JSP pages (continued)

```
        requestedPage += pageLocale.toString();
        requestedPage += JSP_EXTENSION;
        RequestDispatcher rd = httpServletRequest.getRequestDispatcher(requestedPage);
        rd.forward(httpServletRequest, httpServletResponse);
    }

    protected void doGet(HttpServletRequest httpServletRequest, HttpServletResponse
httpServletResponse) throws ServletException, IOException {
        doPost(httpServletRequest, httpServletResponse);
    }
}
```

Example 8-13 gives the appropriate definition of the *web.xml* file.

Example 8-13. Definition of the LocalePageServlet for web.xml in your web application

```
<servlet>
    <servlet-name>LocalePageServlet</servlet-name>
    <servlet-class>com.ora.i18n.servlets.LocalePageServlet</servlet-class>
  </servlet>

  <servlet-mapping>
    <servlet-name>LocalePageServlet</servlet-name>
    <url-pattern>/LocalePageServlet</url-pattern>
</servlet-mapping>
```

In the absence of a more formal or full-scale enterprise application, you use the
setlocale.jsp page to set the user's preferred locale preference (see Example 8-14).
An appropriate URL for setting the user's preferred locale to Hebrew might be *http://
localhost:8080/ora/setlocale.jsp?lang=iw*. Note that the hostname can differ for your
machine.

Example 8-14. setlocale.jsp page used to set the user's preferred locale

```
<%@ page import="com.ora.i18n.LocaleSupport,
                 java.util.Locale"%>
<%@ page session="true" %>
<%
    String language = request.getParameter("lang");
    Locale userLocale = new Locale(language);
    session.setAttribute(LocaleSupport.USER_PREFERRED_LOCALE, userLocale);
%>
<html>
The user's locale has been set appropriately.
</html>
```

In Figure 8-10, you use setlocale.jsp and request the index page. As you can see
from the figure, you are served the appropriate page for your preferred locale,
Hebrew.

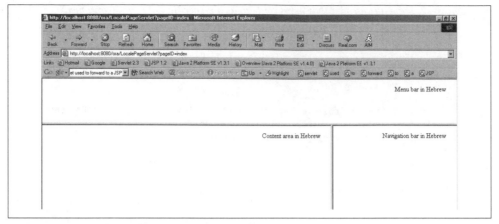

Figure 8-10. Using the LocalePageServlet to request the index page in Hebrew

We included Figure 8-11 to illustrate that the LocalePageServlet is working properly in creating the appropriate JSP page name. However, this particular JSP page does not exist in your application. A more robust controller would handle this situation more gracefully and in a more user-friendly manner.

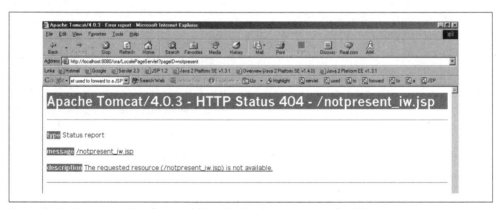

Figure 8-11. Demonstrating the LocalePageServlet that constructs the JSP page name

Data Access Layer

Information that your applications will be presenting to the end user—such as page content, menu items, and error messages—will not always be static. Dynamic data will need to be stored and retrieved from a persistent storage mechanism such as a relational database. There are things you should be aware of that might not be directly evident when setting up your application's data storage, or when operating with this data.

Configure Your Database for Internationalization

Localization support will vary depending on your database vendor. Typically, you will be interested in knowing which character encodings are supported by your database, as this will affect the type of data that you can store in the database. This setting is usually something that needs to be configured at the database level or upon the creation of tables in a particular database.

Oracle, for example, is typically configured to encode data in tables in UTF-8 encoding. This allows you to store a good number of character sets using this particular encoding. In preparing your database for localization, using UTF-8 as the encoding is, to quote Martha Stewart, "a good thing." In presenting the data to the user, the data can be converted from UTF-8 to another character encoding for display.

However, what if you happen to be using PostgreSQL? Out of the box, PostgreSQL does not support localization—this must be enabled when the PostgreSQL server is built from the source distribution into compiled binaries. However, one of the limitations of this database is that, to quote the PostgreSQL documentation on localization,[*] "PostgreSQL uses the standard ISO C and POSIX-like locale facilities provided by the server operating system." Therefore, to achieve proper localization for your application running over a PostgreSQL database, you must involve the system administrator to install the proper language packages.

Another popular database is MySQL. However, by default MySQL uses ISO-8859-1 (Latin-1) and sorts according to the rules of Swedish/Finnish.[†] We will discuss collation at the business object or database level in the next section.

The localization options you choose for your database when it is installed and configured will affect operations such as:

- The sort order when using the ORDER_BY clause
- Operators such as LIKE that do pattern-matching–type operations
- Character conversion or escaping functionality
- Table indexes

If you change localization information about your database, you will typically have to reindex tables.

In summary, be sure to check with your database vendor and database administrator to determine what localization information is configured for the system and for the database on which you will be deploying your application.

---

[*] The localization documentation for PostgreSQL can be found online at *http://www.postgresql.org/idocs/index.php?charset.html*.

[†] The localization documentation for MySQL can be found online at *http://www.mysql.org/documentation/mysql/bychapter/* in Section 4.6, "MySQL Localisation and International Usage."

Use Standard Java Classes (Instead of Database Constructs) for Collation and for Sorting Database Information

Suppose you've properly configured your database to handle the localizations required by your application. As we mentioned in the previous section, the localization information contained within a database can be used to determine things such as the collation or sort order for data returned when the SQL ORDER_BY clause is used to retrieve data.

You might or might not be familiar with the standard Java libraries for collating data. Earlier, in "Design Internationalization-Ready Business Objects," we mentioned the java.text package, which contains the classes that will allow you to control locale-based collation. In applications that you designed to be internationalization-ready, you rely on objects in the business object layer to control the collation and sorting of data. There are a number of reasons why this is advantageous over relying on your database to handle these operations for you.

First, the rules for collation and sorting within the database are typically not configurable. You rely on the operating system or database vendor to investigate the locales it supports to develop the proper rules for collation. However, these rules are not exposed from the database. By allowing your business object layer to perform locale-based collation, you can take advantage of classes such as java.text.RuleBasedCollator for fine-grained control over the rules for sorting.

Another reason is that although most databases today offer the ability to do collation at the database level, some do not. Therefore, if you rely on the database to perform the correct sorting of data returned to the user, you might be in for a surprise. In one instance, your database might not be able to do collation within the database. This dictates that your business object layer must be responsible for performing this type of operation. In another instance, depending on the localizations offered by your database vendor, you might want a particular localization that is not supported by your database. This might require adding the proper language support to the operating system, or it can require a new installation of your database that is configured properly.

Finally, the internal collation operations might not be optimized for performance. For example, the PostgreSQL database documentation states, "The only severe drawback of using the locale support in PostgreSQL is its speed." A frequent performance bottleneck in enterprise applications is in accessing dynamic data from a database. Although, in many instances in which performance degradation in an application is due to the inadequate use of (or lack of) connection pooling mechanisms, issues with database performance such as collation might not be directly evident. Also, classes such as the java.text.CollationKey class allow for faster sorting with certain types of data (e.g., strings).

Design Your Database Schema to Be Internationalization-Ready

Dynamic data such as catalog items present another challenge when designing your application for internationalization. Databases are meant to store large amounts of data that change often, whereas resource bundles are not meant to collect such information. Therefore, it is imperative that you design for internationalization in the data model you choose for the database that will store data for your application.

The simplest example to understand with regard to data modeling is a product catalog. Imagine for a moment a very simplified version of Amazon.com or any web site that sells goods over the Internet. Products in the catalog contain a number of attributes that will vary depending on the locale, such as the product description or product image. If your application is internationalized, each product will have a one-to-many relationship with the localized attributes. In other words, a product will contain a description for each localization instance.

Designing your schema appropriately is a challenge in itself. Let's look at a number of alternatives for modeling items from a catalog. Tables 8-1 through 8-6 offer three different models for a product entity that contains three attributes: a product ID, the quantity on hand, and a description. In this example, the description will need to be localized for the locales supported by your application.

Table 8-1. Product entity data model alternative #1 (PRODUCT)

Attribute	Data type and size
PRODUCT_ID	INTEGER
QUANTITY_ON_HAND	INTEGER
DESCRIPTION_EN_US	VARCHAR2(5000)
DESCRIPTION_FR_FR	VARCHAR2(5000)

Table 8-2. Product entity data model alternative #2 (PRODUCT)

Attribute	Data type and size
PRODUCT_ID	INTEGER
QUANTITY_ON_HAND	INTEGER

Table 8-3. Product entity data model alternative #2 (PRODUCT_DESCRIPTION_EN_US)

Attribute	Data type and size
PRODUCT_ID	INTEGER
DESCRIPTION	VARCHAR2(5000)

Table 8-4. Product entity data model alternative #2 (PRODUCT_DESCRIPTION_FR_FR)

Attribute	Data type and size
PRODUCT_ID	INTEGER
DESCRIPTION	VARCHAR2(5000)

Table 8-5. Product entity data model alternative #3 (PRODUCT)

Attribute	Data type and size
PRODUCT_ID	INTEGER
QUANTITY_ON_HAND	INTEGER

Table 8-6. Product entity data model alternative #3 (PRODUCT_DESCRIPTION)

Attribute	Data type and size
PRODUCT_ID	INTEGER
LOCALE	CHAR(12)
DESCRIPTION	VARCHAR2(5000)

Let's evaluate the alternatives outlined in the preceding tables. In Table 8-1, every attribute is named according to the localizations for the application. This is unattractive from the perspective that each time you want to add a localization to your application, your database schema will change. Also, your application code might change depending on how you retrieve information from the database. Even a sophisticated persistence engine might not accommodate such changes in a database schema. This also means that your schema becomes unwieldy as the number of attributes requiring localization increases.

In Tables 8-2 through 8-4, entities are divided into core attributes and localized attributes. In Table 8-2, the basic product information that will not change regardless of localization is stored. However, Tables 8-3 and 8-4 contain data that is appropriate for the product description in the English and French locales, respectively. This schema design presents many of the same issues already outlined for the previously mentioned alternative. Namely, you should avoid any changes to application code and/or schema design when adding a new localization to your application.

The last alternative for product entity data modeling is shown in Tables 8-5 and 8-6. This is our recommended approach for storing localized information in your database. Here, the product entity is again devided into its core attributes and a description table. However, the product description in Table 8-6 differs from that in Tables 8-3 and 8-4 in that LOCALE is now an attribute for the product description. This table attribute will be used in conjunction with the PRODUCT_ID attribute to form a primary key consisting of PRODUCT_ID, LOCALE. This means that accommodating another localization in your database should be as simple as adding the proper row to the PRODUCT_DESCRIPTION table in Table 8-6 with the appropriate locale identifier.

CHAPTER 9

JSP Best Practices

Hans Bergsten

The JavaServer Pages (JSP) specification was developed to simplify the creation and maintenance of web user interfaces for Java 2 Enterprise Edition (J2EE) applications. A JSP page is a regular web page with markup elements (such as HTML or WML), plus additional JSP elements that control the dynamic parts of the page—for instance, filling a table with data retrieved from a data source at runtime. JSP pages eliminate the need to generate the user interface markup elements with out.println( ) statements in servlets—the approach used in early server-side Java web applications—and make it easier to split the development between *page authors* (user interface developers) and Java programmers.

The basic idea behind JSP is easy to understand, and it's easy to start using the technology, but it's not always obvious how to apply it efficiently, especially for large-scale applications. Because JSP lets you place logic directly in your web pages, it's also easy to abuse the technology; what might seem like time-saving shortcuts early in a project can easily lead to debugging and maintenance nightmares, poor scalability, and an application that's hard to extend as new requirements surface. This chapter offers recommendations for how to use JSP effectively and provides solutions to common issues.

Appropriate Usage of JSP in an Enterprise Application

A JSP page is converted to a servlet before it's called on to serve requests. This means that a JSP page can do anything a servlet can do, but it doesn't mean JSP is appropriate for all tasks.

Favor Using JSP as the View Only

For a very simple application, using JSP for all parts of the application might be acceptable, but in most cases, I recommend following the Model-View-Controller

(MVC) design pattern and using JSP only for the View. If you use JSP for all parts, you typically encounter these types of problems:

- Common features need to be implemented in many places. If logic for access control, logging, and statistics collection is duplicated in most JSP pages, changes in these areas require changes to many parts of the application.

- Business logic is harder to develop, debug, reuse, and maintain if it's implemented as JSP action elements or Java code scriptlets in JSP pages. While some integrated development environments (IDEs) support a rich environment for JSP development and debugging, nonvisual aspects of the application are better done as regular Java classes, in which the full power of the language's object-oriented features and standard program development tools can be leveraged.

- Changes to the database schema or data source type require changes in all JSP pages that access the data source directly.

- The application page flow is hard to visualize and manage because it's spread throughout the application pages.

Combining JSP with other J2EE technologies solves all these problems. The frameworks described in Chapter 3, such as Apache Struts,* can help you develop easy-to-manage web applications. Struts provides a generic Controller server, dispatching requests to simple classes (Action classes) that handle the individual request types and pick the JSP page for rendering the response based on the outcome (and possibly other runtime conditions, such as client type or the user's language preferences). Other component types defined in the servlet specification are suitable for other common tasks—for example, an application lifecycle listener is perfect for initialization of application resources, and a servlet filter can handle application-controlled access control. To isolate the application from data source and schema changes, all access to persistence data should be performed by separate data access objects.

Figure 9-1 outlines the main parts of a product catalog application based on Struts, in which the MVC roles are allocated to these J2EE component types.

When the application starts, the ResourceInitListener creates a single instance of the CatalogDAO class and makes it available to other parts of the application as a servlet context attribute. The CatalogDAO is a data access object, encapsulating all details about how to access product information stored in a database. If the database schema is changed, or if the SQL statements need to be changed when switching to a database from a different vendor, this is the only class that needs to be changed. The data access object contains methods that return a ProductBean representing a specific product or a list of ProductBean instances that match a search criterion.

* Struts is available at *http://jakarta.apache.org/struts/*.

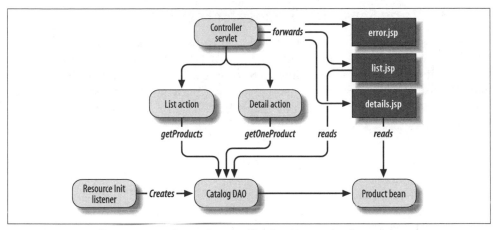

Figure 9-1. An application using JSP combined with other J2EE technologies

All requests are sent to the Struts Controller servlet, which uses a part of the URL to identify the Action subclass responsible for processing the request. Each Action subclass is a simple class with a single method that performs all processing and returns the name of the View that should be used to render the response. In Figure 9-1, the ListAction class is invoked to handle a request for a list of products. It uses a search criterion (e.g., a product category) received with the request to get a list of matching ProductBean instances from the CatalogDAO, saves the list as a request attribute, and returns a View name to the Controller. The Controller maps the returned View name to the URL for the corresponding JSP page—the *list.jsp* page in this example—and forwards the request to the page. The JSP page gets the list of products saved as a request attribute by the ListAction class and renders an HTML list with an entry for each product. Each product entry is rendered as a link with a URL that the Controller recognizes as a request to invoke DetailsAction. This action gets a specific ProductBean from the CatalogDAO, adds a reference to it in the request, and tells the Controller to render the response using the *details.jsp* page. While this description is brief, it hopefully gives you an idea of how the work is distributed between the different components and how they match the Model, View, and Controller roles.

This separation of tasks makes it possible to modify the business logic without touching the user interface, and vice versa. It also means that logging and other central functions can be managed in just one place, and it minimizes the amount of logic needed in the JSP pages. The remaining logic, such as looping through the product list and rendering the product information as HTML elements, can easily be done using the JSP Standard Tag Library (JSTL) actions. JSTL actions or custom actions should be used in favor of Java code scriptlets because the scriptlet syntax is very error-prone and is likely to intimidate nonprogrammers who eventually will change the application user interface layout and style.

Consider Using Separate JSP Pages for Each Role

For a very simple application (for example, up to five web pages and business logic consisting of just reading and writing to one or two database tables), splitting the functionality between different component types can be overkill. If you decide to use only JSP for such an application, I still recommend staying close to the MVC model; use separate JSP pages for the user interface (View) and the nonvisual parts (Controller and Model), as shown in Figure 9-2.

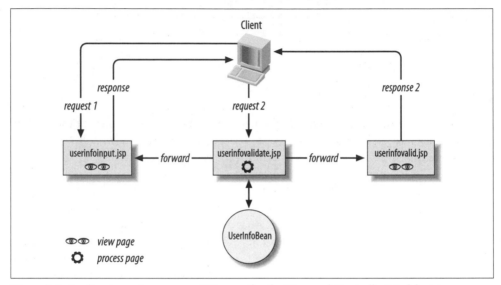

Figure 9-2. Application using separate JSP pages for the View and Controller/Model parts

This makes it easier to maintain the application for the same reasons described earlier, and also makes it easier to replace the business logic implementation with servlets and other Java components later, if needed.

Avoid Using Scripting Elements

Whether you use JSP pages for only the View portion of the application or for other roles as well, avoiding scripting elements (i.e., raw Java code in the pages) is always a good idea. Using scripting elements exposes you to, at least, the following problems:

- Syntax errors are very easy to make and extremely hard to locate because the scripting element code is interleaved with the code generated by the container.
- Scripting code can be reused only through copy/paste.
- To a nonprogrammer charged with maintaining the look-and-feel aspects of the pages, scripting code is very distracting and easy to corrupt by mistake. Some web page authoring tools used by this group of people also remove or corrupt scripting elements.

Before the introduction of custom tag libraries in JSP 1.1, scripting elements were your only choice. Even in the latest JSP version, scripting elements are still supported (because Java specifications go to great lengths to be backward-compatible). But with the introduction of custom tag libraries, and especially the libraries defined by the JSTL specification, there's really no good reason to use scripting elements anymore.

Page Design

This section describes practices related to the overall design of JSP pages for an application, such as flexible solutions for a consistent look and feel, preparing for a multi-lingual user interface, and making the application usable for devices with different capabilities.

Put Shared Page Elements in Separate Files

Most web sites need to maintain a consistent look and layout for all web pages, typically with a common header, footer, and navigation menus, as well as color and font choices. For a static site, site development tools typically let you apply a common template that provides this look and feel to all pages, but they are often not up to the task if the shared parts are dynamic (e.g., a navigation menu hides or exposes submenus depending on the selected page).

Creating the layout and shared content for the first page and then copying it for all the other pages—just changing the main content part—is, of course, one way to provide a consistent look for all pages in an application. It's not a very efficient way, though, because all pages need to be changed when you want to modify the shared parts.

A more efficient way is to first identify all parts that should be shared by all pages and put them in separate files. Using JSP include actions and directives, you can then include them in all pages, as shown in Example 9-1.

Example 9-1. Including shared parts in a JSP page

```
<%@ page contentType="text/html" %>

<%@ include file="/shared/header.htmlf" %>
<table width="90%">
  <tr>
    <td valign="top" align="center" bgcolor="lightblue">
      <jsp:include page="/shared/navigation.jsp" />
    </td>
    <td valign="middle" align="center" width="80%">
      The main content for this page
    </td>
  </tr>
</table>
<%@ include file="/shared/footer.htmlf" %>
```

The shared parts can contain only static content, such as the header and footer files in this example, or JSP elements, as exemplified by the navigation file. None of the files is a complete HTML page. For instance, the *header.htmlf* file contains only the start tags for the <html> and <body> elements, and the *footer.htmlf* file contains the corresponding end tags. The *htmlf* file extension ("f" as in "fractional") is used here to indicate this. Note that the file for the navigation menu uses the standard *.jsp* extension; while it doesn't generate a complete HTML response, it's still a syntactically complete JSP page.

Use a Layout Page to Merge Shared Parts and Main Content

A potential problem with including shared parts in every page is that while you need to change the content of the shared parts in only one place, global layout, color, and font changes are still not easy to make. For instance, if you want to add a "news flash" section on the righthand side of all pages, you must edit every file and add this content.

A more powerful way to provide a consistent look and feel is to turn things around: instead of letting each page include the shared parts, let one layout page include both the shared parts and the main content of each page. Example 9-2 shows what such a layout page might look like.

Example 9-2. A common layout page that includes all parts of the real page (layout.jsp)

```
<%@ page contentType="text/html" %>
<%@ taglib prefix="c" uri="http://java.sun.com/jstl/core" %>

<c:import url="/vars/default.jsp" />
<c:catch>
  <c:import url="/vars/${param.page}.jsp" />
</c:catch>

<%@ include file="/shared/header.jspf" %>
<table width="90%">
  <tr>
    <td valign="top" align="center" bgcolor="lightblue">
      <c:import url="/shared/navigation.jsp" />
    </td>
    <td valign="middle" align="center" width="80%">
      <c:import url="/pages/${param.page}.jsp" />
    </td>
  </tr>
</table>
<%@ include file="/shared/footer.htmlf" %>
```

When this page is invoked with a URL that includes a query string parameter named page with the name of the main content page, it renders a response with all the shared portions as well as the main content for the specified page. The JSTL <c:import> action is used here in favor of the standard <jsp:include> action, primarily to be able to dynamically build the URL for the main content page based on the page request parameter without using Java scripting code.

Another detail of interest is the section at the beginning of the page that imports a page named */vars/default.jsp* and another page in the */vars* directory corresponding to the requested main page. These variable-setter pages add request attribute values that are used to adjust the dynamic content in the shared parts of the page for a specific page. Example 9-3 shows the *header.jspf* file, and Examples 9-4 and 9-5 show how the pages imported from the */vars* directory set the JSTL Expression Language (EL) variables used in the header file.

Example 9-3. Shared header file (/shared/header.jspf)

```
<html>
  <head>
    <title><c:out value="${mainTitle}: ${subTitle}" /></title>
  </head>
  <body bgcolor="white">
    <h1>My Site</h1>
```

Example 9-4. Page setting default values for variables used in the header (/vars/default.jsp)

```
<%@ taglib prefix="c" uri="http://java.sun.com/jstl/core" %>

<c:set var="mainTitle" scope="request" value="Welcome to My Site" />
```

Example 9-5. Page setting page-specific values for variables used in the header (/vars/page1.jsp)

```
<%@ taglib prefix="c" uri="http://java.sun.com/jstl/core" %>

<c:set var="subTitle" scope="request" value="Page 1" />
```

To make the page-specific variable-setting page optional, place the <c:import> action within the body of a <c:catch> element; if the page doesn't exist, <c:import> throws an exception, which the <c:catch> action catches and ignores.

The rest of the layout page in Example 9-2 contains static HTML elements for the layout of the page, and JSP elements for including the shared parts as well as the request-specific main content. If a shared part is added, or if the page layout changed, only the *layout.jsp* needs to be changed. Font styles and colors can also be maintained in the *layout.jsp* page using Cascading Style Sheets (CSS).

Choose an Appropriate Include Mechanism

JSP provides two ways to include content in a page: the include directive (<%@ include file="..." %>) and the include action (<jsp:include page="..." />). As shown earlier, JSTL adds an import action (<c:import url="..." />) to the mix.

The include directive and the include action both include content from resources that belong to the same web application as the including file. The directive includes the source of the specified resource, either a static file or a file with JSP elements. When a JSP file is included this way, it shares the page scope (and all other scopes) as well as all scripting variables with the including file. The included file is rarely a syntactically complete JSP or HTML page, and I recommend that a different file extension be used to highlight this fact. Any extension will do, but good choices are *.jspf* and *.htmlf*, in which "f" stands for "fractional" (as described earlier). The JSP 1.2 specification leaves detecting changes in a file included by the include directive as an optional feature. In a container that doesn't detect these changes, changes to an included file have no effect until you force a recompile of the including file (e.g., by removing the corresponding class file or "touching" the file).

The include action, on the other hand, includes the response produced by executing the specified resource, either a JSP page or a servlet. The included resource has access to the same scopes as the including file (except for the page scope), and the container always detects when the including file changed and recompiles it when needed.

Finally, the JSTL import action includes content from resources in the same web application, a separate web application in the same container, or an external server accessible through a supported protocol (e.g., HTTP or FTP). For a resource in the same web application, it works exactly like the standard include action.

The following rules of thumb help you pick the most appropriate include mechanism:

- Use the include directive (`<% include ... %>`) for a file that rarely changes, which is typically true for things such as headers and footers. Because the including and included files are merged in the translation phase, there's no runtime overhead. Be aware, though, that including large files can cause the generated `_jspService()` method to exceed the size limit for a Java method (64 KB) in some containers. Even in a container with a more sophisticated code-generation algorithm, using the include directive means the file is replicated in the class files for all JSP pages that include it, increasing the overall memory requirements for the application.

- Use the include directive (`<% include ... %>`) if the included file must set response headers, or redesign the application so that included pages never have to do this. The section "Consider Enabling Client-Side Caching for Semistatic Pages" later in this chapter describes this issue in more detail.

- Use either the standard include action (`<jsp:include>`) or the JSTL import action (`<c:import>`) for a file that is likely to change—for instance, a navigation menu or a file containing a shared part with lots of layout and style options (such as a "news flash" box). Of the two, the JSTL import action is more flexible, as it can include both local and external resources, and it supports JSTL EL expressions. It's also more strictly defined in terms of what happens when the include fails, so it can safely be combined with JSTL `<c:catch>` for fine-grained error handling.

Due to its flexibility, it can be slightly less efficient than the standard include action, but not enough to matter in most cases.

Consider Using a Shared Configuration File

Besides shared content, an include directive can also include a file that contains shared page attributes, such as a page directive with an errorPage attribute and taglib directives for all libraries used in the application:

```
<%@ page errorPage="/shared/error.jsp" %>
<%@ taglib prefix="c" uri="http://java.sun.com/jstl/core" %>
<%@ taglib prefix="fmt" uri="http://java.sun.com/jstl/fmt" %>
<%@ taglib prefix="ora" uri="orataglib" %>
```

This way, global changes can be made in one place—for instance, changing a taglib directive's uri attribute when upgrading to a later version.

Consider Using Filters to Simplify URLs

One drawback with the simple templating solution implemented by a layout page is that all links to the JSP pages must include the layout page name plus a query string—e.g., *layout.jsp?page=page1*. Example 9-6 shows parts of the navigation menu page with this type of link.

Example 9-6. Navigation page with links to layout page

```
<%@ taglib prefix="c" uri="http://java.sun.com/jstl/core" %>

<table bgcolor="lightblue">
  <tr>
    <td>
      <c:choose>
        <c:when test="${param.page == 'page1'}">
          <b>Page 1</b>
        </c:when>
        <c:otherwise>
          <a href="<c:url value="layout.jsp?page=page1" />">Page 1</a>
        </c:otherwise>
      </c:choose>
    </td>
  </tr>
  ...
</table>
```

If you want to be able to use more traditional URLs instead, you can use a filter. The filter component type was introduced in the Servlet 2.3 specification. A filter is invoked before a request is delivered to the target servlet or JSP page and is a powerful tool for applying request and response processing to a group of web application resources. The filter shown in Example 9-7 converts URLs of the form *pageName.jsp* to URLs of the form *layout.jsp?page=pageName*, which are behind the scenes at runtime.

Example 9-7. Filter that allows the layout page to be invoked with regular URLs

```java
package com.ora.j2eebp.jsp;

import java.io.*;
import java.net.*;
import javax.servlet.*;
import javax.servlet.http.*;

public class URLConversionFilter implements Filter {

    private static final String LAYOUT_PAGE = "/layout.jsp";
    private static final String PAGE_PARAM = "page";

    private FilterConfig config;

    public void init(FilterConfig config) throws ServletException {
        this.config = config;
    }

    /**
     * Converts the request URL and forwards to the real resource URL
     */
    public void doFilter(ServletRequest request, ServletResponse response,
        FilterChain chain) throws IOException, ServletException {

        HttpServletRequest httpReq = (HttpServletRequest) request;
        HttpServletResponse httpResp = (HttpServletResponse) response;

        String currURL = httpReq.getServletPath( );
        // Strip off the leading slash.
        currURL = currURL.substring(1);
        String pagePath =
            currURL.substring(0, currURL.lastIndexOf(".jsp"));
        String queryString = httpReq.getQueryString( );
        StringBuffer realURL = new StringBuffer(LAYOUT_PAGE);
        realURL.append("?").append(PAGE_PARAM).append("=").
            append(URLEncoder.encode(pagePath));
        if (queryString != null) {
            realURL.append("&").append(queryString);
        }

        ServletContext context = config.getServletContext( );
        RequestDispatcher rd =
            context.getRequestDispatcher(realURL.toString( ));
        if (rd == null) {
            httpResp.sendError(HttpServletResponse.SC_INTERNAL_SERVER_ERROR,
                               "Layout page doesn't exist");
        }
        rd.forward(request, response);
        return;
    }
```

```
    public void destroy( ) {
    }
}
```

The filter gets the URL for the request, extracts the JSP page path, creates a URL for the layout page with the page path as a query string parameter, and forwards to the layout page. Because all this happens on the server, the URL shown in the browser remains unchanged.

The filter must be declared and mapped to the *.jsp* pattern in the web application deployment descriptor (*web.xml*), like this:

```
    <?xml version="1.0" encoding="ISO-8859-1"?>

    <!DOCTYPE web-app
      PUBLIC "-//Sun Microsystems, Inc.//DTD Web Application 2.3//EN"
      "http://java.sun.com//dtd/web-app_2_3.dtd">

    <web-app>
      <filter>
        <filter-name>urlConversion</filter-name>
        <filter-class>
          com.ora.j2eebp.jsp.URLConversionFilter
        </filter-class>
      </filter>

      <filter-mapping>
        <filter-name>urlConversion</filter-name>
        <url-pattern>*.jsp</url-pattern>
      </filter-mapping>
    </web-app>
```

With this filter configuration in place, any request for a JSP page (such as *page1.jsp*) goes through the filter, causing the *layout.jsp* page to be invoked with the original path as the value of the page parameter.

The solution presented here works fine for any web application, but if you use an MVC framework, a templating solution with additional features can be part of the package. For instance, Apache Struts includes a templating package named Tiles. While the principles are the same, Tiles uses an XML configuration file for the type of dynamic values handled by variable-setter pages in the solution presented here, and the tight integration with Struts offers a different solution to the URL naming problem I solved with the filter.

Consider Internationalization from the Start

An Internet web application, and even some extranet and intranet applications, often benefit from internationalization (i18n). If i18n is not considered up front, it's usually a huge effort to retrofit the application later.

As for any application, i18n of a web application starts with identifying all user interface pieces that need to be handled differently for each locale: text, images, number and date formats, etc. The application is then developed to use external, localized versions of these resources instead of hardcoding them in the application. Supporting a new locale simply means adding a new set of localized resources.

When you use JSP for the user interface, you can approach i18n in two ways: use a common set of pages for all locales, dynamically grabbing the localized content from an appropriate resource bundle, or use a separate page for each locale, in effect treating each JSP page as a localized resource. The first approach is preferred for pages with small amounts of content but lots of presentation logic because it's easier to maintain. Using separate pages is a good choice when the layout differs dramatically between different locales, perhaps for Western languages and Asian languages, and for pages with lots of content but little presentation logic. Most sites benefit from a combination of these two approaches—for instance, using separate pages for mostly static content (e.g., product descriptions and white papers) and shared pages for everything else.

Use a Controller servlet to select the locale to be used in the response to each request. It can do so based on information received with the request, such as a parameter or a cookie, or based on profile information in a database for a logged-in user. When separate pages are used for each locale, the Controller forwards to the appropriate page for the selected locale. For a page shared by all locales, the Controller uses a request attribute to record the selected locale and forwards to the internationalized page. The page can use the JSTL i18n actions to get localized text and image URLs from a matching resource bundle, and to format dates and numbers according to the rules for the selected locale.

If an internationalized, shared page needs to contain links to separate pages for each locale, you can use a resource bundle with keys for each locale-specific page and the localized page names as the values, like this:

```
copyright=copyright_sv.jsp
privacy=privacy_sv.jsp
```

You can then use the bundle with the JSTL i18n actions to create a link to the correct page for the current locale:

```
<a href="<fmt:message key="copyright" bundle="${pagesBundle}"/>">
  <fmt:message key="copyright" bundle="${textBundle}" />
</a>
```

For more information about internationalization of a J2EE application, see Chapter 8.

Enable URL Rewriting

Session tracking is necessary for any application that depends on information submitted through multiple requests. While a session ID cookie is usually sufficient for the web container to manage session tracking, it's not guaranteed to work for all clients; some users disable cookie support in their browsers, and cookie support is not a given in browsers for small devices, such as a WML browser.

To handle cookie-less session tracking, web containers provide URL rewriting as a backup mechanism. *URL rewriting* works by embedding the session ID in all URLs in the generated response, ensuring that the session ID is returned to the container when the user clicks a link or submits a form embedded in the response.

URL rewriting requires the page author to encode all URLs pointing back to the web application. It's easy to do with the JSTL <c:url> action:

```
<a href="<c:url value="details.do?id=${prod.id}"/>">
  <c:out value="${prod.name}"/></a>
```

Even for an application in which you can make demands on the browsers being used (e.g., an intranet application), it's a good idea to do this up front to prepare for the day when you no longer have this control.

Caching

As discussed in Chapter 3, a thorough understanding and application of caching techniques is of enormous importance for web applications. This section describes specific things to be aware of when using JSP.

Cache Data Used in Pages

In an enterprise application, how and where data is cached is usually controlled by a servlet. Because JSP uses servlet technology as its foundation, a JSP page has access to the same standard cache repositories as a servlet: sessions for per-user caching and context attributes for application-wide caching. Hence, a JSP page can easily read the cached data maintained by servlets with the standard <jsp:getProperty> action and JSTL EL expressions.

While letting a servlet handle caching is typically the right choice, there are exceptions to this rule. Read-only data that is only of marginal importance to the application is often better managed by the JSP page that renders it. One example of this is an external news feed, used just to make the web application more appealing to its users. A JSP page can retrieve the news in XML from a Rich Site Summary (RSS) service, parse it, and transform it to a suitable format using the JSTL XML actions. With a templating solution such as the one described earlier, the news listing can easily be included in all pages throughout the site without interfering with the main application code.

Caching is, of course, important for this scenario; retrieving and formatting the data is time- and processor-intensive. Incurring this cost for every request is a waste of resources and loads the RSS server unnecessarily. The processed data can be cached using standard and JSTL actions, like this:

```
<c:set var="cachePeriod" value="${60 *60 *1000}"/>
<jsp:useBean id="now" class="java.util.Date"/>
<c:if test="${(now.time - cacheTime) > cachePeriod}">
  <c:import url="http://meerkat.oreillynet.com/?&p=4999&_fl=xml&t=ALL"
    var="xmlSource"/>
  <c:import url="/shared/news.xsl" var="xsltSource"/>
  <c:set var="doc" scope="application">
    <x:transform xml="${xmlSource}" xslt="${xstlSource}"/>
  <c:set>
  <c:set var="cacheTime" value="${now.time}" scope="application"/>
</c:if>
...
<c:out value="${doc}" />
```

Inside the <c:if> block, the data is imported, processed, and saved with a timestamp in the application scope. When a new request is received, the cache timestamp is checked to see if the cache is older than the predefined cache period (one hour, in this example). If it is, a fresh copy is imported, transformed, and saved in the application scope again, along with the timestamp; otherwise, the cached data is used.

Consider Enabling Client-Side Caching for Semistatic Pages

Chapter 3 describes how you can set the Last-Modified and Expires headers to allow clients and proxies to cache a response. In an enterprise application, most JSP pages are invoked through a Controller servlet, so the servlet can set these headers for appropriate client-side caching. You must decide which values to use on a case-by-case basis—for instance, using timestamps associated with all data managed by the application, combined with input received with the request.

The Controller can't be in charge of the headers for all JSP pages, though. Some JSP page requests don't go through the Controller at all—for instance, a request for a company info page implemented as a JSP page just to get the common look and feel. The Controller might also not be aware of caching details for nonessential parts of the pages, such as the "news flash" section mentioned earlier. In cases such as this, the JSP page must manage the headers by itself to enable caching.

It's hard to use the Last-Modified header for JSP page caching because the JSP specification does not include a mechanism for asking the JSP page when it was last modified (i.e., there's no standard way to override the getLastModified( ) method in a JSP page). The Expires header can be put to good use, though. You can use a scriptlet or a custom action that sets this header just as you would in a servlet.

What you need to be aware of is that headers cannot be set by a web resource that is included by another resource using the include( ) method in the RequestDispatcher class. This applies to a resource included with the `<jsp:include>` standard action or the JSTL `<c:import>` action because these actions use the `RequestDispatcher` in their implementations. Templating solutions such as the layout page described in this chapter, or Tiles bundled with Struts, typically use the `<jsp:include>` or `<c:import>` actions to include pieces of the response. One way around this is to let the included page tell the layout page which headers should be set. Example 9-8 shows an extended version of the layout page presented in Example 9-2.

Example 9-8. A layout page that sets the Expires header

```
<%@ page contentType="text/html" %>
<%@ taglib prefix="c" uri="http://java.sun.com/jstl/core" %>
<%@ taglib prefix="ora" uri="orataglib" %>

<jsp:useBean id="exp" scope="request" class="java.util.HashMap" />
<c:import url="/vars/default.jsp" />
<c:catch>
  <c:import url="/vars/navigation.jsp" />
</c:catch>
<c:catch>
  <c:import url="/vars/newsflash.jsp" />
</c:catch>
<c:catch>
  <c:import url="/vars/${param.page}.jsp" />
</c:catch>

<%-- Set the lowest requested expiration date --%>
<c:forEach items="${exp}" var="timeInMillis">
  <c:if test="${empty earliest || timeInMillis.value < earliest}">
    <c:set var="earliest" value="${timeInMillis.value}" />
  </c:if>
</c:forEach>
<ora:setDateHeader name="Expires" value="${earliest}" />

<%@ include file="/shared/header.jspf" %>
<table width="90%">
  <tr>
    <td valign="top" align="center" bgcolor="lightblue">
      <c:import url="/shared/navigation.jsp" />
    </td>
    <td valign="middle" align="center" width="80%">
      <c:import url="/pages/${param.page}.jsp" />
    </td>
    <td valign="middle" align="center">
      <c:import url="/shared/newsflash.jsp" />
    </td>
  </tr>
</table>
<%@ include file="/shared/footer.htmlf" %>
```

At the top of the page, a HashMap* is created in the request scope to hold the expiration date values set by the variable-setter pages corresponding to all dynamically included pages, followed by new `<c:import>` actions for the navigation menu and the news-flash variable-setter pages. JSTL actions then process the values in the HashMap to find the earliest expiration date, and the fictitious `<ora:setDateHeader>` custom action sets the Expires header. (This custom action can be implemented in much the same way as the `<ora:setHeader>` action used in the next section, for which the source code is available at *http://TheJSPBook.com*.) A replacement for the custom action is this combination of standard and JSTL actions plus a one-line scriptlet:

```
<c:if test="${!empty earliest}">
  <fmt:parseNumber var="timeAsNumber" value="${earliest}" />
</c:if>
<jsp:useBean id="timeAsNumber" class="java.lang.Number" />
<%
    response.setDateHeader("Expires", timeAsNumber.longValue());
%>
```

The earliest variable value is of type String, so it's first converted to a Number by the JSTL `<fmt:parseNumber>` action, if it's set. The `<jsp:useBean>` action is needed to make this page scope variable accessible to the scriptlet by creating a Java declaration for the variable and assigning it the Number value, or a new instance of a Number (with the value 0) if the earliest variable is not set. Finally, the scriptlet calls the setDateHeader() method on the HttpServletResponse object exposed through the implicit response scripting variable to set the header value.

Example 9-9 shows the variable-setter page for the news-flash page that adds an expiration value representing the next day.

Example 9-9. A variable-setter page adding an expiration date

```
<%@ taglib prefix="c" uri="http://java.sun.com/jstl/core" %>

<jsp:useBean id="now" class="java.util.Date" />
<c:set var="oneDayInMillis" value="${24 * 60 * 60 * 1000}" />
<c:set target="${exp}" property="newsflash"
  value="${now.time + oneDayInMillis}" />
```

This example creates an instance of java.util.Date, uses it to calculate the number of milliseconds representing the next day, and adds this value to the HashMap created by the layout page. It uses its own page name as the key for the value to ensure it's unique.

Note that setting the Expires header—or the Last-Modified header, for that matter—doesn't work as well as it should when URL rewriting is used because the browser

---

* Some sort of list would have been a better choice, but there's no way to add elements to this type of collection without using scripting elements or developing a custom action. The JSTL `<c:set>` action makes it easy to add elements to a Map, though, so that's what is used in this example.

doesn't realize that two URLs for the same page but with different session IDs refer to the same page. The effect is that the caching is limited to the length of the session. You should still consider enabling client-side caching as described here because even short-term caching is better than nothing. Also, for most clients, cookies can be used for session tracking, so this limitation rarely applies.

Prevent Client-Side Caching for Dynamic Pages

Pages that are very dynamic—for instance, a page showing the result of a search based on user input—must not be cached anywhere. As described in Chapter 3, there's a set of headers you can use to prevent caching of such a response. The problem for JSP pages is the same as described in the previous section, but luckily, the solution is the same as well. let the Controller set the headers for the requests it handles; let JSP pages that are invoked directly set their own headers; and for included pages, let the top-level page set them. Building on the example of a solution for the layout page scenario from the previous section, Example 9-10 shows a variable-setter page that adds caching headers to HashMap collections created by the layout page.

Example 9-10. A variable-setter page that adds caching headers

```
<%@ taglib prefix="c" uri="http://java.sun.com/jstl/core" %>

<c:set var="subTitle" scope="request" value="Page 1" />
<c:set target="${exp}" property="page1" value="0" />
<c:set target="headers" property="Cache-Control"
  value="no-store, no-cache, must-revalidate, post-check=0, pre-check=0" />
<c:set target="headers" property="Pragma" value="no-cache" />
```

The page in this example adds the value 0 to the collection for expiration dates to ensure that the layout page sets it to a date far in the past. Even if another variable-setter page adds an expiration value for a date in the future, the value 0 is still used because it's lower. The Cache-Control and Pragma headers are added to a Map named headers.

Example 9-11 shows the top of a layout page extended to handle the cache headers.

Example 9-11. A layout page that sets the Expires and other cache headers

```
<%@ page contentType="text/html" %>
<%@ taglib prefix="c" uri="http://java.sun.com/jstl/core" %>
<%@ taglib prefix="ora" uri="/orataglib" %>

<jsp:useBean id="headers" scope="request" class="java.util.HashMap" />
<jsp:useBean id="exp" scope="request" class="java.util.HashMap" />
<c:import url="/vars/default.jsp" />
<c:catch>
  <c:import url="/vars/navigation.jsp" />
</c:catch>
<c:catch>
```

Example 9-11. A layout page that sets the Expires and other cache headers (continued)

```
  <c:import url="/vars/newsflash.jsp" />
</c:catch>
<c:catch>
  <c:import url="/vars/${param.page}.jsp" />
</c:catch>

<%-- Set cache headers --%>
<c:forEach items="${headers}" var="header">
  <ora:setHeader name="${header.key}" value="${header.value}" />
</c:forEach>

<%-- Set the lowest requested expiration date --%>
...
```

The HashMap for the headers is created at the top of the page. After processing all variable-setter pages, the page loops through all accumulated header values and sets the corresponding response header. A custom action named `<ora:setHeader>` is used in this example to set the headers. (This custom action is included in the tag library for *JavaServer Pages*, Second Edition, with source code available at *http://TheJSP-Book.com*.) You can, of course, use a combination of standard actions, JSTL actions, and scripting code (similar to Example 9-8), or your own simple custom action, if you prefer.

Error Handling

Even a perfectly designed application can fail now and then, through no fault of its own; external resources such as databases or other servers can become inaccessible due to hardware or network problems, or simply because of regular maintenance activities. It's important that the web application deals with such situations, as well as problems caused by unexpected user input, in an appropriate manner. This section provides ideas for how to do so efficiently.

Use Common Error Pages for the Whole Application

The JSP page directive's errorPage attribute can be used to specify a page to be invoked when an error occurs while processing the page. The page can be a static HTML file, a servlet, or a JSP page. A JSP page used as an error page (designated as such by the page directive's isErrorPage attribute) has access to a Throwable instance that represents the error through the implicit exception scripting variable, or through the EL expression ${pageContext.exception}.

While this mechanism might be suitable for a small application using only JSP pages, it's not appropriate for an enterprise application using a combination of servlets, filters, and JSP pages. Using a shared error handler for all these component types lets you better control error handling and fine-tune it in one place when needed. To use a global error handler, do not use the `errorPage` attribute in the JSP pages. Instead, declare an error handler in the web application deployment descriptor (the *web.xml* file):

```
<web-app>
  ...
  <servlet>
    <servlet-name>errorHandler</servlet-name>
    <servlet-class>
      com.ora.jsp.servlets.ErrorHandlerServlet
    </servlet-class>
    <init-param>
      <param-name>errorPage</param-name>
      <param-value>/shared/error.html</param-value>
    </init-param>
  </servlet>
  ...
  <error-page>
    <exception-type>java.lang.Throwable</exception-type>
    <location>/errorHandler</location>
  </error-page>
  ...
</web-app>
```

Here, I define a servlet as the error handler for all types of exceptions; `Throwable` is the base class for all exception, so all more specific exceptions match this single error handler declaration. You can also define separate error handlers for different exception types (the best match wins), as well as error handlers that are triggered by HTTP response status codes instead of exceptions.

Instead of a servlet, you can specify a static HTML page or JSP page as the error handler. A servlet has the advantage in that it can easily capture information about the error and then forward it to a page (a static page or a JSP page) that just describes the problem in user-friendly terms, so that's what I recommend.

If you still like to use a JSP page instead of a servlet, be aware that the implicit exception scripting variable (and the corresponding value available through an EL expression) that is assigned a reference to `Throwable` when the page is invoked because of an `errorPage` attribute in another JSP page is *not* assigned a value when the JSP page is invoked as a global error handler based on a *web.xml* declaration. This is due to an unfortunate naming mismatch between the Servlet 2.3 and JSP 1.2 specifications: the JSP specification says that a request attribute named javax.servlet.jsp. jspException is used for passing `Throwable` to the error page, while the servlet specification defines the javax.servlet.error.exception request attribute for the same thing when passing it to a global error handler. To get access to `Throwable` in a global JSP error handler, you must therefore extract it from the request attribute yourself—for instance, using this JSTL `<c:set>` action:

```
<c:set var="problem"
  value="${requestScope['javax.servlet.error.exception']}" />
```

Capture Enough Information to Fine-Tune the Application

With a common error handler for both servlets and JSP pages, it's easy to log information about runtime errors. By capturing information detailing where the error occurred, the precise problem, and all (or at least most of) the dynamic data available at the time, you can fine-tune the application to deal more gracefully with common, predictable runtime errors.

A global error handler declared with the <error-page> element in the *web.xml* file has access to all information of interest. First of all, it can get information about which component failed and the exception that was thrown through the following request attributes.

Request attribute name	Java type	Description
javax.servlet.error.status_code	Integer	The HTTP status code that triggered a handler declared as a status code handler
javax.servlet.error.exception	Throwable	The exception that triggered a handler declared as an exception handler
javax.servlet.error.request_uri	String	The URL for the request that triggered the handler
javax.servlet.error.servlet_name	String	The declared name for the servlet or JSP page that triggered the handler, or the class name if no name is declared

In addition to the information available through these request attributes, you should also consider logging request parameter values and application-dependent request, session, and context attributes.

Consider Using <c:catch> to Handle Recoverable Errors

If you discover that a JSP page frequently throws an exception due to unexpected input or because an external resource is occasionally unavailable, you should consider catching the exception in the JSP page using the JSTL <c:catch> action. You can then deal with the problem in a more user-friendly way. Consider this example, in which a JSP page includes an external resource that is not essential for the application's main functionality:

```
<table bgcolor="lightblue">
  <tr>
    <td>
      <c:catch var="error">
        <c:import url="http://www.gefionsoftware.com/jspnews.jsp" />
      </c:catch>
      <c:if test="${error != null}">
        Sorry, the news feed is temporarily unavailable.
      </c:if>
    </td>
  </tr>
</table>
```

By catching the potential exception in the JSP page, a response is generated even when the external resource is unavailable.

Custom Component Development

In addition to the JSP elements, you can develop two types of custom components to use in your JSP pages: custom tag libraries and JavaBeans components.

Choosing Between Beans and Custom Actions

Beans and custom actions (packaged in a tag library) are regular Java classes that just happen to adhere to a few rules. This means they can do anything that any Java class can do. Whether it's best to implement application functionality as an action or a bean might not always be clear. My rule of thumb is that a bean is a great carrier of information, and a custom action is great for processing information.

A bean is a perfect vehicle for making information gathered or created in a servlet available to a JSP page. The standard `<jsp:getProperty>` action and the JSTL EL make it easy to access single-value bean properties, and the JSTL `<c:forEach>` action allows you to iterate through a multivalue property such as an array, a `List`, or a `Map`.

A bean can implement methods other than the property accessors to encapsulate functionality intended for use in many different environments, such as applets, servlets, and JSP pages. Calling such a method in a JSP page, however, requires scripting code and should be avoided. A custom action that internally uses the bean is a better choice. The custom action acts as a JSP-specific adapter for the bean to make it easier for a page author to use.

With the introduction of JSTL, the need for custom actions is significantly lower than it used to be, but occasionally, they are still needed. Examples include custom actions for conditional tests not covered by JSTL (e.g., testing if an authenticated user belongs to a specific role) and application-specific formatting (e.g.,, generating a complex table with various groupings and nested levels). Many custom actions of this type are available as open source or commercial offerings, so it's always a good idea to search the Web for solutions. A good place to start is Sun's JSP page: *http://java.sun.com/products/jsp/*. The examples from *JavaServer Pages*, Second Edition, available at *http://TheJSPBook.com/*, also include generic custom actions that you can use in your application.

Consider Using Immutable Objects

In an enterprise application, JSP pages are typically used only to render the response and should not be allowed to modify business objects maintained by other parts of the application. To ensure that a page author doesn't break this contract—by mistake or intentionally—you should consider passing only immutable objects to the JSP page.

An object is immutable if it doesn't expose direct access to its variables and doesn't provide methods that modify its internal state. Make all variables private and do not implement mutator methods—i.e., methods used to change the property values. If the business logic needs to modify the object before passing it to the JSP page, make the mutator methods package-private or wrap the object in a read-only wrapper before you pass it to the JSP page, as shown here:

```java
public class MutableBean {
    private String name;
    private BigDecimal price;
    ...

    public void setName(String name) {this.name = name;}
    public String getName() {return name;}
    public void setPrice(BigDecimal price) {this.price = price;}
    public BigDecimal getPrice() {return price;}
    ...
}

public final class ReadOnlyWrapper {
    private MutableBean bean;

    public ReadOnlyWrapper(MutableBean bean) {this.bean = bean;}

    public String getName() {return bean.getName();}
    public BigDecimal getPrice() {return bean.getPrice();}
    ...
}
```

If the object's variables hold references to mutable objects that must be exposed through public methods, return a copy of the object or an immutable representation instead:

```java
public final class ReadOnlyWrapper {
    private MutableBean bean;

    public ReadOnlyWrapper(MutableBean bean) {this.bean = bean;}

    public String getName() {return bean.getName();}
    public BigDecimal getPrice() {return bean.getPrice();}
    public Date getPublicationDate() {
        return (Date) bean.getPublicationDate().clone();
    }
    public List getAuthorNames() {
        return Collections.unmodifiableList(bean.getAuthorNames());
    }
    ...
}
```

Consider Using a Reset Property When Capturing Input

In a small application, JSP pages can do more than generate responses. The JSP standard `<jsp:setProperty>` action, for instance, makes it easy to capture user input in a bean:

```
<jsp:setProperty name="myBean" property="*" />
```

The `<jsp:setProperty>` action gets a list of all request parameter names and calls all setter methods for bean properties with matching names. The setter methods for properties that don't match a parameter name are not called, nor are setter methods for properties that match parameters with an empty string value.

For a bean in the page or request scope, this is not a problem, assuming the bean provides appropriate default values for the properties that are not set. If the bean instead is kept in the session scope, and the user is supposed to be able to update its values, you need to be careful. The effect of the setter method calling rules is that if the user deselects all checkboxes in a group or leaves a text field empty in the form that invokes the page with the `<jsp:setProperty>` action, the properties representing the checkbox group and the text field are left untouched, not cleared as would be expected.

A workaround for this problem is to add a setter method for a dummy property named reset:

```java
public class MyBean implements Serializable {
    ...
    public void setReset(String dummy) {
        intProperty = -1;
        stringProperty = null;
        ...
    }
}
```

All the setter method does is reset all properties to their default values. The setter method is used like this in the JSP page:

```
<jsp:setProperty name="myBean" property="reset" value="any value"/>
<jsp:setProperty name="myBean" property="*" />
```

The first `<jsp:setProperty>` action resets all properties, and the second sets all properties matching the request parameters.

Always Include the <uri> Element in the TLD

The `<uri>` element in a JSP Tag Library Descriptor (TLD) is an optional element, intended for defining a default URI for the tag library that an authoring tool can use when generating JSP elements:

```
...
<taglib>
  <tlib-version>1.0</tlib-version>
```

```
<jsp-version>1.2</jsp-version>
<short-name>c</short-name>
<uri>http://java.sun.com/jstl/core</uri>
<display-name>JSTL core</display-name>
<description>JSTL 1.0 core library</description>
  ...
```

The auto-discovery feature introduced in JSP 1.2 relies on the presence of this otherwise optional element, however. During application startup, the JSP container scans all files in the application's *WEB-INF* directory (including the content of JAR files) to locate all TLD files. For each TLD it finds, it looks for a <uri> element and records an implicit mapping between the URI and the location of the TLD file. Therefore, all you need to do to use the library is specify this default URI in the taglib directive; the container figures out from its mappings where the corresponding TLD file is. This dramatically simplifies tag library deployment over the mechanisms available in JSP 1.1, so you should always specify a default URI in the TLD for tag libraries you develop.

Design Tag Handler Classes for Instance Pooling

A JSP container is allowed to reuse a tag handler instance to improve performance, as long as it adheres to the strict rules defined in the JSP specification. Briefly, the rules state that a tag handler instance can be used for more than one occurrence of the corresponding custom action element, in the same or different page, only if the same set of attributes is used for all occurrences. Before reusing the tag handler, the container must call the setter methods for attributes that *differ* between the occurrences (ensuring that the correct values are used for each occurrence), but it's *not* required to call the setter methods for attributes with the same value. You should therefore not do anything fancy in the setter methods; just save the value in an instance value and do all the real work in the doXXX() methods: doStartTag(), doAfterBody(), and doEndTag().

While these rules guarantee consistent treatment of the setter methods, they say nothing about how to deal with variable values that are set through other means during the processing of the tag handler. If you believe the release() method is called between each reuse of the tag handler, giving you a chance to reset the internal state, you're wrong, but don't feel bad—the JSP 1.1 specification was unclear about this, and this misunderstanding about the release() method is very common. There's also no guarantee that the doEndTag() method is called; in case of an uncaught exception while processing the body of the custom action element, or in the tag handler itself, the doEndTag() is not called.

The lifecycle rules are arguably complex and nonintuitive, but all you really need to be concerned about is how to deal with tag handler variables not set by the attribute setter methods:

• A default value for an optional attribute can be set in the instance variable declaration, returned by a getter method that is used internally when the attribute has not been set, or handled as needed by the code in the doXXX( ) methods. The rules described earlier guarantee that a tag handler instance is reused only for custom action elements in which the *identical set* of attributes is used, so there's no need to reset variables to their default values.

- An internal variable value that's valid during only one invocation of the tag handler should be reset in the doStartTag( ) method, or in the doFinally( ) method if the tag handler implements the TryCatchFinally interface. Typically, this is needed when a variable is set by tag handlers for nested action elements, such as nested parameter actions that add parameters to a list used by the parent in its doEndTag( ) method. Another example is when a variable set in doStartTag( ) is needed in the other doXXX( ) methods. Use the doStartTag( ) method (because doEndTag( ) might not be called, as described earlier) to reset the variable when it doesn't matter if the reset is delayed for some time; implement the TryCatchFinally interface and reset the variables in doFinally( ) only if it's critical that the value is reset immediately (for instance, if a value represents an expensive resource that must be closed).

- An instance of a helper class that's expensive to create, such as a java.text. SimpleDateFormat object, can be created in the tag handler's constructor and saved in an instance variable until the tag handler is no longer reused to improve performance. The release( ) method gives you a chance to explicitly close such instances, if needed.

If you don't adhere to these rules (especially the second one), your custom tag library will not work correctly in a container that reuses tag handler instances for multiple custom action elements.

Consider Adopting the JSTL Conventions

The JSTL specification defines a number of conventions you should consider following for your own custom tag library to make it easier for a page author familiar with JSTL to use your library. The following JSTL conventions are generic enough to apply to any tag library:

- Expose data created by an action only through scoped variables (i.e., as attributes of the page context, request, session, or application), never as scripting variables. When a scripting element needs access to the data (which should be rare), the standard <jsp:useBean> action can be used to create a scripting variable and assign it a reference to the scoped variable.

- Provide attributes named var and scope (unless the data has "nested visibility"— see next rule) that the page author can use to define the name and scope for the exposed data. If more than one variable is exposed, use the var and scope attributes for the most commonly used variable and provide additional attributes starting with var and scope—e.g., varDom and scopeDom—for the others.

- If the exposed data has "nested visibility"—i.e., it's available only within the action element's body—the scope attribute should not be provided. Instead, the variable should be placed in the page scope before the body is evaluated and removed at the end of the action processing.

- All attributes except var and scope should accept a dynamic value (a Java or EL expression evaluated at runtime). This provides maximum flexibility, while making it possible to introduce type-checking features in a future JSP or JSTL specification.

- Use the Java variable name capitalization rules for compound words in action and attribute names—e.g., `<xmp:ifUserInRole>` and roleName.

- Wherever possible, handle null attribute values gracefully—e.g., by using a default value instead of throwing an exception. Given the nature of the web application environment, a null value is often just an indication of the absence of an optional request parameter, and forcing tests for null and assignments of default values using JSP elements just complicates the JSP page. An exception must, of course, be thrown when there's no way to handle a null value, as well as for other unrecoverable errors.

- When a tag handler catches an exception that it can't handle, it should rethrow it as a JspException with the original exception assigned as the root cause. Most containers log the root cause exception, making it easier to find the real reason for the problem.

The JSTL libraries provide examples of other, less formal, conventions in addition to these, such as exposing a Reader as a variable with nested visibility to avoid double-buffering in some cases, which allows the main input to an action to be provided as either the action element's body or by an attribute, etc. I recommend that you familiarize yourself with the JSTL actions and mimic their syntax and semantics as much as possible when you design your own custom actions.

The most obvious JSTL convention is not listed in this section—namely, allowing attribute values to be set as JSTL EL expressions. The reason for this omission is that the JSTL specification does not expose the EL evaluation API. You can, however, use the API in the Reference Implementation[*] (RI) to add support for EL expressions in your own tag library, but be aware that you must then bundle the RI (or require that it be installed separately). Another reason why it's hard to recommend supporting the EL in your own libraries as a best practice is that if you do so, you will likely want to remove the code for EL support as soon as support for the next version of the JSP specification is commonplace. In the next version of JSP (currently labeled 2.0), the JSP container will be responsible for evaluation of EL expressions so that no extra code is needed for this in the tag handlers.

[*] Available at *http://jakarta.apache.org/taglibs/doc/standard-doc/intro.html*.

Leverage the JSTL Classes and Interfaces

The JSTL specification includes a number of classes and interfaces you can take advantage of when you develop your own custom tag libraries, including one class that can be used by a servlet or a filter to set configuration data used by the JSTL actions (such as the default locale and resource bundle for the formatting actions). It's beyond the scope of this book to show examples of how to use all these classes and interfaces, but here's a list of them so that you're at least aware of their existence and can study them in detail on your own:

`javax.servlet.jsp.jstl.core.Config`
> This class provides methods for reading, setting, and removing configuration data used by the JSTL actions.

`javax.servlet.jsp.jstl.core.ConditionalTagSupport`
> By extending this base class and providing an implementation of its abstract `condition()` method and your custom attribute setter methods, you get a tag handler that can be used exactly like the JSTL `<c:if>` action either to process its body when the condition is true or save the test result as a scoped variable.

`javax.servlet.jsp.jstl.core.LoopTagStatus`
> An object implementing this interface can be obtained from a tag handler that implements the `LoopTag` interface, such as the JSTL `<c:forEach>` action. It provides a number of methods that tell you the current loop index, whether the first or last element is being processed, etc. This allows custom actions intended for use in the body of an iteration action to different things depending on the current iteration position.

`javax.servlet.jsp.jstl.core.LoopTag`
> This interface provides access to a `LoopTagStatus` instance as well as the current iteration element. It's implemented by the `<c:forEach>` action, and if you implement it in your own iteration actions, nested actions that need to know about the iteration status will work with your custom action as well.

`javax.servlet.jsp.jstl.core.LoopTagSupport`
> This is a base class you can extend to implement your own iteration actions. You need to implement three methods (`prepare()`, `hasNext()`, and `next()`), plus custom attribute setters, to get a fully functional iteration action with support for the same `begin`, `end`, and `step` attributes as the `<c:forEach>` action. And yes, you guessed it: this class implements the `LoopTag` interface, so nested actions that need to know the iteration status are supported as well.

`javax.servlet.jsp.jstl.fmt.LocaleSupport`
> Tag handlers that need access to localized messages can use the static methods in this class. The algorithms for locating the appropriate resource bundle are the same as those for the JSTL i18n actions.

`javax.servlet.jsp.jstl.fmt.LocalizationContext`

> An instance of this class provides information about a locale and resource bundle. A tag handler, or a servlet or a filter, can set a scoped variable (using the `Config` class) to an instance of this class to establish the defaults for the JSTL i18n actions.

`javax.servlet.jsp.jstl.sql.SQLExecutionTag`

> This interface is implemented by the JSTL `<sql:query>` and `<sql:update>` actions. It provides one method that can be used by a nested custom action to set the value of a parameter placeholder in the SQL statement. You can use this in a custom action that merges information from a number of request parameters, or some other source, to create a single value for the database.

`javax.servlet.jsp.jstl.sql.ResultSupport`

> Static methods in this class convert a JDBC `ResultSet` to a JSTL `Result`—i.e., the type of object exposed by the `<sql:query>` action. It's a simple way for a custom action or servlet to create a cacheable version of a query result that might be handy in some applications.

Using these classes and interfaces will help you build tag libraries that follow the JSTL conventions and minimize your work at the same time.

Consider Developing a Tag Library Validator

To make the page author's life as easy as possible, you should consider implementing a tag library validator for your custom tag library. This type of validator was introduced in JSP 1.2, and it can do a much better job verifying that all custom actions are used correctly than the previous mechanism (the `TagExtraInfo` class) could.

You implement a tag library validator by extending `javax.servlet.jsp.tagext.TagLibraryValidator` and provide an implementation for the abstract `validate( )` method:

```
public ValidationMessage[ ] validate(String prefix, String uri, PageData pd)
```

The container calls this method when it translates the page into a servlet. The parameters provide the validator with the tag library prefix, URI (declared by the `taglib` directive in the page), and, most importantly, a `PageData` instance. Through the `PageData` instance, the validator gains access to an XML representation of the complete page (called an *XML view*). With access to the full page in a format that's easy to parse, it can make sure the actions are properly nested and appear in the right order, in addition to what's always been possible: checking the proper use of all attributes for each individual custom action element.

The `validate( )` method returns an array of `ValidationMessage` objects. Each object represents a validation error, containing a text message plus a unique element ID that the container can use to map the error message to the location of the corresponding

---

element in the JSP source file. A JSP 1.2 container is not required to support the ID mechanism, but many do, so this greatly enhances the error-reporting capabilities compared to the old TagExtraInfo mechanism. In the next version of the JSP specification, support for ID mapping will be a mandatory container requirement.

Deployment

JSP pages are typically deployed as is in the public document structure of a web application. The container converts each JSP file to a Java class file the first time it's requested, or possibly as part of the web application deployment process. Deploying the source files is not the only option, though.

Consider Precompilation

An alternative to deploying JSP pages directly is to precompile them into the corresponding JSP page implementation classes and deploy only the class files. The main advantage is that the container invokes the class file immediately instead of going through the JSP container and checking if the source file has changed, resulting in slightly better performance. If you deliver applications to third parties, the fact that the JSP pages cannot be modified can be an advantage, but it can also be a disadvantage because the customer might want to adjust the look and feel of the application.

The class files for the JSP pages can be packaged in a JAR file and dropped in the *WEB-INF/lib* directory. In addition, the *web.xml* file must include mappings for all JSP page URLs to the corresponding class files:

```
<web-app>
  ...
  <servlet>
    <servlet-name>mypage</servlet-name>
    <servlet-class>org.apache.jsp.mypage$jsp</servlet-class>
  </servlet>
  ...
  <servlet-mapping>
    <servlet-name>mypage</servlet-name>
    <url-pattern>mypage.jsp</url-pattern>
  </servlet-mapping>
  ...
</web-app>
```

Most containers include a tool for precompiling the JSP pages in a web application. Tomcat 4, for instance, comes with a command-line tool called JspC, which can be used to compile all JSP pages and generate the required *web.xml* declarations, like this:

```
[tomcat@frontier tomcat]$ cd /usr/local/jakarta-tomcat-4.0.4/bin
[tomcat@frontier bin]$ jspc -d ~/jspsrc -webinc ~/jspsrc/web.inc
-webapp ../webapps/ora
```

The command creates servlet source files for all JSP files in the application located in the directory specified by the -webapp option and saves the generated files in the directory specified by the -d option. It also writes all servlet and URL mapping elements needed for *web.xml* in the file specified by the -webinc option. To compile the source files, you must set the classpath to include all classes that your application uses—for instance, all the tag libraries and beans, as well as the Tomcat JAR files *common/lib/servlet.jar* and *lib/jasper-runtime.jar*. When you deploy the compiled JSP pages, the classes in the Tomcat *lib/jasper-runtime.jar* file must also be deployed because the generated JSP classes depend on them. If you use a different container, read the documentation to see which compile time and runtime classes you need to include, as well as how to use their compilers.

CHAPTER 10

JavaMail Best Practices

William Crawford

JavaMail is the Java 2 Enterprise Edition (J2EE) API that deals with Internet messaging services. While it is normally associated with Internet email, it was designed as a protocol-independent approach to electronic messaging, allowing support for a wide variety of point-to-point message transport mechanisms. JavaMail *service providers* divide the messaging world into *stores*, which hold incoming messages, and *transports*, which launch messages toward a destination. Message objects are used to represent individual emails, and a Session object is used to tie message stores, transports, and messages together. The general capability set of Internet email provides the least common denominator functionality.

The standard JavaMail implementation from Sun provides for POP3 and IMAP message stores, and for SMTP message transport. All three of these protocols support Internet email. An experimental NNTP client is also available from Sun, and various third parties provide support for other messaging systems.* The API is currently at Version 1.2; 1.3 should be finalized and released by the time you read this.

I assume you have some general familiarity with the basic concepts of the JavaMail API. If you've never programmed with JavaMail, this chapter can be seen as the sequel to Chapter 12 of *Java Enterprise in a Nutshell*, Second Edition by myself, Jim Farley, and David Flanagan (O'Reilly).

In this chapter I'll cover strategies for using JavaMail to effectively interact with end users, both to publish information and respond to commands. My real focus is on how email in general, and JavaMail in particular, can be usefully and effectively integrated with J2EE applications.

You'll also see how to use JavaMail to enable connections between different information systems and web services. To get there, we'll start by looking at some different ways of sending messages and managing message content, including how to use the

---

* As of this writing, I have been unable to find any Microsoft Exchange providers for JavaMail. Users who need to access email from an Exchange server via Java need to install the Exchange IMAP bridge.

most effective form of email for the task at hand. We'll then look at how software can effectively retrieve and manage incoming email and address strategies for integrating JavaMail into an enterprise messaging framework. We'll talk about integrating email with web services via the Java API for XML messaging, and finish up by addressing three common JavaMail performance and flexibility bottlenecks.

Understanding Enterprise Email

When developers gather to talk about enterprise development tools, plain old email doesn't come up all that often. Email support wasn't even included in the first editions of the J2EE platform, despite the availability of a relevant Java API. That's surprising: if you're reading this book it's pretty much a given that you use email almost every day. Email is part of the bedrock infrastructure of the Internet, the primary communications conduit for the everyday business of technology (and these days, pretty much everything else). Email traffic between people and computer systems has already hit several hundred billion messages per year, and is expected to double by 2006.

Internet email* has a few very interesting advantages for developers. First, it's simple. Messages start with a sender and end with a recipient. Sometimes there is more than one recipient, but that's about as complex as it gets. The mechanics of delivery are largely abstracted away from the user: the average, avid emailer can't tell you the difference between SMTP, POP, and IMAP, or even Exchange and Lotus Notes, and doesn't care, either. Unlike Enterprise JavaBeans (EJBs), relational databases, or even web links, with Internet email no complex conceptualization is required for end users.

Second, email is ubiquitous. Setting up secure, high-performance email servers can be a bit complex, but participating as a client, whether sending or retrieving messages, is a simple task that can be performed by any network-connected system with a minimal amount of work. Using only the core Java networking support, a programmer can add support for sending email in a few lines of code.

Finally, email is flexible. The original Internet email system was designed to deliver text messages from point to point, but didn't specify anything about the content of those messages. Modern Internet email is essentially the same system that was formalized in 1982 by RFC 822: the only real change made was the introduction of MIME, the Multimedia Internet Mail Extensions, back in 1996. MIME gave email messages the ability to exchange any kind of content, rather than just text, by standardizing the

---

* For the rest of this chapter, we will talk about "email" with the understanding that we're talking about email sent over the Internet using SMTP and retrieved via POP3 or IMAP. This doesn't mean that proprietary email systems, such as Microsoft Exchange, are left out of the strategies developed in this chapter. Vendors saw where the wind was blowing a long time ago, and every proprietary email system now provides a bridge to standard Internet email.

schemes for encoding bytes into text and identifying what those bytes were supposed to be after they were turned back.

Of course, because the Internet email infrastructure is two decades old (and based on even older software), it does not provide some of the features modern systems require. First and foremost, SMTP, the delivery mechanism responsible for shipping messages between systems, provides no quality-of-service guarantees. This has been dealt with somewhat by mail server developers, who typically design their products to return messages to the original sender when a message proves to be undeliverable, but this functionality is neither required nor standardized. And there's no guarantee that the warning message won't get lost in turn.

Message routing is also notably absent. Email has an origin point and a destination point. It can be routed through multiple intermediaries while in transit, but the sender has no way of knowing this in advance, no way to specify it, and no reasonable expectation that the intermediaries will do anything interesting with the message.

Finally, email is insecure. There is no native support for encryption, no support for message signing, and no mechanism for any kind of use authorization. Anyone can easily send a message to anyone, identifying themselves as anyone else. Email messages, without some extension, can be repudiated: the supposed sender can plausibly deny responsibility. It's harder to intercept email meant for someone else, but still very possible.

All three of these drawbacks stem from email's heritage as a person-to-person messaging system on relatively small networks, rather than as a part of the world-girdling Internet of today. Even today these limitations have not proven to be crippling for the original intention, with the notable and infamous exception of the flood of unsolicited commercial email that has become the bane of virtually everyone with a semi-public email address, and the rise of malicious mobile code that uses unsecured email clients as the primary infection vector.

These three issues also limit the use of email as a messaging platform within or between applications. Message-oriented middleware (MOM), accessible from Java via the JMS API and message-driven EJBs, can provide messaging services between systems. But a variety of reasons, including interoperability, availability, and cost, limit the MOM approach, and email can often be used creatively to fill that gap.

Sending Email

JavaMail's mechanism for creating new outgoing email messages is quite simple: instantiate a `MimeMessage` object, add content, and send via a transport. Adding file attachments is only a little more complex: simply create a message part for each component (body text, file attachments, etc.), add them to a multipart container, and add the container to the message. Example 10-1 should act as a quick refresher.

Example 10-1. Multipart mail send

```
import javax.mail.*;
import javax.mail.internet.*;
import javax.activation.*;
import java.io.File;
import java.util.Properties;
...
public class MimeAttach {
...
  public static void main(String[ ] args) {
    try {
      Properties props = System.getProperties( );
      props.put("mail.smtp.host", "mail.company.com");
      Session session = Session.getDefaultInstance(props, null);
      ...
      Message msg = new MimeMessage(session);
      msg.setFrom(new InternetAddress("logs@company.com"));
      msg.setRecipient(Message.RecipientType.TO,
                       new InternetAddress("root@company.com"));
      msg.setSubject("Today's Logs");
      ...
      Multipart mp = new MimeMultipart( );
      MimeBodyPart mbp1 = new MimeBodyPart( );
      mbp1.setContent("Log file for today is attached.", "text/plain");
      ...
      mp.addBodyPart(mbp1);
      ...
      File f = new File("/var/logs/today.log");
      MimeBodyPart mbp = new MimeBodyPart( );
      mbp.setFileName(f.getName( ));
      mbp.setDataHandler(new DataHandler(new FileDataSource(f)));
      mp.addBodyPart(mbp);
      ...
      msg.setContent(mp);
      Transport.send(msg);
    } catch (MessagingException me) {
      me.printStackTrace( );
    }
  }
}
```

This example essentially does everything you might want to do when sending a message: it creates a mail session, creates a message, assigns message headers, and creates multipart content.

Use Dynamic Content Strategies

To get the most out of the power and flexibility of Java and JavaMail when building email-based applications, use dynamic content strategies to reduce coding, increase flexibility, and improve user response.

Many JavaMail applications use email as a publishing medium. Most major web sites, whether magazines, newspaper sites, developer communities, weblogs, or retail, provide some degree of email capability. Some of this information is broadcast: newsletter subscriptions, update announcements, and so forth. Other messages are related to transactions: subscription confirmations, order status announcements, receipts, reports, etc. By reaching from the web site into the user's mailbox, well designed, useful messaging support can make existing applications more valuable by increasing the likelihood that they'll actually be used.

JavaMail can be used to send one message to a large number of recipients, but given the other tools available, it really isn't a particularly efficient mechanism for sending spam. Instead, JavaMail (and Java) are ideally suited to dynamically building extremely rich messages targeted at particular users of an application.

Let's look at some examples on the public Internet and the private intranet. Every morning, the *New York Times* sends me several emails. One of them is a headlines summary, which includes a number of sections that I've indicated interest in. When I registered on the *NYT* web site, I was able to specify that I wanted all the headlines in national news, politics, technology, and Op-Ed. Because I'm not a New Yorker I didn't ask for the Metro section. I kept the Sports section, but asked for only one headline. I also had the opportunity to specify that I wanted to get my headlines in HTML format rather than plain text.

My daily *NYT* email is much more complex than the average newsletter. Rather than sending the same piece of content to every subscriber, as most newsletters do, the *NYT* system looks through the available stories, customizes a set of data according to my preferences, formats it appropriately, and sends it to me. This process is repeated for each subscriber.

Email "push," such as what the *New York Times* offers, is an incredibly useful tool for all kinds of enterprise applications. Beyond the obvious examples (content sites, retailers sending suggestions to customers, and so on), email reports, such as sales forecasts, transaction summaries, and usage statistics, can be valuable on the intranet as well. Building user acceptance is often one of the biggest challenges IT staffs face when rolling out a new system. Bringing the application to the users, in this case by automatically publishing important information, can save users time and increase the likelihood that the application will be used.

Use XML for Content

Content management across multiple sets of user preferences and multiple kinds of content can be a real chore. Building up the contents of most kinds of email messages in Java is a bad idea: you'll need to recompile for every change. To speed up the process, you can use XML to build the content, and define a set of XSL stylesheets to transform it into plain text or HTML based on the users' preferences.

This takes the content and formatting out of the code, and allows redesigns to be implemented by changing the XSL. The XML can be generated by the Java program (which might be the case if the XML input is customized on a per-user basis, such as with receipts or custom newsletters), or it can be generated externally. You can also swap out XSL stylesheets according to user preferences—for example, this would allow you to easily brand a service to particular clients by associating stylesheets with certain users and feeding the XML content through their customized stylesheet.

Here's a brief example of how XSL can be easily integrated with JavaMail via JAXP and a JAXP-compatible XSLT transformer. I've omitted most of the surrounding code for clarity.

```
import javax.xml.transform.*;
import javax.xml.transform.stream.*;
...
// Class support here. These can be cached.
...
TransformerFactory tFactory =
                javax.xml.transform.TransformerFactory.newInstance();
...
Transformer htmlTF = tFactory.newTransformer
        (new StreamSource("contentToHtml.xsl"));
...
Transformer textTF = tFactory.newTransformer
        (new StreamSource("contentToText.xsl"));
...
// Build content, place it in "content.xml", and set useHtml variable to user pref.
...
ByteArrayOutputStream bos = new ByteArrayOutputStream();
Transformer transformer = (useHtml ? htmlTF : textTF);
...
transformer.transform
    (new StreamSource("content.xml"),
     new StreamResult(bos));
...
// Add result to JavaMail message.
message.setContent(bos.toString(), (useHtml ? "text/html" : "text/plain"));
```

Use Templates for Repeated Content

In addition to using XML for content, some applications benefit from using templating engines for content generation. This approach allows easy maintenance of standard email messages (such as notifications, account management messages, and errors) in which the main content remains consistent, but individual details (such as account names, passwords, and confirmations) vary from message to message.

A templating engine takes a plain-text template, replaces placeholding elements with data, and returns the result to the client. The enterprise development world is littered with examples, the most important of which is JavaServer Pages (JSP).

Example 10-2 shows a templated email using the Velocity template system from the Apache Jakarta project (for more information on Velocity, see *http://jakarta.apache.org/velocity*). Velocity takes this template and replaces the $username and $password lines with the data provided for it.

Example 10-2. newuser.vm

```
You have been added to our system!
Your login information is:
...
Username: $username
Password: $password
...
Please do not give these out to anyone. For assistance,
please contact customer support at 212-555-2333
```

Example 10-3 shows a small Java program that starts Velocity, provides the new username and password values, processes the template, and sends the email. For brevity, I accept the new username and password as read, but you can integrate this code into a Java servlet or other environment to easily incorporate standardized mail messages into your applications.

Example 10-3. MailTemplater.java

```
import java.io.*;
import java.util.*;
import javax.mail.*;
import javax.mail.internet.*;
import javax.activation.*;
...
import org.apache.velocity.*;
import org.apache.velocity.app.Velocity;
...
public class MailTemplater {
...
 public static void main(String[] args) throws IOException {
...
    try {
      Properties velocityProperties = new Properties();
      velocityProperties.setProperty(
              org.apache.velocity.runtime.Runtime.FILE_RESOURCE_LOADER_PATH,
              "c:/");

      Velocity.init(velocityProperties);
      ...
      VelocityContext context = new VelocityContext();
      context.put("username", "billg");
      context.put("password", "windows");
      ...
      Properties props = System.getProperties();
      props.put("mail.smtp.host", "mail.attbi.com");
      Session session = Session.getDefaultInstance(props, null);
```

Example 10-3. MailTemplater.java (continued)

```
    ...
    Message msg = new MimeMessage(session);
    msg.setFrom(new InternetAddress("support@company.com"));
    msg.setRecipient(Message.RecipientType.TO,
                    new InternetAddress("user@client.com"));
    msg.setSubject("New User Account");
    ...
    StringWriter messageContent = new StringWriter();
    Template template = Velocity.getTemplate("newuser.vm");
    template.merge(context, messageContent);
    msg.setText(messageContent.toString());
    ...
    Transport.send(msg);

  } catch (Exception e) {
    e.printStackTrace();
  }
}
}
```

Accommodate Various Client Capabilities

Email messages sent by an application must support the widest variety of email clients possible. While the majority of Internet email users have by now upgraded to mail clients that support HTML content, a sizeable minority have not. You've just seen how to send a simple email with a plain-text body and create HTML or plain-text output according to user preferences known ahead of time. The latter is an ideal solution when generating customized content for known users but breaks down a bit when sending more generic messages, such as system announcements or newsletters, to larger groups of users in which user preference information isn't available. Add in the users who can support HTML mail but have intentionally turned off the feature in their client, and it turns out that sending HTML mail exclusively alienates a large portion of your potential audience.

One possible solution is simply to avoid HTML mail entirely and cater to the lowest common denominator. This is the way to go if maximum accessibility is important. However, the MIME standard does offer another option. When a MIME-compliant email program reads a normal multipart message, it treats the first part as the message body, which is displayed to the user, and the subsequent parts as file attachments:

```
    Multipart mp = new MimeMultipart("alternative");
    MimeBodyPart mbp1 = new MimeBodyPart();
    mbp1.setContent("Log file for today is attached.", "text/plain");
    mp.addBodyPart(mbp1);
    ...
    MimeBodyPart mbp2 = new MimeBodyPart();
    mbp2.setContent("Log file for <b>today</b> is attached.", "text/html");
    mp.addBodyPart(mbp2);
    ...
```

Use Multipart/Related for Rich Messages

To ensure that they can be read as easily as possible, richly formatted messages should be completely self-contained, instead of relying on images or resources available on a server. The MIME standard provides another special multipart type: "related". Related parts can refer to each other via URIs pointing to the Content-ID, or "CID," associated with each part. A CID URI takes the form "cid:contentid". You can use the setHeader( ) method of MimeBodyPart to create known content IDs for each message part. Once this is done, HTML parts can, for example, display an image by referring to the message part containing the image data.

The following example contains an HTML part that includes an <img> tag pointing to the "cid:myimage" URI. It also contains a second part containing a GIF image with a content ID of "myimage".

```
...
Message msg = new MimeMessage(session);
msg.setFrom(new InternetAddress("images@company.com"));
msg.setRecipient(Message.RecipientType.TO,
                new InternetAddress("bob.cratchett@company.com"));
msg.setSubject("Image Email");
Multipart multipartRelated = new MimeMultipart("related");
MimeBodyPart mbp = new MimeBodyPart();

mbp.setContent(
  "<html><body><img src=\"cid:myimage\"></body></html>", "text/html");
multipartRelated.addBodyPart(mbp);
...
MimeBodyPart mbp2 = new MimeBodyPart();
mbp2.setDataHandler(new DataHandler(new FileDataSource("c:\\inline.gif")));
mbp2.setFileName("inline.gif");
mbp2.setHeader("Content-ID","myimage");
multipartRelated.addBodyPart(mbp2);

msg.setContent(multipartRelated);
...
```

Using the related type does bulk up the size of your messages, but it allows them to be read when the recipient is offline or when the web server that would otherwise provide the images is inaccessible. It also gives you control over the resource requirements for sending messages (you don't need to be able to support massive numbers of hits on your web site if every recipient decides to read the message at once).*

---

* There are two advantages to embedding links to images on a web server rather than embedding them in the message itself. First, you can reduce message sizes, which is valuable in some situations. Second, you have the opportunity to watch your web server logs to determine whether a message has been read. Use this capability with care, as it requires the user to have a live Internet connection when reading mail and also raises some potentially thorny privacy issues.

Use Related Alternatives

The related MIME type alone does not provide a plain-text alternative for browsers that don't support pretty graphics. If you add a text part to the preceding message, the text will display along with the HTML, rather than instead of it. Fortunately, JavaMail allows you to nest `Multipart` objects, so you can create a top-level "multipart/alternative" and include both a plain-text option and a "multipart/related" section containing HTML and supporting resources.

`Multipart` objects cannot be added directly to each other, but must be wrapped into a `MimeBodyPart` first. You can easily extend the earlier example to do this:

```
Multipart topLevel = new MimeMultipart("alternative");

MimeBodyPart htmlContent = new MimeBodyPart();
htmlContent.setContent(multipartRelated);
MimeBodyPart textAlternate = new MimeBodyPart();
textAlternate.setText("Guidelines");

topLevel.addBodyPart(textAlternate);
topLevel.addBodyPart(htmlContent);
msg.setContent(topLevel);
```

Recipients with HTML capability will now see the HTML version with the embedded graphics, and users with text-only capability will see the text version. Older clients will see everything, but placing the text part at the beginning of the message ensures that they'll be able to make some sense of what's going on.

Of course, the XSL approach can also be used to create the plain text and HTML content for multipart/alternative and multipart/related messages.

Email for System Integration

Most developers are familiar with controlling remote applications via email. Almost anyone who has ever subscribed to a mailing list has emailed a subscription request, a status change, or an unsubscribe to *listserver@somecompany.com*, and received a response indicating that action was taken. More recently, emails to customer service addresses at major companies are read first by software, which attempts to match them to a set of prewritten FAQs, and then are passed to a human only if no relevant FAQ can be found. Even then, the human customer service employees might handle the request via a web interface that serves up each incoming message, allows them to enter a response, and dispatches the result back to the customer.

Consider Email as an Enterprise Bridge

Email can provide an inexpensive, easy-to-implement linkage between multiple applications.

Most email exchanges expect that a human will be on at least one side of the conversion. In a J2EE setting, this is still often true, but not always. The BugZilla open source bug-tracking system, for instance, implements synchronization between installation by sending emails containing XML representations of the data being synchronized. Each instance periodically checks an email address for messages from the other system and uses the contents to update its own database. This implementation allows synchronization between bug databases running on different networks, across firewalls and VPNs, and without system availability concerns because the messages are queued.

This strategy is most effective on internal networks that are already secured, or when the security requirements of the application are minimal. However, when coupled with the security practices discussed later in this chapter, this approach can be used safely and effectively in a wide variety of contexts.

When implementing systems that receive email, consider existing options before creating your own. The James Mail Server, from the Apache Software Foundation, is a pure Java SMTP, IMAP, and POP mail server. James is built around the JavaMail APIs and introduces the concept of a "maillet," which is somewhat like a Java servlet but processes incoming email instead of incoming HTTP requests. If you're considering building advanced mail-handling support into an application, James is worth considering, as it provides mail transport and storage services along with a framework for processing incoming messages.

Retrieve Incoming Mail Efficiently

Inefficient access to email message stores can result in performance degradation.

If you're using messaging middleware, J2EE provides a convenient way to receive incoming messages via message-driven EJBs. The J2EE container will deliver messages to EJBs as they arrive from the external messaging server. While some message queue vendors might have "email bridge" support built into their products, there is no specific J2EE mechanism for receiving messages.

In most cases, including whenever a POP3 message store is involved, you have to explicitly check for mail, and J2EE applications have a few methods for doing so. The first is to check in response to some user activity, either in an EJB session bean or a Java servlet. In most cases, this is not a terribly useful thing to do. Users will not respond well to a three- or four-second (or potentially much longer) wait while the system takes care of housekeeping that is not related to the task at hand.

Instead of holding users hostage to the mail component, most applications deal with mail retrieval by launching one or more background worker threads. This generally has to be done at the application's controller layer, usually by launching a thread from a servlet's initialization method or when the servlet context is being initialized. Remember that EJBs are explicitly forbidden from creating or maintaining threads of any kind. For more information, see the section "Use an Email Management Framework" later in this chapter.

JavaMail supports a listener framework for inboxes, which is discussed in the next section.

A final option involves a standalone application running in its own Java Virtual Machine (JVM), periodically waking up to check mail and then transferring the contents of the incoming messages to another system for processing (such as connecting to an EJB session bean or a simple object access protocol [SOAP] service). You'll see how to quickly ship JavaMail messages off to SOAP-based web services later in this chapter.

Use Inbox Listeners Carefully

JavaMail allows you to assign a listener to a message store, assuming that the server supports adding new messages while a user is connected. IMAP does, but POP3 does not. To be notified when a new message arrives, create a new class implementing MessageCountListener and associate it with a Folder object. The messagesAdded( ) method will be called whenever messages are added to the folder.

In most real-life situations this isn't a great way to go. It requires keeping the connection to the server open, which consumes network resources. The mail server might decide to time you out, or a network problem could knock out the connection. Some servers place a limit on the amount of time one user can be connected. So if you take this approach, implement the ConnectionListener interface and associate it with the folder and message store objects. This will allow you to recreate the connection and folder and assign a new listener.

Choose an Effective Delivery Mechanism

Because JavaMail doesn't provide any provision for having mail delivered to an application, there is an architectural decision to be made regarding how incoming messages will be retrieved. In practice, this comes down to deciding whether you want to retrieve messages from an IMAP mailbox or a POP3 mailbox. In some environments this decision will be made for you, but when possible, it's helpful to evaluate the two options.

POP3 has the advantage of simplicity. It's almost impossible to find a mail server that doesn't support POP, and implementations are very mature. The protocol itself is older and is geared toward listing, retrieving, and deleting messages from a single, undifferentiated pool. For simple process flows, such as when one mailbox is dedicated to a particular application and the application deletes messages after retrieving them, POP is generally the best choice.

POP falls short when dealing with complex message stores. It has no support for folders, no query system, and minimal support for downloading parts of messages. This is where IMAP comes in. Like POP, IMAP allows clients to connect to remote message stores. However, while POP assumes that the client will download messages and store them locally, IMAP assumes that messages will be stored on the server and provides support for multiple mailbox folders to aid in organization. More advanced IMAP implementations can provide a degree of write access to the contents of the message store, as well as server-side queries to find particular messages.

IMAP has been around long enough that it is almost as ubiquitous as POP, and it can offer some real advantages when building email-enabled applications. Mail for multiple applications (or multiple types of messages for a single application) can be directed to IMAP folders via rules on the server, allowing the JavaMail application to read particular folders rather than scan every message. Folders can also be used to store messages after they've been dealt with by an application.

Beware Email in Transactions

Every interface between two applications creates a potential transactional nightmare. Introducing email collection into an application introduces the need to maintain an external resource, i.e., the incoming mailbox. Needless to say, the transaction support in J2EE was not intended to handle this kind of activity. If an EJB session bean uses JavaMail to send email or delete a message from a mailbox, rolling the transaction back will not unsend or restore the messages.

Commercial enterprise messaging systems sometimes have features that allow the sender of a message to control the message after it has been sent. Standard email does not have this capability, so once a message has left the flow of execution it cannot be recalled.

When sending messages, try to hold off until the very end of a transaction, and try to design your transactions so that user input, particularly if provided via email that might arrive at an indefinite time in the future, comes at a break between transactions. If the transaction must send an email to a live user early in the process, it should send the user another message if the transaction is rolled back.

Cut and Run

The best practice for incorporating incoming email into your applications is to get the message out of the email layer as quickly as possible and into a transaction that can be controlled more tightly. The mailbox should never be used as a receptacle for data related to an ongoing process. Instead, the mail should be read out as quickly as possible and loaded into another queue. A database is an obvious choice here.

When retrieving messages, log in, do your business, and log out as quickly as possible. Staying connected and periodically polling for new messages consumes network resources, which is reason enough to try and avoid doing this, but this also makes it much more difficult to write code that will properly handle dropped connections to the mail server.

Connecting to most well-written servers will obtain a lock on the mailbox. If there is any possibility at all that more than one thread (or more than one application) will access a mailbox at the same time, each thread or application should be aware of the possibility of conflict, and should fail gracefully when this happens. For the same reason, applications should be sure to close connections as soon as possible to free up access to the resource. If this can be avoided, so much the better.

Needless to say, information about the state of a mailbox should be considered out-of-date as soon as the connection to the mailbox is closed. This is particularly true of the message IDs provided by the message store, which are not constant or unique beyond the context of the current connection.

Use an Email Management Framework

Single applications should have as few points of contact with the external email layer as possible. This allows the centralization of logic to deal with concurrency issues—only one thread ever accesses the mailbox. To help you out with this, I present a basic framework for handling incoming messages. The framework is based on the Strategy design pattern, which allows you to plug in different kinds of processing behavior.[*] Having this framework will allow you to easily extend your applications to handle different kinds of messages by creating new instances of a monitoring thread pointed at different mailboxes and passing in handler objects that know how to deal with particular message types.

Start by declaring an interface that can be implemented by classes that will be able to handle incoming messages. I will keep it simple for this example, so you will define just one kind of interface, a BlockingMailHandler, which handles a particular message and returns when processing for that message has completed. (See Example 10-4.)

Example 10-4. BlockingMailHandler

```
public interface BlockingMailHandler
{
  public boolean handleMessage(javax.mail.Message message);
}
```

---

[*] For more information on this and other design patterns for software engineering, and on design patterns themselves, check out *Design Patterns: Elements of Reusable Object-Oriented Software* by Erich Gamma, Richard Helm, Ralph Johnson, and John Vlissides (Addison-Wesley).

A more complete implementation would result in a `BlockingMailHandler` from a `MailHandler`, and probably define an `AsynchronousMailHandler` as well.

To handle incoming messages, you create a class that implements the `BlockingMailHandler` interface and does something interesting in the `handleMessage()` method. The handler implementation is responsible for any thread synchronization issues. If the ultimate target of an incoming message (or the information it contains) is a Java object, that object generally shouldn't implement the `BlockingMailHandler` interface directly. Instead, create a new class that acts as an intermediary for the target object. If the target is an EJB, you don't have any choice in the matter—you must implement a wrapper class.

Now, you'll define a `MailMonitor` thread class, which takes a `BlockingMailHandler` and feeds it incoming messages (see Example 10-5). You can construct a new `MailMonitor` when initializing a servlet context, or launch it from a standalone application. Each `MailMonitor` thread will wake up every 30 seconds and retrieve all the messages in a mailbox. Each message is processed by the handler, which returns true or false to indicate whether the message should be deleted.

Example 10-5. MailMonitor

```
import javax.mail.*;
import javax.mail.internet.*;
import java.io.*;
...
public class MailMonitor extends Thread {
  boolean interrupted = false;
  BlockingMailHandler handler = null;

  public MailMonitor(BlockingMailHandler mh) {
    handler = mh;
  }
  ...
  public void stopRunning() {
    interrupted = true;
  }

  public void run() {
    Session session = Session.getDefaultInstance(System.getProperties());
    Store store = null;
    try {
      store = session.getStore("imap");
    } catch (NoSuchProviderException nspe) {
      nspe.printStackTrace();
      return;
    }
    ...
    while(!interrupted) {
      try {
        if (!store.isConnected()) // Should always be true
          store.connect("mail.invantage.com", -1, "carl", "carl@mit");
```

Example 10-5. MailMonitor (continued)

```
        Folder folder = store.getDefaultFolder( );
        folder = folder.getFolder("INBOX");
        if (folder == null) {
          System.out.println("Unable to open INBOX");
          return;
        }
        ...
        // Try to open read/write. Open read-only if that fails.
        try {
          folder.open(Folder.READ_WRITE);
        } catch (MessagingException ex) {
          folder.open(Folder.READ_ONLY);
        }
        ...
        int totalMessages = folder.getMessageCount( );

        try {
          Message messages[ ] = null;
          messages = folder.getMessages(1, totalMessages);
          ...
          for (int i = 0, n = messages.length; i < n; i++) {
            boolean mbDelete = handler.handleMessage(messages[i]);
            // Delete the message.
            if (mbDelete) {
              messages[i].setFlag(Flags.Flag.DELETED, true);
            }
          } // End for
        } catch (MessagingException e) {
        System.out.println("Unable to get Messages");
        }
        ...
        // Close the folder and message store.
        folder.close(true); // Purge deleted messages
        store.close( );
        ...
      } catch (MessagingException e) {
        System.out.println(e.toString( ));
        return;
      }

      try {
        this.sleep(30 * 1000);
      } catch (InterruptedException e) {
        System.out.println("Exiting");
        return;
      }
    }
  }
}
...
```

Enhancements to this framework for a production environment are left as an exercise. Beyond additional configuration options, it would be helpful to support multiple handlers so that one mailbox can receive more than one type of message (remember, it's unsafe to have more than one application routinely accessing the same mailbox). A more complete implementation is available on this book's web site (*http://www.oreilly.com/catalog/javaebp*.

One major concern when implementing a mail monitor in a production system is what do to about messages that aren't recognized. Your implementation deletes only messages that are properly handled. You could set the standard that a handler should delete a message if it doesn't recognize it, but that solution is unnecessarily draconian, particularly if you want to implement the multiple handlers feature. Another option is to implement a handler that deletes unknown messages, but then that handler must be kept up to date on the format for all valid messages.

Ultimately, there's no substitute for human review. With IMAP, you can move messages to other folders after processing, where they can be reviewed by software or by users. A similar approach can be used to handle messages that were not recognized by the system.

Incorporate Security

Remember how, back in the introduction, we went over some areas where Internet email had a few problems? There really isn't much that we can do about lack of support for message routing and quality-of-service guarantees, short of switching over to a heavier-grade messaging system. And for most application-to-application communications problems, that's exactly what you should do.

You can do something about the security problem, however. Most of the intercomponent communications we've discussed in this chapter have been via XML. The W3C has defined standards for using digital signatures both to sign and encrypt XML documents. Provided that your digital signatures are managed in a secure manner, signing documents allows you to prevent other systems or malicious users from providing XML input for your email-enabled applications. Encrypting the XML will prevent its contents from being revealed in transit, even if the message has to leave your private network and cross over onto the Internet.

Signing and encrypting an XML file produces another XML file, which can be attached to a mail message just like any other file. There is no standard Java API for using digital signatures with XML, but several freely available Java tools support the standard, including the XML Security package from the Apache XML Project (*http://xml.apache.org*).

When a human is one end of an email conduit, the S/MIME standard allows digitally signed and encrypted emails that can be managed by an S/MIME-compliant mail reader. JavaMail does not natively support S/MIME, but several commercial toolkits are available that enable you to add S/MIME support to your applications fairly easily.

Use Secure Protocols

Many mail servers now support Secure Sockets Layer (SSL) encryption for particular protocols (including SMTP, POP, and IMAP). If your server supports SSL, your Java-Mail application can use it as well, reducing the likelihood of third parties eaves-dropping on your communications. To do this, you need to create a JavaMail Session object that uses the Java Secure Socket Extension (JSSE) system, which is included in Java Development Kit (JDK) 1.4 or is available as an add-on for earlier Java 2 implementations.

To use JSSE with a particular protocol, you need to install the JSSE provider according to the instructions included with the JSSE installation. You can then create an SSL-aware session by setting the following three properties within the Session objects.

Property	Value
mail.*protocol*socketFactory.class	`javax.net.ssl.SSLSocketFactory`
mail.*protocol*socketFactory.fallback	`true` if the connection should resort to non-SSL if the server does not support SSL; `false` otherwise
mail.*protocol*socketFactory.port	The remote port for the new socket factory

You will also have to set the default port for the protocol if it is not the standard port for the protocol.

If the remote server uses a server certificate not supported by the JSSE implementation, you will need to add the remote certificate to your local set of trusted root certificates. See the JSSE documentation for more information.

Use JAF for Bridging Content

Most JavaMail programmers have built up a passing familiarity with the JavaBeans Activation Framework (JAF). JAF was originally intended as a content-neutral mechanism for handling MIME-formatted data. For several years, JavaMail was the only API that used JAF explicitly. This changed with the introduction of SAAJ, a Java API for handling SOAP messages with attachments. SAAJ provides a standard interface for creating, sending, reading, and receiving messages based on SOAP Version 1.1 and the SOAP with Attachments extension. SOAP messages contain XML content and optional MIME-formatted file attachments, and are usually transported from one system to another via HTTP. For more on SOAP and Java, check out Dave Chappel and Tyler Jewell's *Java Web Services* (O'Reilly).

SAAJ also uses the JAF to handle file attachments. This makes it easy to write email-based frontends for SOAP services, or to transform SOAP messages, complete with attachments, into email. In fact, SMTP can even be used as the transport layer for SOAP, in lieu of HTTP.

For example, imagine a document cataloging system that has been provided with a web services interface. Clients can add documents to the catalog by providing a document ID and the document itself. The web service implements this by accepting a SOAP message containing the ID and header. You can add email support to this application by providing an email address users can send documents to. Your software will read the incoming messages and convert them to SOAP calls.

Example 10-6 extends your `MailMonitor` component by defining a handler that converts incoming email into SOAP messages. The SOAP call is kept simple: the handler just pulls the email subject and inserts it as a document ID.

Example 10-6. SOAPTransferMailHandler.java

```
import javax.activation.*;
import javax.xml.soap.*;
import javax.xml.messaging.*;
import javax.mail.*;
...
public class SOAPTransferMailHandler implements BlockingMailHandler
{
  URLEndpoint soapEndpoint = null;
  ...
  SOAPTransferMailHandler(String epURL) {
    soapEndpoint = new URLEndpoint(epURL);
  }

  public boolean handleMessage(javax.mail.Message message) {
  ...
    try {
      SOAPConnection con =
        SOAPConnectionFactory.newInstance( ).createConnection( );

      SOAPMessage soapMsg = MessageFactory.newInstance( ).createMessage( );
      ...
      // Populate a basic SOAP header.
      SOAPEnvelope envelope = soapMsg.getSOAPPart( ).getEnvelope( );
      Name hName = envelope.createName("header", "ws",
        "http://www.company.com/xmlns/soapservice");
      SOAPHeader header = envelope.getHeader( );
      SOAPHeaderElement headerElement = header.addHeaderElement(hName);
      SOAPElement docIdElem = headerElement.addChildElement("title", "ws");
      docIdElem.addTextNode(message.getSubject( ));
      ...
      Object content = message.getContent( );
      ...
      if (content instanceof Multipart) {
        Multipart multipart = (Multipart)content;
        ...
```

Example 10-6. SOAPTransferMailHandler.java (continued)

```
for (int i=0; i < multipart.getCount(); i++) {
        Part part = multipart.getBodyPart(i);
        if(Part.ATTACHMENT.equalsIgnoreCase(part.getDisposition())) {
          DataHandler attachmentContent = part.getDataHandler();
          AttachmentPart ap =
                    soapMsg.createAttachmentPart(attachmentContent);
          soapMsg.addAttachmentPart(ap);
        }
    }
   }

   con.call(soapMsg, soapEndpoint);

} catch (Exception e) {
  e.printStackTrace();
  return false;
}

return true;
 }
}
```

More advanced systems might pull the XML SOAP body from the email message body. This approach can also be used to bridge web services through firewalls where email services are available.

Performance Optimization

We've looked at performance enhancement techniques throughout this chapter. In this section, we'll conclude our discussion with a few more strategies to make your JavaMail systems more efficient.

Use Fetch Profiles

When performing any network operation, particularly high-volume applications such as downloading email from a message store, it always makes sense to take only what you need. JavaMail supports this by implementing most messages as "lazy" objects. When you call the getMessages() method of a folder, JavaMail does not automatically fetch all the messages in the folder, with all their content. Instead, it creates a set of "lazy-load" objects that access the server as necessary to retrieve particular message components. The efficacy of all this will vary depending on the message store type and implementation.

Sometimes it's desirable to skip the lazy-load and retrieve larger quantities of message information at once. In JavaMail, you can accomplish this via a *fetch profile*. Fetch profiles allow you to specify the components of a message that will be downloaded when the message is initially retrieved from the remote message store. The

FetchProfile.Item object defines three constants: ENVELOPE (for message headers), FLAGS (for mailsystem status flags), and CONTENT_INFO (for headers defining the content of message parts). You can add any or all of these items to a fetch profile, which will instruct the server, where possible, to retrieve all the information in the profile for every message retrieved. This information can then be reviewed without further network access. When you try to access data not included in the fetch profile, the implementation will retrieve it in the normal way.

Here's how to preload all the envelope information for a folder:

```
Message messages[ ] = folder.getMessages( );
FetchProfile profile = new FetchProfile( );
profile.add(FetchProfile.Item.ENVELOPE);
folder.fetch(messages, profile);
```

Fetch profiles affect only message headers, not content, which will be retrieved from the server only upon request. When possible, check the message headers before retrieving the message content and verify that the message is one you're actually interested in processing. This helps minimize the effect of accidental or intentional denial of service attacks levied against your system.

Manage Attachments in Memory

File attachments can be a real drain on system performance. They can be arbitrarily big, and most methods for handling them involve writing them out to disk. This requires access to a directory on the server and can impose all sorts of performance penalties.

JavaMail, oddly, doesn't support nontext MIME parts based on objects in memory. JAF DataHandler objects can be retrieved only from a file or URL. This means that even if you've generated the attachment in memory, you still have to write it out to disk and then attach the ondisk file to your email. The exception, as you've seen, is when you already have a DataHandler object, such as when you receive an incoming SOAP message via JAXM.

Example 10-7 shows how to get around this limitation by subclassing the MimeBodyPart object. The standard MimeBodyPart implementation includes a protected field, contents, that contains the raw content of the MIME part. The JavaMail API also includes a utility class, MimeUtility, that can encode content streams in a variety of ways, including with the base64 and the older UUEncode standards. You can use these two features to create your own MIME encoding system, bypassing JAF altogether.

The StreamBasedMimeBodyPart class has a constructor that accepts an InputStream, a content type, and a filename. The filename is associated with the file attachment so that the recipient can open it easily. Because this is a simple example, the constructor contains all the logic, setting the necessary headers, encoding the input stream into a byte array, and setting the byte array as the content of the MimeBodyPart.

Example 10-7. StreamBasedMimeBodyPart

```java
import javax.mail.*;
import javax.mail.internet.*;
import java.io.*;
...
public class StreamBasedMimeBodyPart extends MimeBodyPart
{
  public StreamBasedMimeBodyPart(InputStream in, String type,
      String filename)
  {
    super();

    try {
      ByteArrayOutputStream bos = new ByteArrayOutputStream();
      OutputStream out = MimeUtility.encode(bos, "base64");
      byte[] b = new byte[1024];
      while(in.read(b) > 0)
        out.write(b);
      this.content = bos.toByteArray();

      setHeader("Content-Type", type + "; name=\""+filename+"\"");
      setHeader("Content-Transfer-Encoding", "base64");
      setDisposition("attachment");
      setFileName(filename);
    } catch (IOException e) {
      // Handle it.
    } catch (MessagingException e) {
      // Handle it.
    }
  }
}
```

Using the class is simple. You just create a new instance of it, passing in your content, content type, and filename, and add the part to a Multipart object just like any other MimeBodyPart (this approach is much more useful, obviously, when the content originates somewhere other than a file because you can just as easily use a regular DataHandler):

```java
FileInputStream fIn = new FileInputStream("c:\\inline.gif");
...
StreamBasedMimeBodyPart bbp = new StreamBasedMimeBodyPart(
        fIn, "image/gif", "inline.gif");

myMultipart.addBodyPart(bbp);
```

Even though you aren't reading a filename from the disk, you still provide a filename to the MIME header; this allows the client displaying the email to provide the user with a way to save the file, and is sometimes required for the client to handle the attachment, even if the content type has been specified.

Before trying this in a production environment, add some error checking.

Use JavaMail to Search

Efficient searching is vital for many email-based applications, particularly when more than one application shares an email address. The simplest way to find a message in a folder is to retrieve all of them and loop through the resulting `Message` object array, examining the relevant fields and selecting the messages that are interesting. Java-Mail provides a mechanism for searching messages from a message store, using `SearchTerm` functionality. The `SearchTerm` object and its descendents are found in the `javax.mail.search` package. The various `SearchTerm` objects perform a particular comparison. `FromStringTerm`, for instance, performs a substring search on a message's `From` header. All string comparisons are case-insensitive.

More complex search terms can be created via the `AndTerm`, `OrTerm`, and `NotTerm` objects, which develop arbitrarily complex search criteria. Here's how I tell when I'm in trouble:

```
SearchTerm t = new AndTerm(new FromStringTerm("editor@oreilly.com"),
                           new SubjectTerm("late book"));
Message[ ] msgs = folder.search(t);
```

What to do after receiving the message is left as an exercise. For maximum performance, search terms should be used wherever possible. This is because more advanced message storage protocols, including IMAP, have native search capabilities. When these are available the JavaMail provider implementation can translate the search terms into a native search command, transmit that command to the server, and have the server do the heavy lifting. For example, if you include a `BodyTerm`, and 1 message in a folder of 200 has a multiple-megabyte file attachment, retrieving all the message bodies and searching on the client will be far less efficient than a search based on the server.

When using message stores (such as POP3) that don't support server-side searching, the implementation will have to download all the messages to perform the search, but it still makes sense to use JavaMail search terms whenever possible, both for convenience and readability and to make upgrades to more capable message stores easier later on.

CHAPTER 11

Enterprise Performance Tuning Best Practices

Jack Shirazi

The enterprise performance-tuning best practices build on the standard Java performance-tuning best practices (which are covered in the performance-tuning chapter in O'Reilly's *Java Best Practices*). In this chapter, I'll summarize the important points from that chapter and provide best practices for Enterprise Java.

Performance Planning

Planning for performance is the single most important indicator of a Java 2 Enterprise Edition (J2EE) project's success. A performance plan does what any other plan does: it optimizes your chance of succeeding in a specific area of a project—in this case, application performance. If you know that successful performance is not necessary for your project, you don't need a performance plan. My experience with projects that have *no* performance requirements is limited to college assignments. In business, I find that the importance of performance is second only to core functionality, and comes ahead of security, robustness, and secondary functionality such as add-ons that differentiate products.

A performance plan puts into place the structures and procedures that ensure you have made every attempt to achieve the performance goals of your project. It also improves the quality of a project, and decreases the risks of project failure. The simple act of defining a performance plan immediately increases the chances that your project will attain acceptable performance. Carrying through your performance plan by setting performance goals, measuring against those goals, and using the feedback to improve performance significantly improves the chances of a project's success.

Perform Initial Performance Planning

To initiate a performace plan for your J2EE application, you should set out the scope and performance objectives and define communications channels between all participating parties.

Performance reaches across all parts of a project. It is necessary to allocate responsibility for performance to one or more people who can look at individual components as well as the overall system. Performance analysis and feedback might require simple code changes, readjustment of the communications structure between components, or even refactoring of the design. This implies that the performance experts might need to communicate with team members about all aspects of the project.

It is not necessary for the performance experts to be project experts as well. Part of performance planning involves setting clearly defined goals (see the next section), and these goals, together with information generated using performance tools, help to clearly identify which aspects of the project are falling short of the targeted performance.

The performance experts should be responsible for maintaining the project's performance goals, and for identifying areas that need improvement. Performance experts should also be responsible for defining alterations to the project that will help to attain the performance goals. In summary, there are three separate performance responsibilities:

- Maintaining the project's performance goals (performance planning)
- Identifying areas of the project that fall short of defined performance goals (performance testing and analysis)
- Suggesting changes to the project that will help achieve the performance goals (performance tuning)

These three sets of responsibilities can be separated; it is not necessary for the same performance experts to be responsible for all of them.

Set Performance Targets

Regardless of where you are in your project, the first step in your performance plan should be to set performance targets. These should cover as many performance aspects as possible. Some of these include expected response times (e.g., "Any button click providing a new page should display in less than 2 seconds, except for queries…"), batch process times (e.g., "Nightly batch processing should not exceed 5 hours"), throughput (e.g., "The system should handle up to 60 transactions per minute within performance targets"), concurrency (e.g., "Up to 500 users can use the application at any one time").

Performance in most projects is seldom consistent. All sorts of procedures can interrupt processes. For this reason, it is usually better to specify a range of acceptable performance targets—e.g., "Button click to page display response times should be less than 2 seconds in 90% of cases, and less than 5 seconds in 99% of cases." When specifying response time ranges for activities initiated by users, pay special attention to the 90% range. Users' perception of the average response times is actually close to the 90% value in the range of measured times. People give more weight to bad news, and their performance perceptions are no different.

Setting the performance requirements of your application is not necessarily a developer-level task. Your customers or business experts need to establish the response time that is acceptable for most functions the user will execute. It can be useful to start by specifying which response times are unacceptable.

With that in mind, let's review the performance-tuning best practices from Java 2 Standard Edition (J2SE):

- Include a performance specification in the project specification.
- Make the performance objectives clear by quantifying them.
- Agree on target times with users before tuning.
- Specify acceptable variations in performance targets.
- Pay attention to the target response time under which 90% of responses should lie, as this is the "average" reponse time perceived by users.
- Specify targets for the scaled system, including variations in user/data/object volumes.

The Performance Environment

The performance environment has several components:

- A client simulation tool (the load-testing tool)
- Java Virtual Machine (JVM) profiling tools
- System and server-side monitoring tools

As with other tools and third-party products used in your project, these tools need to be planned for, evaluated, selected, purchased (or built), trained on, customized, and used. And don't forget to include allocation for literature and developer learning time. Your choices of the right tools and the right approach make a difference in terms of the overall cost and time taken for managing performance.

Use a Client Simulation Tool

The client simulation tool, often referred to as a *benchmark harness* or *load-testing* tool, exercises the application as though one or more users are performing the expected business activity. Some projects adapt their quality assessment testing toolset to create a benchmark harness, other projects build a dedicated harness to exercise the server-side components directly, and others use an off-the-shelf web loading or GUI capture-and-playback tool.

The following three factors are imperative when deciding on a client simulation tool:

- The tool must effectively simulate client activity, including variable pauses in activity such as the time users would take to fill out fields or make selections at decision points.

- The tool should make and record timed measurements of simulated activity between arbitrary points, such as from a simulated user click on a browser to complete page display.
- The tool should not interfere with timing measurements—i.e., it should not add any significant overhead that would measurably affect the times being recorded.

From the J2SE world, here are some tips to keep in mind:

- Build or buy a benchmark harness, which is a tool dedicated to performance measurements and *not* robustness testing.
- Specify benchmarks based on real user behavior.
- Run benchmarks simulating user behavior across all expected scales.

Don't Use JVM Profiling Tools

JVM profiling tools are normally used during development to identify bottlenecks in running Java code. They are suitable for identifying bottlenecks in application sub-components that run in individual JVMs. However, they usually impose a heavy overhead on the JVM. Therefore, they tend to be used infrequently because of the extra time needed to run an application while profiling, and because analyzing the results of the profile can be difficult.

JVM profiling tools do not provide absolute measurements of execution time. The heavy overhead makes the absolute times produced by a JVM profiler irrelevant. Instead, the relative times of execution between methods and threads are measured to provide a profile that can be analyzed to determine the program bottlenecks. Their heavy overheads make JVM profiling tools unsuitable for use as enterprise monitoring tools.

Use Monitoring Tools

Monitoring tools continually measure activity and produce logs that can be analyzed for trends or problems. Your choice of monitoring tools should be guided by three primary requirements:

- The tool should have a low overhead cost for collecting data from the server.
- The tool should provide measurements that are important for your project.
- The tool should be suitable for monitoring in both the development environment and the production environment.

Enterprise monitoring tools provide valuable information for both development performance tuning and production performance monitoring. Ideally, to ensure the success of performance monitoring in production, the skills and knowledge acquired in development should be transferred to the production environment with a minimum of disruption.

Second, monitoring tools should also do the following:

- Scale with the application
- Be easy to configure
- Provide detailed analysis tools
- Provide automatic advisements or warnings whenever possible

A number of commercial J2EE performance-monitoring tools are now available. These tools improve J2EE performance-tuning productivity significantly, and it is worth obtaining one for your project. (A list of such tools can be obtained at *http:// www.JavaPerformanceTuning.com/resources.shtml*). If you want to implement your own tool, you need to add logging to all the main communications interfaces of the application, the transaction and session boundaries, and the lifecycle boundaries (for instance, the creation and destruction of Enterprise JavaBeans [EJBs]) and request initiation and completion. Free logging tools designed to work with J2EE applications, such as Steve Souza's JAMon (see *http://www.JavaPerformanceTuning.com/ tools/jamon/index.shtml*), can assist with this task.

The following are some important lessons learned from the J2SE world that are applicable here:

- Make your benchmarks long enough; more than 5 seconds is a good target.
- Use elapsed time (wall-clock time) for the primary time measurements and a benchmark harness that does not interfere with measured times.
- Run benchmarks in an isolated, reproducible environment before starting the tuning process, and again after each tuning exercise.
- Be sure that you are not measuring artificial situations, such as full caches containing the exact data needed for the test. Account for all the performance effects of any caches.
- Measure all aspects of the system, including operating system statistics (especially CPU, memory, and I/O statistics), and JVM statistics, including the heap, method execution times, garbage collection, and object creation.

Use Test Systems

Every phase of your project should have a testable system. This allows you to continually performance-test your system and quickly identify potential performance problems. The earlier you can identify such problems, the cheaper they are to remedy. Analysis and design stages in particular should include testing of proposed architectures to eliminate possibilities that are functionally adequate but not adequately efficient. Test systems include:

Benchmarks
   The ECperf benchmark is not difficult to install and run, and is representative of what many J2EE applications can do. The Sun Pet Store tutorial is also available

and, although it is not a benchmark, can, after tuning, be used for internal performance testing.

Prototypes and models

Many projects start with a prototype or working model. Such a test system can form a useful core for exercising the main ideas from analysis and design.

Skeleton systems

This type of system provides a core into which components can be slotted as they become available. Temporary simulation components can be used to model behavior and identify potential performance problems even before components are testable.

Partial systems

In many projects with no performance plan, the first time performance is seriously considered is often when a partial system can be tested (usually because performance inadequacies become clear at this point).

Complete development system

When the application has been completed but has not yet passed quality assessment, there is a window of time during which performance testing is possible. Some projects use this window for performance testing simultaneously with quality assessment. However, as the performance planner, you need to be aware that most identified performance problems at this stage will not be fixed in time for the application to pass through quality assessment and be released by the scheduled date.

Potential release system

Subsequent to successful completion of quality assessment, the application is ready for deployment. This system is frequently a target system for intensive performance testing to provide an upgrade to the deployed system that addresses any significant performance problems. There is normally a window of time—after the application has been released to the administration team but before it has been moved into production—during which performance testing can effectively be performed to contribute to an upgrade soon after deployment.

Deployed production system

The production system is the ultimate performance-testing environment. Deploying the application with monitoring in place ensures that valuable performance data is not missed. This data can be analyzed to eliminate any remaining performance problems.

Your performance plan should include some aspects that might not be obvious. First, performance testing should normally be scheduled to take place on systems where no other activity is being performed. Sharing the QA or development system is possible, but in these cases performance testing should be scheduled to run when other activity has died down, typically in the evening or overnight. If this is the case for your environment, it is important that the tools run unattended, and preferably, automatically.

Second, your overall plan must take into account code versioning and release from development to performance environment simultaneously with QA releases. And bear in mind that changes required from both QA and performance testing will need to be applied to both environments. As milestones approach, performance changes are frequently pushed back to the next release, which might be acceptable but should be planned for to avoid confusion.

Proactive Performance Management in Production

Here are some examples of typical performance management problems that crop up:

- Users call with a response time problem.
- The JVM reaches an out-of-memory state and crashes.
- Logging space on the filesystem is exhausted.
- A database table maxes out on the extents.
- The nightly batch runs too long or freezes.

Performance management solutions in production tend to be reactive. For example, here is a standard pattern of activity:

1. A problem occurs and is reported.
2. The system is analyzed to identify what caused the problem.
3. Some corrective action is taken to eliminate the problem.
4. Everything goes back to normal.

Reactive performance management will always be required because it is impossible to anticipate all conditions. However, proactive performance management can minimize situations in which reactive activity is required. Proactive performance management requires monitoring normal activity to identify unusual performance spikes, dips, and trends.

For example, one site with a performance monitoring policy identified a trend that showed long page response time. Analysis of the server indicated that a cache was configured incorrectly. This was fixed and the problem was eliminated. Users noticed nothing. Without the site's proactive policy, administration would not have known about the problem until users complained about increasingly slow performance.

Similarly, another site with a proactive performance management policy monitored JVM memory size. After an upgrade, the JVM memory started to increase slowly. The administrators were able to make controlled restarts of the JVM at times when site traffic was lowest until the object retention problem was fixed. Without heap size monitoring, the JVM would have crashed at some point without warning, and with no obvious cause. The fix would have been delayed until after analysis and, most likely, reoccurence of the problem.

Systems and applications change over time. Monitoring the system and having logs available for analysis helps to minimize reactive problem management.

Plan for Performance Factors

There are five performance factors that you should always plan for:

Workload
> The amount of work that will be performed by the system. This is defined by the number of users, their activity levels, and types of activity, together with any non–user-initiated automatic activity such as background and batch processes. The performance plan needs to take into account how these factors will scale and change over time, and should consider average and peak workloads.

Throughput
> The total amount of work the system can handle. Technically, throughput depends on a composite of I/O speed, CPU speed, and the efficiency of the operating system. Practically, throughput can be considered in terms of factors such as the number of transactions per minute that can be handled by the application, the amount of data or number of objects that can flow through the various subsystems of the application, and the number and sizes of requests that can be handled per minute. The performance plan should highlight expected transaction rates and data flow capacities as targets that need to be met.

Resources
> The system's hardware and software. Within the performance plan you need to anticipate increasing the amount or speed of hardware resources to scale the system, and ensure that the software—e.g., the operating system and middleware— is capable of handling the expected performance.

Scaling
> The ability of the system to handle increasing numbers of users or objects, and increasing amounts of data. A system that scales well is one that can handle almost twice the throughput without performance degradation by doubling the resources available to the system. The performance plan should include performance-testing capabilities for the various scales the system is targeted to reach at various milestones. This includes ensuring that the requisite licensing is available for simulated users and data.

Contention
> When more than one component is attempting to simultaneously use a resource in a conflicting way. Contention is inevitable—for example, there are always times when multiple threads try to use the CPU. Contention limits the scalability

of the application. Minimizing contention is usually a major goal of performance management. The performance plan should target the identification of contended resources at all stages of development and production. Trying to predict which resources will cause contention helps to alleviate contention.

Efficient Distributed Computing Architecture

High-performance architecture for enterprise systems consists of one or more frontend load balancers (the Front Controller design pattern) distributing requests to a cluster of middle-tier web application servers running J2EE, with a database behind this middle tier. Components designed to operate asynchronously with message queues holding requests for the components optimize the throughput of the system (the Message Façade design pattern). Server management of client socket connections should use the `java.nio` package classes, and in particular sockets should be multiplexed with the `Selector` class. Load balancing is efficiently supported using multiplexed I/O (the Reactor design pattern). (Typically, the application server manages sockets transparently in the application, but if your application manages sockets directly, do it with NIO multiplexing.)

In addition, these main architectural components should be supported with caches, resource pools, optimized database access, and a performance-monitoring subsystem, and should have no single point of failure. Caches and resource pools should be made tunable by altering configuration parameters—i.e., they shouldn't require code tuning. Resource pools are recommended only for resources that are expensive to replace or need limiting, such as threads and database connections. Database access optimization is made simpler if there is a separate database access layer (the Data Access Object design pattern).

Know Distributed Computing Restrictions

All forms of distributed computing have two severe restrictions:

Bandwidth limitations
> The amount of data that can be carried per second across the communications channel is limited. If your application transfers too large a volume of data, it will be slow. You can either reduce the volume transferred by compression or redesign, or accept that the application will run slowly. Some enterprise applications provide the additional option of upgrading the bandwidth of the communications channel, which is often the cheapest tuning option.

Latency
> Any single communication is limited in speed by two factors:

- How fast the message can be transferred along the hardware communications channel
- How fast the message can be converted to and from the electrical signals that are carried along the hardware communications channel

The first factor, transferring the actual signals, is limited ultimately by the speed of light (about 3.33 milliseconds for every 1,000 kilometers), but routers and other factors can delay the signal further. The second factor tends to dominate the transfer time, as it includes software data conversions, data copying across buffers, conversion of the software message to and from electrical signals, and, potentially, retransmissions to handle packets lost from congestion or error.

The performance of most enterprise applications is constrained by latency. Data volumes are a concern, but mainly because of the cost of serializing large amounts of data rather than limited bandwidth. The primary mechanism for minimizing latency is to reduce the number of messages that need to be sent across the network, normally by redesigning interfaces to be coarser. That is, you should try to make each of your remote calls do a lot of work rather than requiring many remote calls to do the same work.

Some common techniques help to reduce the number of network transfers:

- Combine multiple remotely called methods into single wrapper methods (Session Façade and Composite Entity design patterns).
- Cache objects (Service Locator design pattern and its variations), in particular JNDI lookups (EJBHome Factory design pattern and variations).
- Batch messages and data.
- Move execution to the location of the data.

The Value Object design pattern also helps to reduce the number of message transfers by combining multiple results into one object that requires only one transfer. You can reduce serialization overheads by using transient fields and implementing the `java.io.Externalizable` interface for classes causing serialization bottlenecks.

There is also one common case in which data volume is an issue: when large amounts of data can be returned by a query. In this case, the Page-by-Page Iterator design pattern (and variations of that pattern, such as the `ValueListHandler` pattern) should be used to ensure that only the data that is actually needed is transferred.

Tuning Procedure

The overall tuning procedure for enterprise projects follows the strategies for J2SE projects. The main difference is contention. Eliminating contention in J2SE applications is mostly a matter of identifying and eliminating deadlocks, or balancing the occasional shared resource. Contention in enterprise systems tends to occur throughout the system, arises quite easily, varies as the application scales, and can be difficult to identify. Contention for multiuser resources is usually the factor that limits the theoretical performance of an enterprise system, which means that if you can tune away the implementation bottlenecks, you will probably be left with the contention bottlenecks.

Again, here are some best practices from the J2SE world that are applicable here:

- Measure the performance using logging, monitors, profilers, and benchmark suites, and by instrumenting code.
- Don't tune any benchmarks that have already reached the target performance.
- Identify the main bottlenecks (look for the top five bottlenecks, but go higher or lower if you prefer).
- Determine whether bottlenecks are related to CPU, memory, or I/O problems, and try to accurately identify their cause.
- Choose the quickest and easiest bottleneck to fix and address it. Target only one bottleneck at a time.
- Think of a hypothesis for the cause of the bottleneck.
- Consider any factors that might refute your hypothesis.
- Create a test to isolate the factor identified by the hypothesis.
- Test the hypothesis.
- Alter the application to reduce the bottleneck.
- Test that the alteration improves performance and measure the improvement (regression-test the affected code).
- Make sure that the tuning exercise has improved speed. The most common tuning mistake is to assume that a change has improved performance without testing it, only to find at some point later that the change actually decreased performance.
- Document optimizations fully in the code. Retain old code in comments. Tuned code can sometimes be difficult to understand.
- Quality-test the application after any optimizations have been made. An optimization is not fully valid until it has passed QA.
- Repeat the whole tuning procedure for the next bottleneck.

User Perceptions

In J2SE applications, all that really matters is the user's perception of performance. Giving the user the perception of faster performance *does* make the application perform faster. User perceptions are also important for enterprise applications, but overall throughput is equally important. Enterprise applications have to balance optimal response times for individual users against optimal total work done by the system.

Some practices can slow down response times to increase the throughput of the server. If some users have higher performance requirements than others, the enterprise system should be built around multiple-priority queues, with higher-priority users or services processed before lower-priority ones.

In addition, enterprise applications need to handle communications failures and client screen display optimally. All client display technology, including browser-based technology, display some screens more effectively than others. For example, some browsers display some types of screens quicker if size tags are included in the markup, if tables are avoided, and so on. Most clients (including browsers) can be built or configured to display information before the full download is completed, which gives the perception of good performance. If your clients connect to the server with varying communications bandwidths, you need to test and design for this variety, bearing in mind that users with larger bandwidths expect to see screens display faster.

Communications failures are a fact of life for enterprise systems. Handling communications failures gracefully—i.e., requiring the user to perform as little extra work as possible to recover his last state—gives the impression of better performance.

As a basic guideline to good enterprise performance, 1 million requests per day, 24/7, is equivalent to 12 requests per second. The vast majority of servers receive requests unevenly around some periodic patterns. Peak traffic can be an order of magnitude higher than the average request rate. For a highly scaled popular server, ideal peak performance targets would probably consist of subsecond response times and hundreds of (e-commerce) transactions per second. These are basic guidelines to help you calculate target response times appropriate for your application. Note that Java-based Internet applications have scaled to this level of traffic, and beyond.

Here is a summary of some applicable J2SE performance guidelines as they pertain to user perceptions:

- What really matters is the user's perception of performance.
- Keep the application interface responsive at all times. Allow the user to abort ongoing tasks and carry on alternative tasks.
- Long response times make a bigger impression on memory than shorter ones.
- Try to provide the appearance of better performance.
- Don't give users a false expectation that a task will be finished sooner than it will.
- Use threads to separate functions that could block the user interface.
- Anticipate user actions to precalculate results.
- Provide any partial data for viewing as soon as possible.
- Cache items that the user might want to reuse.

Tuning Techniques

Java Enterprise performance-tuning techniques include J2SE tuning techniques, as well as a variety of others. Here is a summary of the J2SE best practice techniques:

- Improve CPU limitations with faster code, better algorithms, and fewer short-lived objects.
- Improve memory limitations by using fewer objects or smaller long-lived objects.
- Improve I/O limitations by reducing the number of I/O operations with targeted redesigns, or by speeding up I/O by reducing the amount of data requiring I/O, or perhaps by multithreading the I/O. Buffer I/O where possible (usually almost everywhere).
- Switch to an optimizing compiler.
- Use a JIT-enabled JVM.
- Test other JVMs to find a faster one.
- Turn off any JVM options that slow down the application (e.g., `-Xrunhprof` and `-verbose`).
- Tune the heap.
- If a bottleneck consists of a slow method, make it faster.
- If a bottleneck consists of many calls to a fast method, reduce the number of times that method is called.
- Tune object-creation and garbage-collection bottlenecks by reusing objects and reducing the number of objects used.
- Target loops. Minimize the time executed in the loop by moving any code you can outside the loop, avoiding repeated operations and inlining method calls.
- Target strings. Only internationalized text needs to use `String` objects. All other string use can probably be optimized with your own character handling.
- Try to use primitive datatypes directly. Avoid wrapping them.
- Use or build the fastest collection possible. Traverse collection elements directly where possible.
- Exceptions are time-consuming to create, so avoid creating them.
- Minimize casting by specializing algorithms and data structures to the required datatype.

Choose the Right Data Structure

Enterprise systems typically have requirements for handling very large datasets. The data structures delivered with the Java SDK are not necessarily ideal for efficiently manipulating very large datasets. The efficiency of the data structures is closely related to the data being manipulated by the structure and the algorithms used to do the manipulation. You need to consider carefully how large datasets will be used and queried, and try to match the scaling characteristics of the structures and algorithms against the volumes of data likely to be applied.

Sometimes no single data structure is ideal for your data. In these cases, you have three choices:

Compromise data structure

Use a compromise data structure that is not ideal but provides adequate performance for the most important functions. This option is the easiest to implement and maintain, but performance is compromised. As an example, use a `TreeMap` for holding key/value pairs that also need to be ordered.

Aggregate data structure

Use more than one data structure holding the same set of data, with each data structure providing optimum performance for different functions. This option can be a little complex, though aggregating preexisting data structures under a single class and hiding the underlying complexity provides a maintainable solution. For example, you could use a `HashMap` and an `ArrayList` holding the same data in an aggregate class when you want to hold key/value pairs that need to be ordered. Iteration using the `ArrayList` is fast, but there is more overhead in maintaining the repeated dataset in the two structures held by the aggregation class.

Hybrid data structure

Use a hybrid data structure that combines the structures and algorithms you need for your dataset and data manipulation algorithms. Because you usually need to build this complex solution from scratch, this option can be difficult to implement and maintain, but it potentially provides the best performance. Using the example of holding key/value pairs that also need to be ordered, the exact functionality required would need to be analyzed, and a specialized solution proposed, built, debugged, and maintained.

Transactions

Transactions have many overheads. If you can avoid them, do so for performance reasons. Handle the nontransactional part of your application differently from the parts that require transactions. Where transactions are necessary, tune transactions using the following guidelines:

- Try to use optimistic transactions (the Optimistic Locking design pattern) for transactional systems in which accesses predominate updates.

- Minimize the time spent in any transaction, but don't shorten transactions so much that you unnecessarily increase the total number of transactions. Combine transactions that occur within a few seconds of each other to minimize the overall time spent in transactions. This can require manually controlling the transaction—i.e., turning off auto-commit for JDBC transaction or using TX_REQUIRED for EJBs.

- J2EE transactions are defined with several isolation modes. Choose the fastest transaction isolation level that avoids corrupting the data. Transaction levels in order of increasing cost are: TRANSACTION_READ_UNCOMMITTED, TRANSACTION_READ_COMMITTED, TRANSACTION_REPEATABLE_READ, and TRANSACTION_SERIALIZABLE.

- Don't leave transactions open, relying on the user to close them. Inevitably, there will be times when the user does not close the transaction, and the very long transaction that results will significantly decrease the performance of the system.

- Bulk or batch updates are usually more efficiently performed in larger transactions.

- Optimize read-only transactions. EJBs should use read-only transactions in the deployment descriptor, while JDBC should use read-only connections.

- Lock only where the design absolutely requires it.

Miscellaneous Best Practices

Finally, here is a set of miscellaneous best practices that have not been mentioned anywhere else in the book. Keep these in mind when creating the various parts of your enterprise system.

Design

- Design objects so that they can be easily replaced by a faster implementation.
- Use interfaces and interface-like patterns (e.g., the Factory pattern).
- Design for reusable objects.
- Use stateless objects.
- Consider whether to optimize objects for update or for access.
- Minimize data conversions.

Monitoring

- Constantly monitor the running application.
- Retain performance logs. Choose one set as your comparison standard.
- Monitor as many parameters as possible throughout the system.
- Note every single change to the system.

- Listen to the application users, but double-check any reported problems.
- Ensure that caching effects do not skew the measurements of a reported problem.
- Train users to use the application efficiently.

Parallelism

- Design parallelism into the application wherever possible. Identify what cannot be parallelized. Watch out for too much parallelism. There are diminishing returns from parallelism overheads.
- Balance workloads. Unbalanced parallel activities can limit the performance of the system.
- Split up the data among many different files (preferably on separate disks).
- Support asynchronous communications.
- Decouple activities so that no activity is unnecessarily blocked by another activity.
- Minimize points where parallel activities are forced to converge.

Distributed Computing

- Minimize the communication between distributed components.
- Avoid generating distributed garbage.
- Reduce transfer costs by duplicating data.
- Cache distributed data wherever possible.
- Minimize the synchronization requirements of duplicated data.
- Use compression to reduce transfer time.

JMS

- Close resources (e.g., connections, session objects, producers, and consumers) when you're finished with them.
- Start the consumer before the producer so that the initial messages do not need to queue as they wait for the consumer.
- Use separate transactional sessions and nontransactional sessions.
- Use nonpersistent messages, as they are faster than persistent messages.
- Use shorter messages, as longer messages take longer to deliver and process.
- Specify the lowest redelivery count and time-to-live that the application can accept.
- Maximize message throughput by tuning the delivery capacity.
- Use asynchronous reception of messages with the `MessageListener` interface.

- Process messages simultaneously with ConnectionConsumers and ServerSessionPools.
- Throttle very high-volume message delivery to a rate the consumers can handle. Use load-balanced message queues if necessary.
- Duplicate-delivery mode is the fastest possible delivery mode, followed by auto-acknowledgment mode. Try to avoid client acknowledgment mode.
- Use publish-and-subscribe for large numbers of active listeners, and point-to-point connections for few active listeners.

List of Contributors

Hans Bergsten is the founder of Gefion Software, a company focused on server-side Java services and products based on J2EE technologies. Hans has been an active participant in the working groups for both the servlet and JSP specifications from the time they were formed. He also contributes to other related JCP specifications, such asJSP Standard Tag Library, and helped get the Apache Tomcat reference implementation for servlet and JSP started as one of the initial members of the Apache Jakarta Project Management Committee.

William Crawford is Principal Software Architect at Perceptive Informatics, Inc. He was previously Chief Technology Officer at Invantage, Inc. and is the co-author of *Java Enterprise in a Nutshell*, as well as several other titles. His next book will be available in 2003 from O'Reilly & Associates. He can be reached at *http://www.williamcrawford.info*.

Dave Czarnecki is is a computer scientist in the Advanced Computing Technologies organization at GE's Global Research Center in Niskayuna, NY. Professionally, he has been involved in the application of Java technology to diverse areas such as e-commerce, evolutionary computation, and natural language algorithm design. David has also presented on software internationalization and general Java topics at local Java user groups and national conferences such as JavaOne. In his spare time, he achieves artistic expression through playing guitar, painting, and writing.

Andy Deitsch manages the Advanced Computing Technologies organization at GE's Global Research Center in Niskayuna, New York. He has been working with computers since 1978 when he first learned to program in BASIC on a PRIME mainframe—and has been hooked ever since. Educated in England, Israel, and the United States, Andy holds a B.S. degree in computer science and an M.B.A. When he's not working, Andy enjoys SCUBA diving and traveling the world with his wife Marie.

Robert Eckstein enjoys dabbling with just about anything related to computers. In fact, most of his friends agree that Robert spends far too much time in front of a computer screen. At O'Reilly, Robert mostly edits Java books, and in his spare time has been known to provide online coverage for popular conferences. Robert holds bachelor's degrees in computer science and communications from Trinity University in San Antonio, Texas. In the past, he has worked for the USAA insurance company and for Motorola's cellular software division. He now lives in Round Rock, Texas with his wife Michelle and their talking puppy, Ginger.

William Grosso spends his days designing and building software. Since 1995, he has focused mainly on distributed systems and artificial intelligence. Most recently, he's been working at Hipbone Incorporated, where he serves as both the Chief Architect and the Director of Quality Assurance. In his spare time, he serves on the Board of Directors for the Software Development Forum and helps run its Emerging Technologies Group. In his other spare time, he's a wine enthusiast, an avid hiker, and a pretty good hex player. He is also the author of *Java RMI*.

Jason Hunter is the author of *Java Servlet Programming* and is a prolific speaker on various Java and open source topics. As an Apache member, he served as Apache's representative to the Java Community Process Executive Committee and played a critical role in the establishment of a landmark agreement for open source Java. He is the publisher of Servlets.com, a frequent contributor to many magazines and online publications, one of the original contributers to Apache Tomcat, and a member of the expert groups responsible for Servlet/JSP and JAXP API development. With Brett McLaughlin, he co-created the open source JDOM library (*http://jdom.org*), which enables optimized Java and XML integration. These days, he particularly enjoys his work on CountryHawk and BrowserHawk from cyScape (*http://cyscape.com*).

Brett McLaughlin has been working in computers since the Logo days (remember the little triangle?). He currently specializes in building application infrastructure using Java and Java-related technologies. He has spent the last several years implementing these infrastructures at Nextel Communications and Allegiance Telecom, Inc. Brett is one of the cofounders of the Java Apache project Turbine, which builds a reusable component architecture for web application development using Java servlets. He is also a contributor to the EJBoss project, an open source EJB application server, and Cocoon, an open source XML web-publishing engine. His projects all focus on using XML and the J2EE platform in mission-critical, high-performance, distributed systems. Together with Jason Hunter, he has defined the JDOM API for manipulating XML in Java programs. When he's not bathed in the glow of a computer screen, Brett can usually be found playing the guitar or being dragged around the block by his five dogs.

Sasha Nikolic is a software consultant specializing in web services and enterprise integration applications. His work has focused mainly on architecting and implementing systems using J2EE. In the past few years, he has worked with Research In Motion, The Middleware Company, and other smaller companies. Other than Java, his interests include AI, computer graphics, physics, and soccer. He currently lives and works in Toronto, Canada.

J. Steven Perry has been a software developer for over 10 years, having worked as a maintenance programmer, systems analyst, and architect. This has given him the opportunity to see firsthand how critical a need there is for management technologies such as the Java Management Extensions (JMX). Steve has been working with JMX for nearly two years and is a member of the JMX Expert Group (JSR 160), and is the author of *Java Management Extensions*. He works as an architect in the Chief Technology Office at ALLTEL Information Services in Little Rock, Arkansas.

George Reese has taken an unusual path into business software development. After earning a B.A. in philosophy from Bates College in Lewiston, Maine, George went off to Hollywood, where he worked on television shows such as *The People's Court* and ESPN's *Up Close*. The L.A. riots convinced him to return to Maine, where he finally became involved with software development and the Internet. George has since specialized in the development of Internet-oriented Java Enterprise systems and the strategic role of technology in business processes. He is the author of *Database Programming with JDBC and Java*; co-author of *Managing and Using MySQL*; and designer of the world's first JDBC driver, the mSQL-JDBC driver for mSQL. He currently lives in Minneapolis, Minnesota with his wife, Monique, and three cats, Misty, Gypsy, and Tia. He makes a living as the National Practice Director of Technology Strategy in Imaginet, J. Walter Thompson's digital branch in Minneapolis.

Jack Shirazi is the director of JavaPerformanceTuning.com, the premier resource site for information on all aspects of performance-tuning Java applications, and is the author of *Java Performance Tuning*.

Index

A

Accept-Language header, 171
AccessException, 129
Action class, 35, 196
actions
    <c:catch>, 214
    <c:forEach>, 215, 221
    <c:if>, 221
    <c:import>, 209
    <c:url>, 207
    include, 199, 202
    <jsp:getProperty>, 207, 215
    <jsp:setProperty>, 217
    <jsp:useBean>, 210, 219
    <mt:parseNumber>, 210
    <sql:query>, 222
    <sql:update>, 222
addAttribute() method, 156–158
addHeader() method, 55
addNotification() method, 159
addOperation() method, 156, 158
aggregate data structure, 261
AlreadyBoundException, 129
AndTerm object, 247
Ant build environment, 29
Apache Struts, 36, 196
Apache Turbine, 36
API format conversion, 106–108
application controller and locale handling, 187–190
application layers, 8
application logic
    separating from database logic, 63
    separating from marshalling code, 110
architecture
    distributed computing, 256, 263
    shopping-cart, 48
    standard, 8
ArrayList, 261
asynchronous remote message calls, 138–141
AsynchronousMailHandler interface, 239

attributes
    errorPage, 212
    isErrorPage, 212
    null, 220
    scope, 219
    var, 219

B

BackgroundCallQueue method, 138
BackgroundCallQueueImpl method, 138
bandwidth limitations, 256
batch methods, 136
benchmark harness, 250
bidirectional languages, 175–183
binary data, 83
bind() method, 129
BlockingMailHandler interface, 238–241
BMP/CMP entity beans, 25–27
bootstrapping DOM, 98–101
Bouncer class, 126
browser setting and localization preferences, 170
build environments, 29
business delegates, 24
business interfaces, 14
business logic layer, 8
business object layer, 185–190
byte arrays, 120–122
byte data type, 37–40

C

Cache-Control header, 53–55, 211
caches, 51–55
caching
    client-side, 208–211
    content, 50–55
    data used in pages, 207
    dynamic pages, 211
    with JSP, 207–212
    return values, 135
    stubs to remote servers, 133

We'd like to hear your suggestions for improving our indexes. Send email to *index@oreilly.com*.

-verbose option, 260
versioning, 110
VMID class, 124

W

wasNULL() method, 82
web applications, 33
WHERE clauses, 82
workflow logic, encapsulating, 10
workload and performance plan, 255
write() method, 39
writeExternal() method, 117
writeObject() method, 117
Writer Class, 37

X

XML
    attributes, 88–90
    authoring, 85–90
    elements, 88–90
    entity references, 85
    for email content, 229
    and localization, 183–185
    parsing speed, 93
    processing, 105–108
    used for MBean management interface
        definition, 161–166
    validation, 95
XMLReader object, 95
-Xrunhprof option, 260
XSL stylesheets, 229

Colophon

Our look is the result of reader comments, our own experimentation, and feedback from distribution channels. Distinctive covers complement our distinctive approach to technical topics, breathing personality and life into potentially dry subjects.

The animal on the cover of *Java Enterprise Best Practices* is the common sand dollar (*Echinarachnius parma*). This species of sand dollar can be found on the shores of the North American East coast north of New Jersey. It is circumpolar and can also be found in Alaska, British Columbia, Siberia, and Japan.

A sand dollar can be anywhere from 5–10 centimeters when fully grown and can weigh 10–25 grams. The hard shell (called a "test" since it is not really a shell because it is sheathed in skin) contains several small perforations that form a five-part, petal-like configuration. The animal is covered in brown spines, which gives it a furry appearance. Spines on its flat underside help it move through the sand. Hair-like strands called cilia cover the spines. Coated in mucous, cilia capture and move food to the sand dollar's mouth, which lies in the middle of the star-shaped grooves on the animal's underside. Sand dollars feed on algae and small pieces of organic material found on the ocean floor.

Because of their hard shells and minuscule bodies, sand dollars are relatively safe from predators. Also, they further protect themselves by burrowing into the sand on the sea floor. After a storm, their skeletons will often wash up on beaches.

Matt Hutchinson was the production editor and proofreader for *Java Enterprise Best Practices*. Audrey Doyle was the copyeditor. Emily Quill and Tatiana Apandi Diaz provided quality control. Judy Hoer provided production assistance. Lynda D'Arcangelo wrote the index.

Hanna Dyer designed the cover of this book, based on a series design by Edie Freedman. The cover image is a 19th-century engraving from the Dover Pictorial Archive. Emma Colby produced the cover layout with QuarkXPress 4.1 using Adobe's ITC Garamond font.

David Futato designed the interior layout. This book was converted to FrameMaker 5.5.6 with a format conversion tool created by Erik Ray, Jason McIntosh, Neil Walls, and Mike Sierra that uses Perl and XML technologies. The text font is Linotype Birka; the heading font is Adobe Myriad Condensed; and the code font is Lucas-Font's TheSans Mono Condensed. The illustrations that appear in the book were produced by Robert Romano and Jessamyn Read using Macromedia FreeHand 9 and Adobe Photoshop 6. The tip and warning icons were drawn by Christopher Bing. This colophon was written by Matt Hutchinson.